Sport, Events, Tourism and Regeneration

Investments in sport, events and tourism in cities and wider regions are part of nascent regeneration strategies linked to transitioning economic bases and place images. While it is important to consider physical regeneration, there is a range of subsequent benefits and opportunities brought about through regeneration that considers social impacts, communities and how investments and developments influence how people interact in transformed spaces.

This book brings together a collection focusing on the diverse range of approaches and perspectives of regeneration. Twelve chapters outline and bring together critical perspectives of regeneration from scholars in different parts of the world. This collection critically assesses some of the key factors impacting upon regeneration initiatives in relation to sport, events and tourism. By doing so, this book assesses if new opportunities have arisen from developments, increasing the demands and needs of locals and tourists, or if transformations result in exclusion – thus challenging who regeneration is for.

This book will be valuable reading for students and academics interested in tourism studies, events planning, sport and leisure studies or development studies, as well as the wider social sciences.

Nicholas Wise is a Senior Lecturer in the Faculty of Education, Health and Community at Liverpool John Moores University. He specialises in international sport, events and tourism studies.

John Harris is Associate Dean of Research in the Glasgow School for Business and Society at Glasgow Caledonian University, Scotland.

Contemporary Geographies of Leisure, Tourism and Mobility
Series Editor: C. Michael Hall, Professor at the Department of Management, College of Business and Economics, University of Canterbury, Christchurch, New Zealand

The aim of this series is to explore and communicate the intersections and relationships between leisure, tourism and human mobility within the social sciences.

It will incorporate both traditional and new perspectives on leisure and tourism from contemporary geography, e.g. notions of identity, representation and culture, while also providing for perspectives from cognate areas such as anthropology, cultural studies, gastronomy and food studies, marketing, policy studies and political economy, regional and urban planning, and sociology, within the development of an integrated field of leisure and tourism studies.

Also, increasingly, tourism and leisure are regarded as steps in a continuum of human mobility. Inclusion of mobility in the series offers the prospect to examine the relationship between tourism and migration, the sojourner, educational travel, and second home and retirement travel phenomena.

For a full list of titles in this series, please visit www.routledge.com/series/SE0522

The series comprises two strands:

Contemporary Geographies of Leisure, Tourism and Mobility aims to address the needs of students and academics, and the titles will be published in hardback and paperback. Titles include:

Routledge Studies in Contemporary Geographies of Leisure, Tourism and Mobility is a forum for innovative new research intended for research students and academics, and the titles will be available in hardback only. Titles include:

Sport, Events, Tourism and Regeneration

Edited by Nicholas Wise and
John Harris

LONDON AND NEW YORK

First published 2017
by Routledge
2 Park Square, Milton Park, Abingdon, Oxon OX14 4RN

and by Routledge
711 Third Avenue, New York, NY 10017

Routledge is an imprint of the Taylor & Francis Group, an informa business

British Library Cataloguing-in-Publication Data
A catalogue record for this book is available from the British Library

Library of Congress Cataloging-in-Publication Data
A catalog record for this book has been requested

ISBN: 978-1-138-64281-2 (hbk)
ISBN: 978-1-315-62972-8 (ebk)

Typeset in Times New Roman
by codeMantra

MIX
Paper from
responsible sources
FSC
www.fsc.org   FSC® C013056

Printed and bound in Great Britain by
TJ International Ltd, Padstow, Cornwall

Contents

List of figures

List of tables

List of contributors

Sixte Abadía is Associate Professor at Ramon Llull University (URL) and researcher at the Research and Innovation Group on Sport and Society (GRIES). Recently, he participated in several editions of the International CESH Congress, European Association for Sociology of Sport (EASS) and Spanish Association of Social Research Applied to Sport (AEISAD).

Alberto Amore is at the University of Canterbury, New Zealand and Università degli Studi di Milano Bicocca, Italy. He recently completed his graduate research on tourism governance in post-earthquake Christchurch. He conducts research on tourism policy and planning, post-disaster regeneration, heritage conservation, tourism governance, and tourism and resilience.

Tanja Armenski is Assistant Professor at the University of Novi Sad, Serbia. Her research areas are destination competitiveness, consumer behavior, cross-cultural studies and applied statistics. She is a member of several research projects, and a member of the organizational board of contemporary trends in tourism, an international scientific meeting.

Brandi Baker is a sociology student at Georgia College & State University. Baker is interested in the role of culture in urban development and her work has been presented at the Southern Sociological Society Conference.

C. Michael Hall is Professor in the Department of Management, Marketing and Entrepreneurship at the University of Canterbury, New Zealand; Docent, Department of Geography, University of Oulu, Finland; and Visiting Professor, Linnaeus University School of Business and Economics, Kalmar, Sweden. He has published widely on tourism, regional studies and environmental change.

Gareth Hall is Senior Lecturer in Social Psychology at Aberystwyth University. His research asks how and why physical cultures and practices including sports participation and spectating impact upon social identities, well-being and quality of life. He is interested in the social impacts sport has on participant and non-participant communities.

John Harris is Associate Dean Research in the Glasgow School for Business and Society at Glasgow Caledonian University, Scotland. He is Leisure and Events Subject Editor for the *Journal of Hospitality, Leisure, Sport and Tourism Education* (JoHLSTE) and author of *Rugby Union and Globalization* (Palgrave Macmillan).

Joan C. Henderson is Associate Professor at Nanyang Business School in Singapore where she teaches on the Tourism and Hospitality Management programme. She has published work in various journals and current research interests include aspects of tourism development in South East Asia and the Middle East.

Christine Herzer is Lecturer and Project Manager in the Institute of Tourism at the Lucerne University of Applied Sciences and Arts. She also leads the Bachelor of Science in Business Administration with Major in Tourism and Mobility. She worked several years in a Swiss sport association focusing on international events.

Jung Woo Lee is Lecturer in Sport and Leisure Policy at the University of Edinburgh. He is associate editor of *Asia Pacific Journal of Sport and Social Science* and a founding member of the Edinburgh Critical Studies in Sport research group. His research interests include sport media/communication, semiotics, mega-event studies and globalisation.

Sangkwon Lee is Assistant Professor in the Department of Kinesiology at Texas Woman's University. His research interests are economic effect of sport, events, tourism development, economic impact analysis, and public subsidy in the sport, events and tourism industry.

Brij Maharaj is an urban political geographer at the University of KwaZulu-Natal, Durban, South Africa, who has received widespread recognition for his research on mega-events and social impacts, segregation, local economic development, xenophobia and human rights, migration and diasporas, and has published over 150 scholarly papers on these themes.

Glenn McCartney is Associate Professor in Hospitality & Gaming Management, University of Macau. His background is in tourism/event management and he supervises the MSc International Integrated Resort Management. Glenn specialises in the marketing and development of Asia's integrated resorts and works with the casino and entertainment industry and related government sectors.

Candace Miller is a sociology student at Georgia College & State University. Miller is interested in urban issues and her work has been presented at the Southern Sociological Society Conference.

Sacra Morejon is Associate Professor at Ramon Llull University (URL) and researcher at the Research and Innovation Group on Sport and Society (GRIES). She is Architect (UPC) and PhD in sports science (URL). Her research focuses on the design of sport facilities and the study of sport and physical activity in the urban space.

Marko Perić, PhD, is Associate Professor and Head of the Department of Management at the Faculty of Tourism and Hospitality Management, University of Rijeka. His fields of interest include strategic management, project management, and sports management. He has co-authored 4 books and over 35 papers on management issues.

Xavier Pujadas is Associate Professor at the Ramon Llull University (Barcelona) and director of Research and Innovation Group on Sport and Society. He specialises in social history of sport and physical activity in contemporary Europe. He is Vice Dean of Graduate Studies and Research at the FPCEE Blanquerna (URL).

Heinz Rütter studied economics at Zurich University focusing on value creation. In 1988, he founded the socio-economic research and consulting company Rütter Soceco AG. Heinz has extensively researched and published in the field of value added- and sector-analysis, regional analysis, economic impact studies, and education as well as innovation and technology policy.

Costas Spirou is Professor of Sociology & Public Administration and Chair of the Department of Government and Sociology at Georgia College & State University. His most recent book *Building the City of Spectacle: Mayor Richard M. Daley and the Remaking of Chicago* (with D. Judd) was published by Cornell University Press.

Jürg Stettler is Head of the Institute of Tourism (ITW), Head of Research and Services and Vice Dean of the Business School at the Lucerne University of Applied Sciences and Arts. Apart from teaching, his activities include heading up research and consulting projects in the areas of sport economy, destination management, leisure and tourism mobility as well as health tourism.

Anna Wallebohr is Research Associate in the Institute of Tourism (ITW) at the Lucerne University of Applied Sciences and Arts (since 2013). Her main tasks at the institute are in the areas of sports tourism as well as analysis of events and health tourism.

Nicholas Wise is a human geographer focusing on sport, events and tourism, looking specifically at social regeneration, sense of place and community. His research focuses primarily on the Balkans and Latin America. His current research looks at social regeneration linked to community change and local impacts.

Introduction

Framing sport, events, tourism and regeneration

Nicholas Wise and John Harris

Why regeneration?

Regeneration is a widely debated holistic concept among social science, development and management scholars (e.g. Spirou, 2011; Smith, 2012; Poynter *et al.*, 2016). The topic has been the focus of research across a range of disciplines. Some studies looked at peoples' outlooks, attitudes, impact and support, whilst other works focus more on economic conditions and encouraging cohesive involvement in communities. The development literature is concerned with spatial planning and transformations (e.g. Jones, 2002; Thornley, 2002), whereas entrepreneurial and management perspectives focus on encouraging people to create new enterprises (Hall, 2006; Richards *et al.*, 2013). There are a number of other broad areas that we could highlight here and the majority of these will be covered within this book. Scholars were identified and invited to contribute to this collection on the basis of their regional expertise and our quest to provide an international and interdisciplinary analysis of regeneration in relation to sport, events and tourism. This collection will demonstrate the extent of current research to consider management agendas, economic development strategy, public policy and social impacts. Moreover, the aim of this book is to stimulate further research into this expanding area of academic study and to identify critical approaches and future challenges linked to an integrated focus on sport, events and tourism-led regeneration strategies.

Forms of niche tourism such as sport tourism or event tourism are becoming increasingly important to help a destination distinguish itself from its competitors in what is often described as an increasingly competitive and global marketplace. Getz (2003, p. 49) noted that "events are a major component of sport tourism." Deery *et al.* (2004) argued that the field of sports tourism and events tourism are part of similar management and planning initiatives, with the difference based on consumer participation and involvement. These fields are gaining popularity because many people seek new experiences and can actively or passively engage in sport as they desire (Perić & Wise, 2015). Weed and Bull (2009) discuss sport tourism as the interaction of activities, people and places. While traveling away from an individual's familiar environment they are attracted to destinations to participate in and/or watch sporting events based on meeting their own demands.

Therefore, regeneration planning needs to meet the demands of consumers by making use of the existing environment and amenities along with seeking ways to benefit and involve local communities.

While accepted definitions of such forms of sport tourism and event tourism exist, the purpose of this collection is to look at the role and impact of regeneration on sport, events and tourism in a more holistic way. Each of the chapters focuses on regeneration in relation to the three areas of sport, events and tourism. When we consider regeneration, in relation to the above, the motive to change spaces and develop new infrastructures, facilities and amenities for sport are often a result of a bid to host or attract an event along with the intention to publicise a destination to increase tourism. Numerous regeneration initiatives have attempted to utilise events based on sport and the promotion of tourism to achieve this goal (see Getz, 2003; Raj & Musgrave, 2009; Smith, 2012), resulting in a range of new enterprise and entrepreneurial opportunities (Hall, 2006; Richards *et al.*, 2013). Enterprise opportunities are especially important as this links to perceived social benefits: employment, training, and a greater sense of well-being. When there are public-led initiatives, they often require private investment. Therefore, the promotion of urban regeneration initiatives has been accompanied by public-private partnerships in a range of different places across the world.

Regeneration is often regarded as the process of change (also referred to as renewal, revitalisation or redevelopment). One of the main motivations of regeneration is to create new opportunities in destinations for investors, stakeholders and local communities. The sport, events and tourism industries are driving regeneration, change and new developments in cities and regions around the world today. Investments in sport, events and tourism in post-industrial cities and wider regions are part of ongoing regeneration strategies linked to transitioning economic bases (Richards & Palmer, 2010; Tallon, 2010; Cowan, 2016). In emerging economies, the approach may be different. Some places may be attempting to regenerate a national image, or develop a new destination using sporting events to attract tourists to diversify and expand other economic activities. Emerging economies such as South Africa and Brazil, two places that are the focus of case studies included in this book, are developing their cities in an attempt to define their place in the international events arena. Given the global endeavours to attract tourists and host sporting events, there is a need to focus on change to keep up with the shifts in demand in the global economy in order for places to maintain a competitive advantage. Moreover, places need to keep up with the pace of global change or they risk stagnation and decline as increased competition is resulting in new products and more opportunities and choice for consumers (Richards & Palmer, 2010; Spirou, 2011; Smith, 2012). There exists an extensive literature focusing on the regeneration of facilities and infrastructures. While it is important to consider physical regeneration, there is a range of subsequent benefits and opportunities brought about through regeneration that considers social impacts, communities and how investments and developments influence how people interact in transformed spaces (e.g. Spirou, 2011; Deery *et al.*, 2012; Richards *et al.*, 2013). The purpose of this book is to bring together a series of chapters addressing interdisciplinary perspectives of regeneration with a particular focus that reflects on the interconnectedness of events, sport and tourism around the globe.

Sport, event and tourism-led development and regeneration in the 1970s, and into the 1980s, was primarily public sector-led using taxpayer money to fund infrastructure projects (Smith, 2012). By the late-1980s, and even more so into the 1990s, public-private partnerships rapidly emerged—thus changing how urban infrastructure projects were funded and financed—resulting in increased profits among private investors (see Smith, 2012; Perić & Wise, 2015). The establishment of partnerships between the public and private sectors resulted in investment clustering. Earlier intentions were to build on the strengths of shared resources and knowledge transfer to contribute added value to a range of sport, events and tourism products being offered and delivered for the purpose of economic regeneration (Rosentraub, 2003). Investing in sport, events and tourism helps with establishing, or enhancing, a destination's reputation. Moreover, these industries are now seen as drivers that add further value to destinations (Smith, 2012), but a number of social issues around notions of inclusion and exclusion are also clearly visible (Minnaert, 2012). Scott (1999) noted that whilst a range of new products are offered and infrastructures upgraded, the facilities and opportunities need to be made available not only to tourists but for local communities as well. There are often suggested or perceived opportunities for local residents to benefit from employment, enterprise and new leisure opportunities, but many developments are not resulting in benefits being as far-reaching as intended (e.g. Curi *et al.*, 2011; Wise, 2016). The extent of private sector financing and (expected) profit margins often conforms to neoliberal agendas—especially in cases that address larger scale events (Hall, 2006). The focus on perceived/ predicted economic impacts therefore overshadows social benefits as destinations and private investors seek to profit on investments. Chalip's (2006) work attempted to shift practical and conceptual perspectives by identifying how social outcomes were leveraged—addressing how communities are impacted and can benefit from change. A number of chapters in this book build on the critical points addressed by the above-mentioned authors who outline impacts and directions of regeneration based on major organisations, policy makers and investors involved in sport, events and tourism directed regeneration.

An outline of the book

This book includes 12 chapters covering international cases and interdisciplinary perspectives. In some chapters, sporting events will be the primary focus with tourism linked to wider discussions. In other chapters, attention is centred on the role of tourism, and the ways sport and events help support urban and regional policy agendas. Another focus is framed around sport tourism and the increasingly important role of events. As noted, while regeneration can refer to physical and tangible change, the chapters in this book focus more on image, policy and intangible impacts that require strategic management agendas that respond to contemporary social, political and economic issues concerning regeneration, change and development. Practices, approaches and understandings differ around the world, and this collection showcases how regeneration approaches and strategies are not prescriptive. An ongoing challenge or situation in South Africa will differ greatly from planning approaches in Middle Eastern countries, and by no means can be assumed to work in Brazil or the United States. Therefore, moving beyond the interdisciplinary nature of this book, the international focus shows how regeneration is approached differently, with cases from North America, South America, Europe, Africa, the Middle East, East Asia and the South Pacific. The chapters in this book address the range of perspectives pertaining to regeneration with the intent to challenge scholars and students to think about regeneration holistically.

Chapter 1 by Joan C. Henderson presents the role of sporting events and tourism on the new images and visions of Middle Eastern destinations, focusing on Abu Dhabi, Dubai and Qatar. Regeneration as discussed in this chapter puts the emphasis on image alongside mega-scale developments and the creation of ultra-modern cities. The dependence issue on oil in the Middle East and the role of mega-events and tourism is driven by the need to diversify industries in these destinations going forward. Henderson argues that prestigious sporting events are both a manifestation and instrument of the contemporary development processes to showcase power and wealth. All too often our perspectives of regeneration direct us towards post-industrial cities devastated by economic restructuring where investments in the sport, event and tourism industries is needed to establish a new economic foundation (Cowan, 2016). However, the Middle East presents us with a different scenario, one where the dominant oil industry has defined the wealth and these destinations, and arguably sporting events and tourism represent a nascent economic base alongside the more dominant industry. Other chapters in this book also frame how emerging and newly established destinations challenge approaches to regeneration. Regeneration in this case and in several of the following chapters addresses widely accepted modernisation and/or destination branding trends. However, there are critical questions around sustainability based on the serious challenges ahead.

Questions of sustainable regeneration are no more prevalent than in the case of Brazil, the focus of Chapter 2. In the last decade Brazil has hosted the 2007 Pan American Games, 2014 Fédération Internationale de Football Association (FIFA) World Cup and 2016 Summer Olympic Games. Nicholas Wise and Gareth Hall recognise that Brazil is already a popular destination in South America, but the country has faced much criticism having just hosted two mega-events. Given the vastness of Brazil, with the country's primary tourism markets oriented to the coast, hosting events and competitions in remote peripheral areas lend to challenges of sustainable regeneration and development. Wise and Hall offer a geographical analysis of Brazil's host cities by addressing notions of scale, core and periphery, followed by a discussion addressing sustainable regeneration and directions for future research following the country's sporting decade. In Chapter 3, Brij Maharaj critically assesses Durban's FIFA 2010 beachfront beautification, especially in terms of its implications for the city's poor. Maharaj argues that the legacy of FIFA 2010 in Durban was the regeneration of the city's beachfront. Durban's beachfront regeneration served as a catalyst for subsequent major investments and to upgrade infrastructures and facilities. However, this chapter highlights how these projects displaced informal traders and subsistence fishermen from the beachfront through efforts to create a more modern beachfront image based on consumption and to promote Durban (and South Africa) as a global destination.

The Incheon Asian Games in 2014 is arguably the most controversial sporting event South Korea has ever hosted. In Chapter 4, Jung Woo Lee notes how hosting the Asian Games is often interpreted as a desperate attempt by Incheon to host a mega-event in order to rebrand the city. Attempts to develop Incheon into a popular destination in Asia left the city with a large economic deficit and a brand new stadium now rarely used. A legacy of the event was Incheon's international sport development programme known as Vision 2014—which created additional financial burden. Incheon, regarded for its strong industrial past and historical tradition, saw this past association overshadowed by contemporary performances of Korean pop culture in the opening and closing ceremonies. This chapter addresses much of the critique and scepticism brought on by the Asian Games considering Incheon's desire to brand a new destination driven by popular culture to attract regional visitors.

In Chapter 5, John Harris looks at the somewhat peculiar place of Cardiff. Cardiff is the capital city of Wales, and is focusing on increasing its international visibility by hosting large-scale sporting events, but is also increasingly visible in sporting events hosted by neighbouring England. The Cardiff Bay project and the ultra-modern Millennium Stadium were at the centre of regenerating the city's infrastructure and image of (post)modernity, driving a new urbanity that promises progress and something for the future of Cardiff. By critically assessing the complex relationship between Wales and England in international sport, Harris uses the work of the cultural theorist Raymond Williams to explore the interplay of sport, events and tourism within a particular locale. Jürg Stettler, Christine Herzer, Anna Wallebohr and Heinz Rütter continue this discussion linking the important role of sporting events and destination promotion by looking at the case of Switzerland in Chapter 6. While the arguments discussed by the authors of this chapter are in line with the two preceding chapters, their conceptual and methodological approach contributes another way of understanding and approaching sport, events and tourism by outlining a calculation model called 'Event-Scorecard' to measure the sustainable and regenerative effects of events. The case of Switzerland looks at both one-time and recurring major sporting events each evaluated using the Event-Scorecard. This approach allows for a comparison of different impacts associated with major sporting events, supported and presented with the 'Event-Management-System' and the 'NIV-concept.' The main focus of this chapter is on the sustainable realisation of event and longer-term legacies, and seeks to better understand what destinations need to do to stay competitive in an increasingly diversified events landscape.

Christchurch, New Zealand was a destination devastated by earthquakes in 2010 and 2011. In Chapter 7, Alberto Amore and C. Michael Hall address the number of challenges and policy issues associated with sport and event-led regeneration strategies following a major natural disaster. City officials began looking at options to develop infrastructures and venues to support leisure and tourism in Christchurch's central business district, the central core of city faced 70% destruction from the earthquakes. The building of a new stadium was contested, but it was encouraged by New Zealand's national government as a way to promote the future of sport and events. Moreover, a stadium acts as an anchor project to promote subsequent economic development. Amore and Hall raise a number of issues associated with the regeneration process and the development of a new stadium, and they offer critical reflection on governance, the policy process and planning practices through a review of policy documents and interviews. Continuing with a focus on policy and recreating an urban destination, Chapter 8, by Costas Spirou, Candace Miller and Brandi Baker, looks at the city of Atlanta. The authors outline the aggressive downtown regeneration efforts by city officials in Atlanta to position the destination as a global city to solidify its standing as the commercial and transportation centre in a rapidly developing region of the United States. Tourism and events were at the forefront of this regeneration policy, with much of the focus on sport linked to new stadia developments for the city's professional sports franchises. Spirou, Miller and Baker focus specifically on the Central Atlanta Progress, the Atlanta Convention and Visitors Bureau and the Atlanta Downtown Improvement District, presented as three interconnected change agents leading Atlanta's ambitious regeneration strategy. They suggest that the outcome for Atlanta has resulted in a socially and economically reconstituted centre.

Chapter 9 by Glenn McCartney continues with a focus on the global prominence of integrated resorts across Asia. This chapter offers insight into the situation in Macao and Singapore more specifically. The Chinese consumer market and their increasing mobility are driving the development of integrated resorts across East Asia, with more integrated resorts hosting vast event portfolios able to attract larger audiences. This increasingly competitive demand guided market is driving service-based regeneration across many destinations that are expecting to see clients staying longer with repeated visitation. In addition, major international event and entertainment companies are using the opportunity to brand their businesses by hosting popular events and sports (such as boxing matches) which are contributing to the appeal and image of integrated resort destinations.

The final three chapters in this book pay particular attention to public policy and social impacts. In Chapter 10, Sacra Morejon, Sixte Abadía and Xavier Pujadas, looking at Barcelona, address the regeneration of certain urban spaces focusing on the impacts of physical activity undertaken within these spaces. The authors argue that urban waterfronts, in particular, are targeted by city planners and policy makers because they are seen as dynamic spaces. In Barcelona, the use of the waterfront has changed over time, and more recent regeneration endeavours have created spaces ideal for sport. The analytical approach is undertaken here to gain an in-depth understanding of regenerative impacts specific to the elements facilitating sport and physical activity, with the intention of informing and promoting the development of similar urban experiences elsewhere in the city. The public authorities responsible for regeneration initiatives have the opportunity to improve the quality of life of urban residents by fostering physical activity. In Chapter 11, Sangkwon Lee recognises that sport, events and tourism are popular catalysts for regeneration in urban areas used to stimulate economic growth. Focusing on five cities in the United States (Arlington, Texas; Cleveland, Ohio; St. Louis, Missouri; Indianapolis, Indiana; and Santa Clara, California), Lee looks at the relationship between sport, events and tourism development and urban regeneration from an economic perspective. There are several levels of scale at play discussed in this chapter based on policies promoted by different levels of government, but each are focused on achieving economic growth. However, the role of public investment plays an important and critical role in such strategies given the economic consequences that impact communities.

In the final chapter of this book, Nicholas Wise, Marko Perić and Tanja Armenski look at regeneration based on insight from tourism managers, planners and stakeholders. By surveying those working to develop the sport industry in Medulin and Pula, Croatia, this chapter attempts to address evolving sports tourism and events strategies following the recent regeneration of sporting venues and facilities. While training facilities have been in operation in Croatia's Istria Region since the 1970s, the upgrading of sports facilities aims to attract more clubs to further develop sports tourism. Croatia is a popular summer destination, and new investments in sport, tourism and events are part of a strategy to promote and attract off-season tourism. Moreover, these industries are an attempt to sustain the destination year-round. This chapter also offers a discussion of potential social impacts that consider encouraging support and more involvement among local residents. A short conclusion brings the collection together and identifies the main themes and looks at future research directions.

References

Chalip, L. (2006). Towards social leverage of sport events. *Journal of sport & tourism*, *11*, 109–127.
Cowan, A. (2016). *A nice place to visit: Tourism and urban revitalization in the postwar rustbelt*. Philadelphia, PA: Temple University Press.
Curi, M., Knijnik, J. & Mascarenhas, G. (2011). The pan American games in Rio de Janeiro 2007: Consequences of a sport mega-event on a BRIC country. *International review for the sociology of sport*, *46*, 140–156.
Deery, M., Jago, L. & Fredline, L. (2004). Sport tourism or event tourism: Are they one and the same? *Journal of sport tourism*, *9*, 235–245.
Deery, M., Jago, L. & Fredline, L. (2012). Rethinking social impacts of tourism research: A new research agenda. *Tourism management*, *33*, 64–73.
Getz, D. (2003). Sport event tourism: Planning, development and marketing. In S. Hudson (Ed.) *Sport and adventure tourism*. New York, NY: Haworth Hospitality Press (pp. 49–85).

Hall, C.M. (2006). Urban entrepreneurship, corporate interests and sports mega-events: The thin policies of competitiveness within the hard outcomes of neoliberalism. *The sociological review, 54*, 59–70.

Jones, C. (2002). The stadium and economic development: Cardiff and the Millennium Stadium. *European planning Studies, 10*, 819–829.

Minnaert, L. (2012). An Olympic legacy for all? The non-infrastructural outcomes of the Olympic Games for socially excluded groups (Atlanta 1996–Beijing 2008). *Tourism management, 33*, 361–370.

Perić, M. & Wise, N. (2015). Understanding the delivery of experience: Conceptualising business models and sports tourism, Assessing two case studies in Istria, Croatia. *Local economy, 30*, 1000–1016.

Poynter, G., Viehoff, V. & Li, Y. (Eds.) (2016). *The London Olympics and urban development: The mega-event city*. London, England: Routledge.

Raj, R. & Musgrave, J. (Eds.) (2009). *Event management and sustainable regeneration*. London, England: CABI.

Richards, G., de Brito, M. & Wilks, L. (Eds.) (2013). *Exploring the social impacts of events*. London, England: Routledge.

Richards, G. & Palmer, R. (2010). *Eventful cities: Cultural management and urban revitalisation*. London, England: Elsevier.

Rosentraub, M. (2003). Indianapolis: A sports strategy and the redefinition of downtown redevelopment. In D. Judd (Ed.) *The infrastructure of play*. New York, NY: M.E. Sharp (pp. 104–124).

Scott, A. (1999). The cultural economy: Geography and the creative field. *Media, culture and society, 21*, 807–817.

Smith, A. (2012). *Events and urban regeneration*. London, England: Routledge.

Spirou, C. (2011). *Urban tourism and urban change*. London, England: Routledge.

Tallon, A. (2010). *Urban regeneration in the UK*. London, England: Routledge.

Thornley, A. (2002). Urban regeneration and sports stadia. *European planning studies, 10*, 813–818.

Weed, M. & Bull, C. (2009). *Sport tourism: Participants, policy and providers* (2nd ed.). Oxford, England: Elsevier/Butterworth Heinemann.

Wise, N. (2016). Outlining triple bottom line contexts in urban tourism regeneration. *Cities, 53*, 30–34.

1 Sports events, tourism, development and regeneration

A perspective from Gulf states of Abu Dhabi, Dubai and Qatar

Joan C. Henderson

Introduction

Sports events can be a major tourist attraction and destinations vie with each other to host what are perceived to be the most prestigious. Events can bring appeal to destinations and have potential to generate new revenue. Competitions and other sporting occasions thus become a tool in tourism development and marketing policies, but are often harnessed to wider strategies and serve social and political as well as economic purposes. These issues are discussed in this chapter with specific reference to the Gulf States of Abu Dhabi and Dubai in the United Arab Emirates (UAE) and Qatar, which have been very active in expanding their programmes of sports events and supporting infrastructure in recent years. They are illuminating instances of small and wealthy globalising states in the Muslim world with ambitious plans for the future where tourism is central. Limited conventional tourism resources have led to heavy investment in new amenities, including events of assorted types and requisite facilities, in a bid to attain and sustain growth. This chapter analyses and compares experiences with regard to sports-related events and tourism. Attention is given to other objectives and the extent to which official interest reflects broader agendas pertaining to development and regeneration and prevailing circumstances at home and overseas. While the cases are distinctive, especially regarding the financial and political power of governments and socio-cultural conditions, their study affords more general insights into the role of sports events in modernising states seeking to assert identities and enhance standing internationally.

Sports events and tourism

Events as a whole are the subject of a growing literature (Mair & Whitford, 2013) and one key form is sports events, which is also an essential component of sports tourism (Weed, 2009), encompassing active and passive modes of participation (Gibson, 2005). Academic and practitioner interest has increased in recent decades as certain events such as the Fédération Internationale de Football Association (FIFA) World Cup have become larger and of greater commercial significance, involving substantial amounts of money and reaching a global audience of millions. Effects are not confined to tourism and premier events are welcomed by authorities as a catalyst of infrastructure and economic development alongside regeneration. A widely studied example is the Olympic Games (Roche, 2006), which are exceptional because of their size and contests of smaller scale may be a more realistic option for many locations, perhaps packaged with complementary entertainment to lengthen visitor stay and spending. Although prestigious sporting tournaments are acknowledged to be a tourism resource with the ability to attract visitors, including recipients of corporate hospitality, there is less agreement about whether actual returns justify the high levels of investment (Weed, 2014). A destination's regular tourism may be disrupted and visitors displaced or discouraged by fears of price hikes and overcrowding. Surpluses of accommodation and venue capacity can result, as well as opportunities for corruption, and funding can be directed away from areas deemed more worthwhile for resident communities (Euromonitor International, 2011). There are additional adverse political, social and environmental impacts to take into account, which confound authoritative conclusions about whether benefits outweigh costs in the tourism and broader economies (Henderson *et al.*, 2010).

Events do not only function as a visitor attraction or strategic economic tool. They are instrumental in place branding, which is now commonly employed by national and subnational administrations (Chalip & Costa, 2005). Moreover, events help transmit officially endorsed representations to foreign and domestic audiences in accordance with aspirations if not realities. China, for example, saw the 2008 Summer Olympics as a vehicle for articulating the country's status as a global leader and bolstering a sense of pride and accomplishment amongst the Chinese people. Authorities in South Africa too allied the 2010 FIFA World Cup to the vision of a land of promise where crime and poverty were diminishing (Cornelissen & Swart, 2006). For newly emerging and less developed countries, a successful bid and event demonstrates and inspires confidence in the financial and other capabilities of government which can yield political capital internally and abroad. It is a reminder that modernisation is occurring, challenging conventional stereotypes, and a sign of membership of the international community (Horne & Manzenreiter, 2006). Events can provide a rationale for environmental improvements and promote the well-being of citizenry by motivating them to take up healthy sports (Preuss, 2007) and such positive legacies are increasingly prominent in hosting bids. Once largely confined to the Western world where destinations were more likely to be able to meet funding and infrastructural demands, events are acquiring a more prominent position in Asia and the Middle East (Weber & Ali-Knight, 2012) as their tourism industries mature and socioeconomic development occurs. Some of the wealthier states in the Gulf have been at the forefront of this movement, exemplified by UAE members and Qatar as recounted below after some background information about the territories in order to set the scene.

The United Arab Emirates and Qatar in context

The UAE lies to the east of Qatar, the southern borders of which have been disputed between the two and adjacent Saudi Arabia. The UAE occupies 83,600 square kilometres, almost all of which is desert, and has a coastline of 64 kilometres. The majority of the population of 7.9 million live on the coast where summer temperatures and humidity can reach 46°C and 100%, respectively, with average rainfall of 42 millimetres. Inland, the desert has cool winters and hot dry summers. Abu Dhabi is the largest of the seven autonomous sheikhdoms, followed by Dubai and Sharjah. Much of the landscape of Qatar, an Arabian Gulf peninsula of 11,251 square kilometres, is also desert with areas of rolling dunes in the southeast and more elevated ground in the northwest. The coastline is sandy and stretches 563 kilometres. Summer temperature too can surpass 45°C, accompanied by humidity of over 85%, but fall to 10°C and 20°C in the winter and yearly precipitation averages 39 millimetres. Most of the population of 2 million reside in the capital of Doha.

Once part of the Ottoman Empire and then a British Protectorate, Qatar rejected affiliation with the UAE on independence and became a republic in 1971. The government has been headed by Sheihk Tamin bin Hamad al-Thani since 2013 when he took over from his father and the family has long been influential in the territory. There is an Advisory Council which is wholly appointed and a cabinet, but these do not have legislative responsibilities and political parties are illegal. The UAE is governed by a Supreme Council comprising all leaders of the families ruling individual emirates, which are granted a degree of autonomy, and the emir of Abu Dhabi (Sheik Khalifa bin Zayed al Nahyan) is the President. The administration also includes an advisory Federal National Council, half of whom are appointed and the remainder elected. Oil and gas industries have catalysed modernisation and urbanisation and citizens had an estimated GDP per capita of $73,266 (all monetary figures in US dollars) in 2015; hydrocarbon deposits are not distributed evenly, however, and Abu Dhabi is the richest (EIU, 2016a). Reserves are also found in Qatar and have given Qataris one of the world's highest GDP per head, at $143,343 in 2015 (EIU, 2016b). There is awareness of the need for economic diversification to lessen reliance on finite supplies of oil and gas; this underlies UAE efforts to develop as a hub for finance, trade, transport and tourism (EIU, 2016a) and the 2030 Qatar National Vision which envisages Qatar as a leading centre for business and finance (EIU, 2016b).While Islamic, levels of orthodoxy vary and Dubai in particular exhibits a cosmopolitanism unusual in the Middle East. The presence of migrant workers from expatriate professionals to manual labourers cannot be overlooked and more than 75% of Dubai's inhabitants and those of Abu Dhabi are from overseas (Henderson, 2014) while only around 12% of Qatar's inhabitants are nationals. Qatari society has traditionally been conservative and adheres to the Wahhabist school of Islam propounded in Saudi Arabia, although an easing of some constraints has been observed in Doha (Henderson, 2015).

Tourism arrivals and attractions

Tourism in the UAE is dominated by Dubai and Abu Dhabi, and an estimated 8.4% of the whole federation's GDP was earned directly and indirectly by the industry in 2014 (World Travel and Tourism Council, 2015a). Dubai's hotel revenue was $6.5 billion for 2014 when foreign hotel guests numbered 11.6 million. Saudi Arabia was the main market followed by India, the United Kingdom, the United States, Iran, Oman, China, Kuwait, Russia and Germany (ETN, 2015). Leisure is the primary reason for visiting and the official website (DTCM, 2015a) divides offerings into three themes of discover (world famous attractions, festivals, events and exhibitions), shop, dine, relax (shopping, cuisine, spas, beach and beach clubs) and see, thrill and play (adventure, sport, entertainment and the arts, nature, heritage and culture). Dubai is a transport hub served by Emirates Airlines, which has an increasingly comprehensive global route network and work underway will raise airport capacity from 60 million passengers to 80 million passengers by 2018 (Dubai Airports, 2015).

Abu Dhabi recorded 3.49 million tourists in 2014, 1 million of whom were from other emirates, and revenues of $272 million. India, the United Kingdom, Germany, China and the United States were other principal generators (The National, 2015). Business travel predominates, yet Visit Abu Dhabi (2015a) promises attractions and landmarks (family, iconic, cultural), experiences and activities (summer season, golf, motor sports and karting, water sports, sports and clubs, tours, cultural experiences, horse riding, activities), shopping and lifestyle (luxury retail, shopping malls, lifestyle and community, centres and bargain outlets, traditional markets and souks) and leisure (wellness and spa, dining, events). It too has a very ambitious airline, Etihad, which is adding new routes and an airport being enlarged to handle 30 million passengers annually by 2017 (Abu Dhabi Airports, 2015).

A total of 2.8 million visited Qatar in 2014 and injected $7.6 billion into the economy, contributing 5.1% of GDP overall (World Travel and Tourism Council, 2015b). Other Gulf Cooperation Council (GCC) members of Bahrain, Kuwait, Oman, Saudi Arabia and the UAE accounted for 40% of the total with 28% from Asia and Oceania and 15% from Europe (Bqdoha, 2015). Business travellers account for most visitors and vacationers make up only 10% of demand (Cighi & Gandhi, 2011). Advertised leisure attractions are outdoor pursuits, entertainment, dining, shopping and sightseeing at natural and cultural heritage locations (QTA, 2015a). Doha is the centre of activity and its modern cityscape is a striking illustration of Gulf urban transformation (Rizzo, 2013). It is the place of entry for most air passengers and the airport, base for the rapidly expanding Qatar Airways, has become a stopover and transit point. Airport capacity recently was augmented to 30 million passengers annually and was planned to reach 50 million in the next phase, although the 2015 deadline was not met (Civil Aviation Authority, 2015).

Tourism policy making

There is a National Council of Tourism Antiquities, dating from 2009, which represents the UAE collectively under the slogan of 'Seven Emirates One Destination.' It acts as a coordinator and supports expansion alongside conservation (NCTA, 2015). Promotion and development are largely carried out at an emirate level by the Abu Dhabi Authority for Tourism and Culture (TCA), formed in 2012 by a merger between tourism and culture agencies, and the Department of Tourism and Commerce Marketing in Dubai which had its origins in the late 1980s. The latter's vision is of Dubai as a "leading destination for global travel, business and events by 2020" with an economy strengthened by tourist spending and inward investment (DTCM, 2015b). For the TCA, the goal is "evolution into a world-class, sustainable destination which makes a unique contribution to the global cultural landscape while conserving its singular character and ecosystem" (TCA, 2015). Tourism is an ingredient of wider development strategies and features in Abu Dhabi's 2030 Economic Vision (Abu Dhabi Council for Economic Development, 2008) and Dubai's 2021 Strategic Plan (The Executive Council, 2014), the latter also possessing a Tourism Vision 2020 (DTCM, 2015c).

Amongst common elements are emphasis on business and higher-end leisure travellers as well as education and healthcare, but Abu Dhabi is distinguished by an interest in culture. This is demonstrated by the new Zayed National Museum and branches of the Guggenheim and Louvre under construction and designed by star architects (Ponzini, 2011; McClellan, 2012). Dubai's approach has been described as one of "bigger, better, brasher" (Stephenson & Ali-Knight, 2010, p. 280) evidenced by large-scale purpose-built attractions such as shopping malls and theme parks. The Mall of the World is one of several ongoing projects and slated to have the "world's largest mall, largest indoor park, cultural theatres and wellness resorts" with over 100 hotels in an area of 740,000 square metres (Dubai Holding, 2014). The staging of the 2020 World Expo is stimulating new development, the government allotting $8 million to related infrastructure (HSBC Global Connections, 2014), in pursuit of a targeted 20 million tourists that year (Euromonitor International, 2015).

The Qatar Tourism Authority (QTA) was founded in 2007 to promote the country as a "quality tourism destination for leisure, business, education and sports" (QTA, 2015b). These markets are referred to in a 2004 tourism master plan which highlights the importance of luxury travellers (Akkawi, 2010). Spending has correspondingly taken place and the government is reported to have allocated $20 billion to the tourism sector in the period 2008–2014 (Khodr, 2012). Qatar is eager to stress its role as a centre of learning and diplomacy as well as business (Rizzo, 2013), investing in conference facilities and attracting foreign universities. Attention has also been given to cultural amenities and regional and global marketing (Euromonitor International, 2012, 2013). Projects worth $8.48 million are currently in progress and include a convention centre, shopping mall, museum and marina (Bqdoha, 2015). The industry is acknowledged to play a part in economic diversification and thereby attainment of the National Vision.

The pro-tourism stances of governments and their willingness and ability to spend on physical plants are major factors underlying the recent expansion in tourism in Abu Dhabi, Dubai and Qatar (Euromonitor International, 2014). Limitations of climate and inhospitable terrain have been partially overcome and cities have been erected which are "monuments of modernity, progress and national prestige" (Khalaf, 2006, p. 257), the outcome of what Adham (2009, p. 218) terms a "confluence of strategies of consumerism, entertainment and global tourism." Dubai has been a pioneer in the process of destination development (Henderson, 2006), engaging also in aggressive marketing which reaches out beyond the region. The emirate has thus become something of a model, the successes of which other states may seek to emulate. However, and while there are ambitious plans for the future in all three instances, questions of long-term sustainability arise and continued investment is required if manmade attractions are to retain their appeal to first-time and repeat visitors. Funding in the UAE is heavily dependent on credit and real estate markets, which could have destabilising consequences for economies at large (Euromonitor International, 2014). The effect was apparent in Dubai after the global financial crisis which commenced in 2008 when many schemes were interrupted. Analysts have warned of cost over-runs, a surplus of property and heavy debt burdens in the case of the 2020 World Expo compounded by the dramatic slump in oil prices which commenced in 2014 and is expected to be prolonged.

Other shortcomings are discernible pertaining to destination attributes and tourism policies. For example, Qatar is given a low score for its natural and cultural resources in the World Economic Forum's travel and tourism competitiveness index (World Economic Forum, 2015). It is rated 43 out of 141 globally and limited knowledge of the place internationally is another possible drawback. The country may have negative associations related to human rights issues, religious dictates and regional uncertainties (Morakabati *et al.*, 2014). I will return to these issues in the section on the World Cup. Although concerns about political stability and threats to personal safety do not seem to have had a significant impact on arrivals yet, the activities of groups such as ISIS are a cause of anxiety in Qatar and the UAE. The UAE was placed 24th in the World Economic Forum index, but it too does not possess an abundance of outstanding heritage and the harsh climate at certain periods is a deterrent. Like Qatar, Abu Dhabi and Dubai have focused on affluent visitors in a manner which has resulted in an imbalanced accommodation stock. Length of stay is relatively short at 3.5 nights in Qatar (Travel Weekly, 2014), 3.4 nights for hotels and 5.7 in the hotel apartment favoured by Arabian visitors in Dubai (HSBC Global Connections, 2014) and just over 3 nights in Abu Dhabi (Gulf News, 2014) in 2013. There is also mounting competition from nearby and distant alternative destinations, as well as each other, and rivalry is manifest in the field of sports events programmes which are now considered.

Sports events in Abu Dhabi, Dubai and Qatar

Opportunities for visitors to participate in and watch sports are highlighted in the Abu Dhabi marketing as observed earlier. Perhaps the premier event is the Formula 1 Etihad Airways Abu Dhabi Grand Prix, which was inaugurated in 2008 and is billed as the "world's only twilight race," distinguished from Singapore's night race. Over 60,000 spectators attended in 2014 when the race was accompanied by satellite events such as pop concerts (Visit Abu Dhabi, 2015b).

The airline sponsors several Abu Dhabi sports associations as well as a number overseas; for example, Manchester City Football Club. A noteworthy occasion is the Mubadala World Tennis Championship, which takes its name from the sponsoring government-owned strategic investment company. It is a men's singles professional exhibition tournament attended by top players, the winner receiving $250,000 in 2015. The venue is Zayed Sports City, which was built in the 1980s and remains the main stadium. The Abu Dhabi Sports Council, the Chairman of which is the Crown Prince, recently entered into a partnership with the International Triathlon Union (ITU) whereby the emirate will be the location of the season opener from 2015 to 2019. It also backed the 2015 Abu Dhabi Tour, part of the men's professional cycling calendar—making reference in announcements to the intention that these occasions will stimulate popular engagement in sport. The tourism authorities were instrumental in initiating the five-day motor sports Abu Dhabi Desert Challenge, endorsed by the FIM (International Motorcycle Federation) and FIA (World Motor Sport Council), and the Class-1 and UIM Formula 1 Powerboat World Championship.

Dubai is commended by officials for its sports culture, embracing residents and tourists, which is marked by the growing number of sports federations (Dubai Sports Council, 2015) and a 20-page Sports Events Guide to happenings throughout the year (Government of Dubai & Dubai Sports Council, 2015). There is an active Sports Council and an Events Division in the DTCM also explores hosting possibilities. A popular venue is the 25,000 seat Dubai Sports City stadium at the heart of the $6 billion Sports City complex, the full completion of which was delayed by post-2008 financial uncertainties (Smith, 2010). Another site is The Sevens, home to the Emirates Airlines Dubai Rugby Sevens, which is owned and operated by the airline and accommodates 50,000 while the Meydan Racecourse can hold 60,000 and includes a luxury hotel and IMAX theatre (Government of Dubai & Dubai Sports Council, 2015). Regular competitions drawing the world's leading players are the Association of Tennis Professionals (ATP) Dubai Duty Free Tennis Championship, with a winner's prize of $505,000 in 2015, and golf's Omega Dubai Desert Classic which had prize money of $2.65 million in 2015. The World Cup horse race is touted as the largest and most expensive globally with a total purse in 2015 of around $10 million and Dubai hosts the annual FINA Swimming World Cup. The International Cricket Council (ICC) has its headquarters in Dubai and the Pakistan cricket team is based in the UAE for security reasons so that home internationals are staged in both Dubai and Abu Dhabi. Provision is not confined to formal competitions as illustrated by the friendly football match in late 2014 between AC Milan and Real Madrid, which was arranged by the DTCM and Emirate Airlines, the latter the sponsor of the famous European clubs as it is of Arsenal's stadium in London.

Sports tourism policy in Qatar is perhaps the most ambitious of those of all the Gulf States with an interest in the field (Foley *et al.*, 2012). Its priority is indicated in the work of the QTA which boasts of attracting the "biggest sporting events in the world" and government investment of $2.8 billion in athletic competition infrastructure (QTA, 2015c). The Asian Games is the second largest such assembly after the Summer Olympics and Qatar was the first Middle East country to hold it in 2006 with a budget of $28 billion (Khodr, 2012). The 2016 and 2020 Summer Olympics bids failed, but securing the 2022 FIFA World Cup, which is discussed in the next section, has been critical to positioning as a sports tourism destination. The Arabian Drag Racing League, Horse Games, Islamic Triathlon Championship, Asian Football Confederations Asia Cup and Pan Arab Games in 2011 in addition to camel racing are amongst events with a regional or Asian focus. More international events include the 2010 IAAF (International Association of Athletics Federations) World Indoor Championship, Qatar Masters which is part of the European professional golf tour and ATP Qatar Open (with a champion's prize of $195,000). A major venue is Qatar Sports City (or ASPIRE Zone), which has athletics, entertainment, other recreation and wellness facilities and was built for the 2006 Asian Games. Its objectives, apparent in the name, are to inspire local athletes as well as those from overseas representing Qatar to perform better (Campbell, 2010; Smith, 2010) and encourage citizens to exercise, which is regarded as critical in view of the incidence of obesity and physical unfitness (Brannagan & Giulianotti, 2015).

The 2022 FIFA World Cup

The awarding of 2022 FIFA World Cup rights to Qatar in late 2010 was vital to efforts to brand itself as a premier sports events destination. It also justified investment in the installation of extensive and expensive amenities and infrastructure, the intended purposes of which transcend the competition. The event can therefore be regarded as a key instrument of planned development and regeneration, central to the strategy of modernising Qatar and raising its international profile in general as well as boosting the tourism industry in particular. However, the award has proved highly controversial and revealed the challenges concomitant upon such hosting (Henderson, 2016). There have been allegations that bidding procedures were marred by bribery and corruption involving officials from FIFA which the organisation has found difficult to refute (Pielke, 2013), especially in light of subsequent enquiries and disclosures, tarnishing the sport's governing body and the event. Qatar's weather rendered it an unexpected choice as aforementioned summer conditions could be life threatening to players and extremely uncomfortable for spectators. Authorities promised that stadia would be furnished with solar-powered cooling, but there was some scepticism about its effectiveness (Sofotasiou *et al.*, 2015) and a decision was taken in early 2014 to move the event to November-December. Alcohol is another problem given that consumption is prohibited by the Islamic Sharia Law applying in Qatar, although it is available to non-Muslims through strictly regulated schemes. World Cup fans travelling to Qatar are likely to anticipate drinking and there have again been formal assurances about provision. However, details about practical arrangements have not been released and there are possibilities of resistance from more conservative elements in the administration and offended citizens who shun alcohol and spaces where it is imbibed (Dun, 2014).

An additional topic of controversy has been the welfare of the migrant labourers upon whom the construction industry relies and who are building the new arenas and supporting infrastructure. They come primarily from less developed South Asian nations and work very long shifts throughout the year for relatively low pay, surrendering their passports to employers under the kafala system. The agencies that have recruited them charge substantial fees and the men are often accommodated in poorly maintained dormitories away from the public gaze. While health and safety laws exist, these are not necessarily enforced and workers risk being exploited (Human Rights Watch, 2012). Some steps to better protect the workforce have been taken by the Supreme Committee responsible for the World Cup, but human rights campaigners have dismissed these as inadequate (The Guardian, 2016). The regime has also been heavily criticised for its authoritarianism, treatment of women and homosexuals, and links to certain militant Islamic groups. The stories suggest how much of Western reporting of the FIFA World Cup has been antagonistic and not always about football (Dun, 2014), leaving officials unused to public censure struggling to handle communications (Dorsey, 2015).

There has been less debate about the ability of Qatar to fund and execute the physical development demanded by World Cup hosting, although government revenue has declined in parallel with slumping oil prices. There has been speculation about cutbacks in spending on World Cup infrastructure, but this is likely to be privileged over other areas because of the importance attached to the event's success (EIU, 2016b). Development planned is indicative of the potential for mega-events to change and perhaps enhance the built environment. In its bidding documents, Qatar proposed constructing eight and upgrading four existing stadia across seven host cities with total costs of $3 billion. The new arenas are designed to be dismantled and donated to less developed countries. Road and railway improvements are part of the plan, notably a metro designed to relieve overcrowding and reduce dependence on the car as well as serve World Cup venues (Furlan & Faggion, 2015). These are complemented by airport expansion and the World Cup has been a catalyst for other public and private sector projects (Cighi & Gandhi, 2011; Scharfenort, 2012). Work started in late 2011 and 40–60 hotels are also set to open in the years leading up to the event (Euromonitor International, 2013). They hope for tourism returns that are an influx of between 500,000 and 700,000 visitors, which will boost annual arrivals to 3.5–4 million, greater awareness of Qatar as a destination, and widening of the market (Skift, 2015).

Summary and conclusion

The perceived capacity of sports events to act as an agent of development and regeneration in both tangible and more intangible forms is conveyed in Khodr's (2012) comments about Qatar. She writes of a policy driven by "economic sustainability and diversification, tourism image and branding" alongside "development of the society, globalisation and modernisation and regional competition"

(Khodr, 2012, p. 89). The largest events necessitate expenditure on structures and infrastructure directly and indirectly related to the occasion which contributes to the transformation of the physical landscape in and outside cities; in turn, this is believed to benefit various economic sectors, including tourism. Greater leisure opportunities are afforded to citizens, cultivating healthier lifestyles so that development and regeneration may occur at a more personal level. Amongst wider goals which also have development and regeneration implications are the amassing of soft power whereby size does not prevent small countries from being respected international community members that are globally influential (Grix & Lee, 2013; Ginesta & San Eugenio, 2014; Brannagan & Giulianotti, 2015). Championship sports events, many of which organisers strive to endow with an aura of glamour and sophistication, additionally inspire favourable images. These counter stereotypical ideas of the Middle East as a region given over to turbulence and religious fanaticism, disseminating officially sanctioned impressions of an Arab world in which localising and globalising forces meet and the traditional and modern comfortably coexist (Fox *et al.*, 2006).

Abu Dhabi, Dubai and Qatar have been shown to possess certain advantages regarding sports events tourism such as government support, wealth and access to sponsorship, high quality accommodation and connections by air to the rest of the world. Ruling families exercise power unconstrained by political opposition or electorate opinion which enables rapid decision making and accelerated infrastructural construction, even if condemned by some outsiders as anti-democratic (Hvidt, 2009). Disadvantages are the weather, inhibiting outdoor activities in summer so that events are best held in winter or indoors, and shortage of mid-price and budget hotels. Hosting very large events also draws attention to the states' dictatorial and Islamic aspects, as well as position in a zone of some instability and insecurity, which might deter potential tourists and especially those from longer haul markets. There is a chance of clashes between the secular and hedonist attitudes and behaviour of visitors connected to the event and the religious and conservative principles and practices of the host community.

Rapid urbanisation and the pace of development overall is another concern with possible adverse environmental and social consequences unless properly managed. Despite a commitment to urban planning (Abu Dhabi Urban Planning Council, 2007; Qatar Foundation, 2013), there are deficiencies in execution. Sprawling and fragmented spaces are being created comprising monumental buildings of an international character without reference to local identities. The private car tends to dominate and there is serious traffic congestion. Any remaining built heritage is at risk and cities are in danger of losing their attractiveness to residents and tourists as they become less liveable (Elsheshtawy, 2008; Viewpoints, 2010; Salama & Wiedman, 2013). Unprecedented matters of financial barriers to government policy implementation may also arise in the future because of shrinking oil revenues; for example, Qatar recorded its first deficit in 15 years in 2016 and analysts have spoken of the 'end of a golden era' for oil-rich states (EIU, 2016b). The implicit social contract by which citizens have acceded to authoritarian rule in return for the material gains supplied could thus come under pressure if the latter are significantly curtailed, engendering political and social as well as economic uncertainties.

With regard to the tourism function of sports events specifically, whether tourists from the Middle East and beyond share official enthusiasm for Gulf sports events is unclear. More research is required into their capacity to motivate visitation, together with popularity amongst residents, to allow proper assessment. One evaluation incorporating Qatar and the 2006 Asian Games estimates that domestic tourist expenditure fell by 16.5% in 2006 and by 16.8% the following year while incoming tourism receipts dropped by 20.9% and 17.8%, respectively (Euromonitor International, 2011). Expectations of the value of sports events in boosting tourist arrivals and advancing the wider goal of diversification of the economy and reduced reliance on the hydrocarbon industries may thus be over-optimistic. Financial rewards were perhaps less of a consideration in the past for these prosperous countries engaged in erecting ultra-modern cityscapes, but have now become more urgent during times of volatile oil prices. Although still wealthy and contrasting markedly in circumstances and experiences, they may be moving closer to the stance of some urban authorities in Europe and North America where events are viewed as a means of reversing decline and revitalising ageing infrastructure and deprived inner city cores.

It seems likely that sports events will continue to be given a relatively high priority in Abu Dhabi, Dubai and Qatar as their tourism industries evolve and development and regeneration proceeds. Nevertheless, the success of the strategy within a tourism context and beyond is not guaranteed and the states are exposed to new internal and external economic, social and political forces which are unpredictable in operation and effects. Conditions merit ongoing study and the subject is a rich field for further enquiry in pursuit of a better understanding of the dynamics of sports events and tourism—particularly in the Gulf States.

References

Abu Dhabi Airports. (2015). Overview. http://www.adac.ae/ebglish/capital-development/development/overview.

Abu Dhabi Council for Economic Development. (2008). *The Abu Dhabi economic vision 2030*. Abu Dhabi: Abu Dhabi Council for Economic Development.

Abu Dhabi Urban Planning Council. (2007). *Plan Abu Dhabi 2030. Urban structure framework plan*. Abu Dhabi: Urban Planning Council.

Adham, K. (2009). Rediscovering the island: Doha's urbanity from pearls to spectacle. In Y. Elshestawy (Ed.) *The evolving Arab city: Tradition, modernity and urban development*. London, England: Routledge (pp. 218–257).

Akkawi, M.H. (2010). Resident attitudes towards tourism development in conservative cultures: The case of Qatar (Unpublished MA thesis). Waterloo: University of Waterloo.

Bqdoha. (2015). Tourism adds USD7.6 billion to Qatar's economy. http://www.bqdoha.com/2015/03/tourism-in-qatar.

Brannagan, P.M. & Giulianotti, R. (2015). Soft power and soft disempowerment: Qatar, global sports and football's 2022 World Cup finals. *Leisure studies, 34,* 703–719.

Campbell, R. (2010). Staging globalisation for national projects: Global sports markets and elite athletic transnational labour in Qatar. *International review for the sociology of sport, 46,* 45–60.

Chalip, L. & Costa, C.A. (2005). Sport event tourism and the destination brand: Towards a general theory. *Sport in society, 8,* 218–237.

Cighi, C.I. & Gandhi, H. (2011). *Qatar: The race for 2022.* Dubai: HVS.

Civil Aviation Authority. (2015). About CAA. http://www.caa.gov.qa/en/about-caa.

Cornelissen, C. & Swart, K. (2006). The 2010 Football World Cup as a political construct: The challenge of making good on an African promise. *Sociological Review, 54,*108–123.

Dorsey, J.M. (2015). How Qatar is its own worst enemy. *The international journal of the history of sport, 32,* 422–439.

DTCM. (2015a). Discover. http://www.visitdubai.com/en/discover.

DTCM. (2015b). About us. http://www.visitdubai.com/en/department-of-tourism_new/about-dtcm.

DTCM. (2015c). Tourism Vision 2020. http://www.visitdubai.com/en/department-of-tourism_new/about-dtcm/tourism-vision-2020.

Dubai Airports. (2015). Dubai airports strategic plan 2020. http://www.dubaiairports.ae/corporate/media-centre/fact-sheets.

Dubai Holding. (2014). Mohammed Bin Rashid launches Mall of the World, a temperature-controlled pedestrian city in Dubai, Press Release. http://dubaiholding.com/media-centre/press-releases/2014/407.

Dubai Sports Council. (2015). About sports and tourism. http://www.dubaisportscouncil.ae/en/sportsandtourism/Pages.

Dun, S. (2014). No beer, no way! Football fan identity enactment won't mix with Muslim beliefs in the Qatar 2022 World Cup. *Journal of policy research in tourism, 6,* 186–199.

EIU. (2016a). *Country report United Arab Emirates.* London, England: Economist Intelligence Unit.

EIU. (2016b). *Country report Qatar.* London, England: Economist intelligence unit.

Elsheshtawy, Y. (Ed.) (2009). *The evolving Arab city: Tradition, modernity and urban development.* London, England: Routledge.

ETN. (2015). Dubai hotels welcomed 11.6 million guests in 2014. http://www.eturbonews.com/56211/dubai-hotels-welcomed-116-million-gests-2014.

Euromonitor International. (2011). *Sports and mega-events tourism: Big rewards but high risks.* London, England: Euromonitor International.

Euromonitor International. (2012). *City travel briefing: Doha.* London, England: Euromonitor International.

Euromonitor International. (2013). *Travel and tourism in Qatar.* London, England: Euromonitor International.

Euromonitor International. (2014). *Travel and tourism in the United Arab Emirates.* London, England: Euromonitor International.

Euromonitor International. (2015). *City travel briefing: Dubai.* London, England: Euromonitor International.

Foley, M., McGillivray, D. & McPherson, G. (2012). Policy pragmatism: Qatar and the global events circuit. *International journal of events and festival management, 3,* 101–115.

Fox, J.W., Mourtada-Sabbah, N. & al-Mutawa, M. (2006). The Arab Gulf region: Traditionalism globalised or globalisation traditionalised? In J.W. Fox, N. Mourtada-Sabbah & M. al-Mutawa (Eds.) *Globalisation and the Gulf.* London, England: Routledge (pp. 3–31).

Furlan, R. & Faggion, L. (2015). The development of vital precincts in Doha: Urban regeneration and socio-cultural factors. *American journal of environmental engineering, 5,* 120–129.

Gibson, H. (2005). Sports tourism: Concepts and theories. An introduction. *Sport in society, 8,* 133–141.

Ginesta, X. & San Eugenio, J. (2014). The use of football as a country branding strategy. Case study: Qatar and the Catalan sports press. *Communication and sport, 2,* 225–241.

Government of Dubai and Dubai Sports Council. (2015). *Dubai sports events guide 2015.* www.dubaisc.ae.

Grix, J. & Lee, D. (2013). Soft power, sports mega-events and emerging states: The lure of the politics of attraction. *Global society, 27,* 521–536.

Gulf News. (2014). Abu Dhabi hotel guests up 30% from January to May. http://gulfnews.com/business/sectors/tourism/abu-dhabi-hotel-guests-up-30-from-january-to-may-1.1354050.

Henderson, J.C. (2006). Tourism in Dubai: Overcoming barriers to destination development. *International journal of tourism research, 8,* 87–99.

Henderson, J.C. (2014). Global Gulf cities and tourism: A review of Abu Dhabi, Doha and Dubai. *Tourism recreation research, 39,* 107–114.

Henderson, J.C. (2015). The development of tourist destinations in the Gulf: Oman and Qatar compared. *Tourism planning and development, 12,* 350–361.

Henderson, J.C. (2016). Hosting the 2022 FIFA World Cup: Opportunities and challenges for Qatar. *Journal of sport and tourism, 19,* 281–298.

Henderson, J.C., Foo, K., Lim, H. & Yip, S. (2010). Sports events and tourism: The Singapore Formula One Grand Prix. *International journal of event and festival management, 1,* 60–73.

Horne, J. & Manzenreiter, W. (Eds.) (2006). *Sports mega-events: Social scientific analyses of a global phenomenon.* Oxford, England: Blackwell.

HSBC Global Connections. (2014). Trends in Dubai's tourism industry. https://globalconnections.hsbc.com/uae/en/articles/trends-dubais-tourism-industry.

Human Rights Watch. (2012). *Building a better World Cup; protecting migrant workers in Qatar ahead of FIFA 2022.* Washington, DC: Human Rights Watch.

Hvidt, M. (2009). The Dubai model: An outline of key development-process elements in Dubai. *International journal of Middle East studies, 41,* 397–418.

Khalaf, S. (2006). The evolution of the Gulf city type, oil and globalisation. In J.W. Fox, N. Mourtada-Sabbah & M. al-Mutawa (Eds.) *Globalisation and the Gulf.* London, England: Routledge (pp. 244–265).

Khodr, H. (2012). Exploring the driving factors behind the event strategy in Qatar: A case study of the 15th Asian Games. *International journal of event and festival management, 3,* 81–100.

Mair, J. & Whitford, M. (2013). An exploration of events research: Event topics, themes and emerging trends. *International journal of events and festival management, 4*(1), 6–30.

McClellan, A. (2012). Museum expansion in the twenty-first century: Abu Dhabi. *Journal of curatorial studies, 1,* 271–293.

Morakabati, Y., Beavis, J. & Fletcher, J. (2014). Planning for a Qatar without oil: Tourism and economic diversification, a battle of perceptions. *Tourism planning and development, 11,* 415–434.

NCTA. (2015). Patterns of tourism: National Council of Tourism and Antiquities. http://www.uaetourism.ae/web/guest/patterns-of-tourism.

Pielke, R. (2013). How can FIFA be held accountable? *Sport management review, 16,* 255–267.

Ponzini, D. (2011). Large scale development projects and star architecture in the absence of democratic politics: The case of Abu Dhabi, UAE. *Cities, 28,* 251–259.

Preuss, H. (2007). The conceptualisation and measurement of mega sporting event legacies. *The journal of sport and tourism, 12,* 207–227.

Qatar Foundation. (2013). Realising a vision to develop a sustainable future. http://www.qf.org.qa/content/qf-telegraph/issue-99.

QTA. (2015a). Things to do. http://www.qatartourism.gov.qa/.

QTA. (2015b). Qatar Tourism Authority. http://portal.www.gov.qa/wps/portal/directory/agency/qatarourismauthority.

QTA. (2015c). Sports. http://www.qatartourism.gov.qa/en-us/thingstodo/activities/sports.aspx.

Rizzo, R. (2013). City profile: Metro Doha. *Cities, 31,* 533–543.

Roche, M. (2006). Mega-events and modernity revisited: Globalisation and the case of the Olympics. *Sociological review, 54,* 25–40.

Salama, A.M. & Wiedman, F. (2013). *Demystifying Doha: On architecture and urbanism in an emerging city.* Farnham, England: Ashgate.

Scharfenort, N. (2012). Urban development and social change in Qatar: The Qatar national vision 2030 and the 2022 FIFA World Cup. *Journal of Arabian studies, 2,* 209–230.

Skift. (2015). Interview: Qatar's tourism chairman positions his country for big growth. http://skift.com/2015/01/20/interview-how-qatars-tourism-chairman-positions-his-small-country-for-big-growth.

Smith, A. (2010). The development of sports city zones and their potential value as tourism resources for urban areas. *European planning studies, 18,* 385–410.

Sofotasiou, P., Hughes, B.R. & Calautit, J.K. (2015). Qatar 2022: Facing the FIFA World Cup climatic and legacy challenges. *Sustainable cities and society, 14,* 16–30.

Stephenson, M. & Ali-Knight, J. (2010). Dubai's tourism industry and its societal impact: Social implications and sustainable challenges. *Journal of tourism and cultural change, 8*(4), 278–292.

TCA. (2015). Abu Dhabi Tourism and Culture Authority: About us. http://tcaabudhabi.ae/en/about/Pages/about-us.aspx.

The Executive Council. (2014). *2021 Dubai plan.* Dubai: The Executive Council.

The Guardian. (2016). FIFA faces 'tough decision' over Qatar World Cup if human rights abuses continue, 14 April. http://www.theguardian.com/football/2016/apr/14/fifa-qatar-world-cup-report.

The National. (2015). Abu Dhabi visitor numbers expected to keep growing. 15 February.

Travel Weekly. (2014). WTM: Qatar Tourism Authority hails trade support. http://www.travelweekly.co.uk/Articles/PFDetails/50994.

Viewpoints. (2010). Architecture and urbanism in the Middle East. Special edition. http://www.mideasti.org.

Visit Abu Dhabi. (2015a). See and do. http://www.visitabudhabi.ae/en/see.and.do.

Visit Abu Dhabi. (2015b). Formula 1 Etihad Airways Abu Dhabi Grand Prix. http://www.visitabudhabi.ae/en/see.and.do/leisure/events/2015.

Weber, K. & Ali-Knight, J. (2012). Events and festivals in Asia and the Middle East/North Africa (MENA) region: Opportunities and challenges. *International journal of event and festival management, 3,* 4–8.

Weed, M. (2009). Progress in sports tourism research? A meta-review and exploration of futures. *Tourism management, 30,* 615–628.

Weed, M. (2014). After 20 years, what are the big questions for sports tourism research? *Journal of sport and tourism, 19*, 1–4.

World Economic Forum. (2015). *The travel and tourism competitiveness report 2015.* Geneva, Switzerland: World Economic Forum.

World Travel and Tourism Council. (2015a). *Travel and tourism economic impact 2014 UAE.* London, England: World Travel and Tourism Council.

World Travel and Tourism Council. (2015b). *Travel and tourism economic impact 2014 Qatar.* London, England: World Travel and Tourism Council.

2 Transforming Brazil

Sporting mega-events, tourism, geography and the need for sustainable regeneration in host cities

Nicholas Wise and Gareth Hall

Introduction

The relationship between sporting mega-events, host cities and regeneration has developed a burgeoning cross-disciplinary literature. Discussions are almost entirely shaped by potential legacies of mega-events, including increased sports participation, social benefits though transformation, and economic returns on investments by host nations and cities. Much work has looked primarily at Western developed nations but a shift in hosting mega-events is turning attention to developing emerging economy countries. Broadly, however, there are still no satisfactory conclusions for clear positive development and legacies that occur for nations or cities hosting sporting mega-events (Coakley & Souza, 2013), but it is important to look at and compare situations in the cities that host events. Yet, sporting mega-events are legitimate strategies and catalysts for social and economic development in emerging economies such as India, China, South Africa and Brazil (Curi *et al.*, 2011; Darnell, 2012). Moreover, such events serve to enhance these nation's power, economic competitiveness, and prestige in global relations (Maharaj, 2015) with the presumed outcome of attracting international investment, positive media and increased tourism (Curi *et al.*, 2011; Coakely & Souza, 2013).

Until 2007, Brazil had not hosted any mega or major international sporting events since the 1950 Fédération Internationale de Football Association (FIFA) World Cup and the 1963 Pan American Games. The 44-year hiatus ended following a series of successful bids to host the 2007 Pan American Games and the 2014 FIFA World Cup. The 2016 Summer Olympics in Rio de Janeiro closed out Brazil's sporting decade (see Gaffney, 2010; Reis *et al.*, 2013). Given Brazil's success in being awarded recent hosting rights for one sporting major-event and two mega-events, it comes as no surprise then to see to an emerging (English-language) literature addressing a number of critical impacts including development and regeneration (e.g. Reis *et al.*, 2013; de Menezes & de Souza, 2014; Millington & Darnell, 2014; Maiello & Pasquinelli, 2015; Gaffney, 2016; Wise, 2017). While Brazil is already regarded as a popular tourism destination in South America, the hosting of two sporting mega-events is expected to increase the nation's exposure internationally and physically develop or regenerate cities across the country with renovated or new sports facilities and venues – including new amenities for tourism. The aim is to make Brazil a more competitive destination in the global events arena and increase mobility to the country and within. Given the vastness of Brazil as a country and with the primary tourism markets oriented to the coast, hosting events and competitions in remote peripheral areas lend to challenges of sustainable regeneration and development. Past and on-going development initiatives in Brazil focus on developing cities and regions away from the coast as part of the country's attempt to modernise peripheral cities and regions (see Clawson, 2011). A key challenge here concerns the social, environmental and economic sustainability of peripheral regions if they are exposed to rapid increases in industries such as events and tourism. It can be a challenge to host mega-events in peripheral regions due to transportation and supplementary services that are needed may suffer later if the short-term demand has no long-term impact. This chapter offers a geographical analysis of 2014 FIFA World Cup and 2016 Summer Olympics host cities by addressing notions of scale, core and periphery, followed by discussions addressing sustainable regeneration and directions for future research in Brazil during this time.

Sport and geography, core and periphery

Mega-events are described as large-scale mass cultural gatherings attracting a significant international audience (Roche, 2000). Sporting mega-events such as the Summer Olympic Games and the Men's FIFA World Cup attract much attention and publicity in the media and represent an opportunity to showcase a destination (Stevenson, 2013). There is a need to offer a geographical analysis of sporting mega-events that looks specifically at figures concerning sport events and tourism in each host city. In recent years, geographers have contributed new and critical perspectives of sport (e.g. Koch, 2013; Conner, 2014; Lawrence, 2016; Wise, 2015a,b). These debates have focused on differentiated power relations, ideas of inclusion and exclusion, and the role of everyday interactions in reproducing social, political and economic processes (Wise, 2017). From another perspective, spatial land-use planning for new stadium venues also impacts local populations, through both positive and negative regeneration efforts (Henry & Gratton, 2001; Turner & Rosentraub, 2002; Smith, 2012; Wise, 2015a). Another perspective emphasises that places and countries are imagined based on particular sports (see Bale 2003; Conner, 2014). Our knowledge of places are communicated to us through newspapers, television, film, photographs and more recently social media (Shears & Fekete, 2014). Nations, regions and cities are each places that are imagined through various cultural elements, political situations or economic bases, and we can look at cities in relation to each other by acknowledging geographical scales of core and periphery.

To address sporting mega-event host cities, regeneration and development in Brazil, this chapter considers conceptual notions of scale, core and periphery.

Noticeable spatial divides exist in geography (MacKinnon 2011), and this is especially common when looking at the hosting of sporting mega-events. Smith (2000, p. 724) acknowledges scale refers to "one or more levels of representation, experience, and organisation of geographical events and processes." Geographers are concerned with understanding how processes are structured (Smith, 1990; Swyngedouw, 1997; Herod & Wright, 2002; Herod, 2011; MacKinnon, 2011), with much focus on positioning political and economic complexities of power, control and hierarchies (Delaney & Leitner, 1997; Storper, 1997; Gibson-Graham, 2002). The points expressed by these political and economic geographers focus on interplays of power to understand how certain countries or cities dominate a particular region. Research has addressed sport and scalar relations looking at where power and governance is concentrated, based on established hierarchies (see Harris & Wise, 2011; Wise, in press). As we become aware of power relations and hierarchies, two scalar spectrums have emerged (Herod, 2011) based on Wallerstein's (1974) world systems theory that identifies global cores and peripheries. Scholars also argue that it is important to consider the semi-periphery (Taylor & Flint, 2000; Barton *et al.*, 2007; Harris & Wise, 2011) because some places are rapidly emerging, growing or gaining new influence – which results in closer ties with the core. From an urban studies context, semi-peripheral cities would be considered second-tier cities. Taylor and Flint (2000) mention that core and periphery is a 'static phenomenon' where established cities benefit from strategic geographical advantages based on location, ease of access and regional influence. When a country bids for and is awarded a mega-event, it often proposes particular cities. For the FIFA World Cup, the host country will identify particular cities. For the Olympics, a country will propose a host city where the games will be held. In Brazil, São Paulo and Rio de Janeiro would represent the core, as these are well-known global destinations; however, the nation's political power is centred in Brasilia. Brazil is attempting to spread development, open new destinations and regenerate established destinations to show the world its power as an emerging economy. Some cities in Brazil's periphery may not have been so well-known before the event, but it is through mega-events the media broadcasts that make people aware of new destinations – such as Cuiabá.

When looking at sport, events and tourism, it is important to note that cores and peripheries are based on influence, regeneration and development; some destinations will benefit more than others based on exposure and place perceptions. Referring to such points from the perspective of sport, an analysis of interactions highlights particularities and differences across different economic, political and social contexts. Wise (in press) looked at the countries that competed in the Rugby World Cup and examined a number of factors where the established core countries that controlled the sports governance were limiting the sports expansion. Also observed in sports research, and as discussed next, core and periphery play a role in understanding the impact of sporting events by looking at destinations in relation to each other.

Mapping Brazil's sporting mega-event host cities

Countries have established urban hierarchies, or core cities – may they be mega-cities (with populations above 10 million inhabitants), capital cities or financial centres. While social and political factors are key to understanding (and reproducing) what might be understood as the core and periphery, more needs to be made of the social fabric that exists within all cases. There are then a number of cities that are emerging or gaining in power or reputation based on new influences, or in this case mega-event host cities. When we look at a number of inter-related cases, using scale, core and periphery, these conceptualisations challenge us to rank places based on influence and established hierarchies. Such conceptual understandings of 'place' mean locating cities in relation to other cities based on process and practice (Agnew & Duncan, 1989; Cresswell, 2004). Table 2.1 and Figure 2.1 rank and position Brazil's 12 host cities. The core-periphery model presented in this chapter only focuses on Brazil's sporting mega-event host cities in 2014 and 2016. The cities included are compared and assessed accordingly, and it is possible to argue that these cities have an advantage and may benefit from regeneration and development strategies or a new image given their exposure as a mega-event host destination. With any wave of regeneration or development, there are places that are included and others excluded.

Looking at Table 2.1, officials in Brazil selected 12 cities to host matches for the 2014 FIFA World Cup. Herod (2011) argues that there needs to be more emphasis on connectivity regarding scalar relations. Therefore, this chapter attempts to look at the 12 cities in Brazil based on a range of factors specific to sport, events and tourism to inform discussions of different perspectives of regeneration. Based on Figure 2.1, of the 12 cities that hosted FIFA World Cup matches, 11 are among the top 14 ranked destinations in Brazil and among the top 20 most populated cities in the country. Cuiabá is the only outlier among the 12 host cities. It is argued that hosting involves much investment in regeneration and new developments to prepare for a mega-event (see Smith, 2012). Therefore, new infrastructures are needed in cities that do not have venues and facilities that meet demand and capacity requirements. In such instances, cities with larger populations are more likely to see new venues built because there is more likely anticipated demand. But if we look back to South Africa, a new large venue built in Cape Town was criticised due to future use and demand (Maharaj, 2015). Similarly, Manaus, a peripheral city in Brazil, has received much criticism because the city also had a new venue built for the FIFA World Cup. Local competitions do not require such a large stadium, leaving the future use of the venue in question.

A wide range of media outlets portrayed images of economic recession, political turmoil and social distress across Brazil to international audiences (Millington & Darnell, 2014). While it is important to acknowledge the range of economic, political and social issues and critique surrounding Brazil and the country's hosting of two sporting mega-events, this chapter is interested in addressing and understanding geographical notions of core and periphery, sustainability and

Table 2.1 Sporting event and tourism content about each host city

Brazil's mega-event host city	2014 FIFA World Cup				2016 Summer Olympics	Tourism		Rank/ urban population	Score/core-periphery rank
	Matches held	Venue status	Venue capacity	Total event attendance		Type of airport	Dest. rank		
Belo Horizonte	6	Renovated	58,170	345,350	Football	Intl*	11	5/2,373,224	72/4
Brasilia	7	New	69,349	478,218	Football	Intl*	5	6/2,207,718	79/3
Cuiabá	4	New	41,112	158,717	–	Domestic	–	33/521,934	21/12
Curitiba	4	Renovated	39,361	156,991	–	Regional	12	7/1,718,421	30/10
Fortaleza	6	Renovated	60,342	356,896	–	Intl*	10	4/2,400,000	65/6
Manaus	4	New	40,549	160,227	Football	Intl*	8	8/1,598,210	51/7
Natal	4	New	39,971	158,167	–	Intl*	13	19/763,043	30/10
Porto Alegre	5	Renovated	43,394	214,969	–	Intl*	6	11/1,372,741	51/7
Recife	5	New	42,610	204,882	–	Intl*	14	9/1,478,098	39/9
Rio de Janeiro	7	Renovated	74,738	519,189	Host City	Intl*/Dom	1	2/6,023,699	95/1
Salvador	6	New	51,900	300,647	Football	Intl*	4	3/2,711,840	72/4
São Paulo	6	New	63,321	375,593	Football	Intl*/Dom	2	1/10,021,295	83/2

Note: Only domestic flight destinations listed at the time of research, the name of Cuiabá airport is Marechal Randon International Airport.
(Sources: www.citymayors.com/gratis/brazilian_cities.html; FIFA.com; http://exame.abril.com.br/estilo-de-vida/noticias/os-destinos-brasileiros-mais-visitados-pelos-estrangeiros)

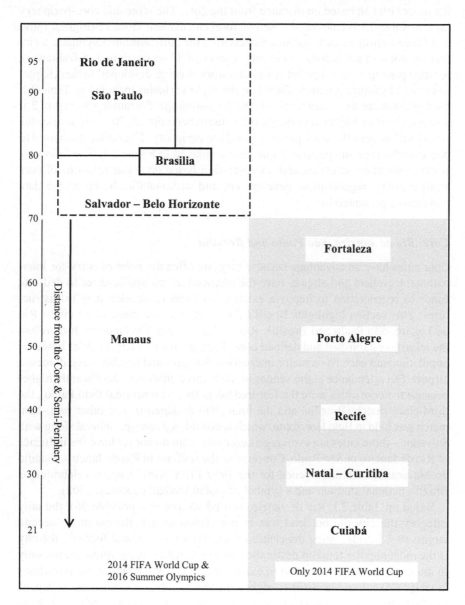

Figure 2.1 Conceptualising the core and periphery of Brazil's mega-event host city destinations.

regeneration to identify future research directions. The 12 cities selected to host 2014 FIFA World Cup matches arguably benefit from exposure, which impacts each city through various forms of regeneration – may it be economic, physical or image related. Figure 2.1 shows the 12 host cities. It depicts an accurate range of the core cities at the top based on the rankings from Table 2.1 to locate where the other cities sit based on distance from the core. The score and core-periphery rank in Table 2.1 is calculated based on total calculations from 12 (highest rank) to 1 (lowest rank) for each column. Concerning the 2016 Summer Olympics, a city that did not host any matches or events, a score of '0' was assigned. A framework for interpreting core and periphery in this work is being developed in this chapter to expand in future research. Based on the eight variables included in Table 2.1, the highest score a city can receive is 96. To distinguish the ranking in Figure 2.1, a score of 80 or higher represents the established core. A 70 score marks the threshold between the semi-periphery and the periphery. The rank is then used to organise the core and periphery mapping displayed in Figure 2.1. The following subsections offer reflection and interpretation based on scalar relations of core and periphery, regeneration, development and sustainability based on the data and figures presented here.

Core: Rio de Janeiro, São Paulo and Brasilia

Core cities have an advantage because they are often the point of entry for international travellers and already have the financial means and investor to dedicate funds to regeneration to improve existing facilities or develop new infrastructures. This section highlights Brazil's three defined core mega-event cities: Rio de Janeiro, São Paulo and Brasilia. Rio de Janeiro and São Paulo both represent the (clearly) established and defined core. They are the two largest cities based on population and each has a major international airport and another large domestic airport. Fan attendance at the venues in these three cities was significantly higher because the core cities were the featured hosts for one semi-final (São Paulo), the third-place match (Brasilia) and the final (Rio de Janeiro). The other semi-final match was held in Belo Horizonte, which is considered semi-peripheral along with Salvador – these cities are evolving as core cities but do not yet have the influence of Rio de Janeiro or São Paulo. Concerning the stadium in Rio de Janeiro, Estádio do Maracanã, built and opened for the 1950 FIFA World Cup, is celebrated as Brazil's national stadium and a symbol of global football (Gaffney, 2008).

Based on Table 2.1, Rio de Janeiro scored 95 (out of a possible 96); the only category the city did not lead was in population as it is the country's second largest city. Besides being the centre of Brazilian international football, the city is the most popular tourism destination in Brazil with tourists attracted not only to major- and mega-events but to experience the city's iconic natural harbour (a UNESCO cultural landscape), night atmosphere, attractions such as the 'Christ the Redeemer' statue atop Corcavado, and the popular beaches of Copacabana and Ipanema. The touristic features that Rio de Janeiro possesses not only make the city an important destination in Brazil (and South America), but also a major international/global tourism centre. As the host city of the 2016 Summer Olympics, the city saw a number of new development projects and much more extensive investment as compared to the other 11 cities assessed in this chapter. It is important that public, private and community stakeholders in Rio de Janeiro plan for sustainable legacies for the newly developed and revitalised venues. Since the city is the top tourism destination in Brazil, they are at a strategic advantage over markets that are not as developed and do not receive the volume of tourists or ability to host national, regional and international events.

Of the 12 cities, five had stadiums renovated and seven cities had new stadiums built. Twelve points were awarded to cities with existing venues that were upgraded as they had the necessary infrastructure ahead of the event. The other seven cities with new stadiums received a score of 7 as this was a needed infrastructure and development ahead of the 2014 FIFA World Cup. Of the core cities, São Paulo and Brasilia received new stadiums. It was fitting for the nation's largest city and capital, respectively, to receive new venues, but the largest stadium in Latin America was renovated ahead of the World Cup and no new stadium has a capacity higher than Estádio do Maracanã. Estádio Nacional Mané Garrincha in Brasilia and the Arena de São Paulo became the second and third largest host stadiums in Brazil, with all three core cities with venue capacities of over 63,000. São Paulo's stadium was built for the FIFA World Cup, but with a capacity of just over 63,000 for the event, it can be regarded as one of the new venues that will be regularly used in the future. One of Brazil's largest football clubs, Sports Club Corinthians Paulista, owns and operates this venue now referred to as Corinthians Arena. São Paulo is one of the world's largest urban areas and the country's financial centre (Clawson, 2011). Relating São Paulo to Wallerstein's (1974) world systems theory, the city is clearly a global core based on its influence, financial and commercial power globally. The city is a centre for trade, global commerce, finance and international air passenger and cargo traffic, but the city does not have the same touristic appeal as Rio de Janeiro as São Paulo is not immediately on the coast and population growth has put much environmental strain on the city.

Rio de Janeiro and São Paulo receive much attention as the two core cities in Brazil; however, it is important to acknowledge Brazil's capital city because Brasilia's rank and position in this study displayed in Figure 2.1 is unique. Most major urban centres in Brazil are oriented to or within close proximity of the coast. Brasilia's geographical location is unique given it is the nation's capital city. In 1960, the Brazilian government relocated the capital from Rio de Janeiro to Brasilia to open up, encourage economic development and modernise more remote peripheral areas of the country (Clawson, 2011). Looking at any highway map of Brazil, Brasilia is a gateway to Amazonia, with numerous highways radiating out towards Amazonia. The capital city is still very much connected to the coast with growth corridors established to act as a hub between the coast and this important entry point to Amazonia. By developing and modernising Brasilia in the 1960s and undergoing events-led regeneration ahead of 2014, this was another attempt to increase the attraction of the capital city and promote travel inland towards Amazonia. It can be argued that Brasilia is a core city by default as the main political centre of the country, but the city's rank in Table 2.1 still puts the capital city ahead of the semi-peripheral cities by seven points.

Semi-periphery: Salvador and Belo Horizonte

Concerning research on core and periphery, Harris and Wise (2011, p. 378) note "a more contemporary train of thought has been to look at the semi-periphery."

To support this idea, Barton *et al.* (2007) advocate that increased competition and places (in this case cities) that position themselves with the established core can differentiate themselves from other peripheral cities as emerging economics, or what this work would consider as destinations with emerging reputations as mega-event host cities. The two cities that fit the semi-periphery label based on this case are Salvador and Belo Horizonte. Both received a score of 72 in Table 2.1 (2 of only 5 cities to score above 70, which was the competitive threshold dividing the semi-periphery from the periphery). With both cities receiving the same score, it is important to highlight the differences among them. Both held six 2014 FIFA World Cup matches – with Belo Horizonte at a slight advantage here having hosted a semi-final match. The group stage matches tend to attract attendees (including many international sports tourists) and viewers through the media based on what countries happen to compete in a particular host city. As countries enter the round of 16 and the quarterfinals, then closer to the finals, cities that host these matches not only attract more attendees (increasing the total event attendance in a city), but global viewing audiences increase – arguably increasing recognition of the host city among viewers around the world. Therefore, Salvador (hosting a round of 16 and a quarter-final match) and Belo Horizonte (hosting a round of 16 and a semi-final match) gained increased exposure as sporting mega-event destinations. Belo Horizonte's much larger and renovated stadium (Estádio Mineirão) allowed it to attract approximately 45,000 more attendees to the six matches hosted compared with Salvador's new Arena Forte Nova.

Belo Horizonte and Salvador were both featured in the 2016 Summer Olympics by hosting football matches. Only five cities outside Rio de Janeiro had venues involved in the Olympics, and four of these five are part of the core and semi-periphery. Manaus was the only exception here and will be discussed in the next subsection. Looking at the population figures for Belo Horizonte and Salvador, they are comparable second-tier cities ranked third and fifth, respectively. Concerning tourism related comparisons of the two semi-peripheral host cities, both have international airports with direct flights operated to Europe and North America. The most significant difference is as a tourism destination, Salvador ranks fourth nationally whereas Belo Horizonte is ranked at 11. Salvador is renowned for its annual Carnival celebration which attracts tourists to the state of Bahia. Bahia is the state of Brazil where Carnival is said to have started (see Schelling, 1998). While Salvador has attracted much attention as a host city for the 2014 FIFA World Cup, the city is once again overshadowed by Rio de Janeiro. Similarly, Rio de Janeiro attracts tourists from around the world to its Carnival celebration – but the event in Rio de Janeiro is the world's largest Carnival (Farias, 2014).

Periphery: Fortaleza, Manaus, Porto Alegre, Recife, Natal, Curitiba and Cuiabá

The core and the semi-periphery (often only a few cases) show where the power is concentrated – in this case mega-event host cities in Brazil. No matter the context of study, the majority of cases will be located in the periphery (see Wallerstein,

1974; Barton *et al.*, 2007; Wise, in press). This study only assesses 12 cities. But in a sporting events and tourism context, all 12 of these Brazilian cities are at an advantage. However, when compared all together, seven are identified as peripheral to the established core and emerging semi-periphery. Fortaleza just sits below the semi-peripheral threshold, and there is a noticeable score difference between each city, or pair of cities, as you move away from the core. As Brazil's fourth largest city, where Fortaleza lacks as a major city in this case is the city was not included to host football matches during the 2016 Olympics. At tenth in Brazil based on the destination ranking, if Fortaleza sees increases in tourism over other cities, the city has potential to move into the semi-periphery.

Of the seven peripheral cities, only Fortaleza hosted six matches. In fact, all cities that hosted six or more matches have stadium capacities over 50,000. Fortaleza's Estádio Castelão has a capacity of just over 60,000. Estádio Beira-Rio (Porto Alegre) and Arena Pernambuco (Recife) each hosted 5 matches and the stadiums in these cities are both larger than the sports venues in the other four cities that only hosted four group stage matches; these being: Arena da Amazônia (Manaus), Arena das Dunas (Natal), Arena de Baixada (Curitiba) and Arena Pantanal (Cuiabá). Based on the data displayed in Figure 2.1, the ranking of venue capacity has a direct correlation with the number of matches held – which also closely corresponds with total event attendance. The exception based on total event attendance is Manaus, which has a slightly smaller stadium than Cuiabá, but approximately 1500 more people attended matches in Manaus compared with Cuiabá.

Each of the seven peripheral cases is listed accordingly in Figure 2.1 based on distance from the core. Looking at the score/core-periphery rank in Table 2.1, peripheral scores range from 65 to 21. The differences are quite vast among these seven peripheral host cities. It was thought that the peripheral cities would have each received a new stadium in an attempt to modernise and show a country's ability to build new modern venues. In Brazil, three cities (Fortaleza, Porto Alegre and Curitiba) had existing venues renovated, but the bottom three ranked tourism destinations each did receive new stadiums (Natal, Recife and Cuiabá). The outlier here is Manaus, which is a strategic city in terms of the nascent promotion of economic development in Amazonia. Manaus, however, is the only non-core and non-semi-periphery city to host football matches for the 2016 Summer Olympics. Arguably, Manaus is one of the cities that will benefit most as an emerging sporting events destination, but as discussed next, the city's distant and very peripheral location will likely create challenges for growth and further development. Another interpretation considering why the Arena da Amazônia in Manaus hosted six football matches for the 2016 Olympics is based on criticisms officials received when they planned and built a new 40,000 seat capacity venue in the remote state of Amazonas. There was arguably a need to feature Manaus' Arena da Amazônia in another event; however, the other peripheral city (geographically), and lowest ranked city in this chapter, Cuiabá, did not host any matches for the Olympics.

With the exception of Fortaleza, all peripheral cases have urban populations outside the top five, and Cuiabá ranking farthest from the core at 33rd. Again, the need to build a new stadium in a remote destination in a city with a relatively small population as compared to other cases links to this attempt to promote economic development in areas away from the coast. While Manaus is located on the Amazon River, Cuiabá in the state of Mato Grasso adjacent to Bolivia is approximately twice the distance from the coast as Brasilia and is isolated with only a few transportation networks to other inland urban areas, including a direct highway to Brasilia. Cuiabá also has a domestic airport, so its connections internationally are through major international gateway cities. Moreover, no tourism destination rank could be identified for Cuiabá. The other peripheral cities were all ranked among the top 14 destinations in Brazil, with three (Fortaleza, Natal and Recife) of the seven cities with direct access to the coast – Porto Alegre and Curitiba are both within 100 kilometres from the Atlantic Ocean. The final section offers insight into the need to focus on and measure sustainable regeneration in Brazil's host cities – especially in these seven identified peripheral host cities.

The need to address *sustainable* regeneration and development in host cities

Geographers and social scientists are concerned with places' sustainable futures, regeneration and development in destinations that have recently hosted mega-events (Darnell, 2012; Gaffney, 2016; Wise, 2017). Regeneration, development and modernization bids and investments are having significant economic, political and social impacts across Brazil. Rising wealth gaps and increasing competition means disadvantaged communities in Brazil are further excluded from perceived or intended benefits of sporting event and tourism-led regeneration surrounding these two sporting mega-events (see Gaffney, 2010, 2016; Reis *et al.*, 2013). Scholars are particularly interested in how sports, events and tourism are being utilised economically, politically and socially to drive regeneration and development. This section will discuss impacts and the need to address sustainable regeneration in host cities. Discussions of sustainability emerged early on when new stadia were planned and built in remote locations (Manaus and Cuiabá). These destinations are remote, and therefore constructing new stadia and amenities to support the events was a costly endeavour. For instance, in Manaus, materials to construct Arena da Amazônia were transported via the Amazon River. Arguably, having such peripheral host cities represents an attempt to open the Amazonian interior to increased tourism and future sporting events. Perhaps this is also an extended reach inland. As mentioned, Brazil relocated the country's administrative capitol to Brasilia from Rio de Janeiro in an attempt to extend economic development into Amazonia in 1960 (Clawson, 2011). With more growth and investment in Brazil's interior, allocating host cities in Manaus and Cuiabá extends economic development into Amazonia to gain exposure and promote tourism after the events.

The hosting of the FIFA World Cup and Rio 2016 has been highly contested due to economic recession, social protests and political turbulence. The previous section addressed the complexities of core and periphery using insight from human geography, but to make recommendations we must also draw on understandings from sociology, social-psychology and urban planning because a multidisciplinary approach will enable researchers to not only collaborate but also make informed and meaningful assessments of people, places and impacts of change. There are a number of critical research conditions to consider when looking at sports, events, tourism and regeneration (Chalip, 2006; Smith, 2012; Getz; 2013), including: the involvement and support of the local population, opportunities and experiences for local residents, existence of mentorship and educational programmes, encouragement of local enterprise opportunities, inclusion and exclusion, plans to assist people from underprivileged communities, pride in place/satisfaction and sense of community/identity, the co-management of venues and facilities to support local resident use, and local understandings of policies concerning legacy. The International Olympic Committee (IOC) (2013) recognises and is concerned with how sports contribute to positive lifestyle choices. However, these organisations focus on the athletes, and there is a need to further consider social transformations by focusing on the residents of the very host cities where mega-events are held. FIFA and the IOC are focusing on change and transformation based on United Nations Development Goals and international development agendas (see Darnell, 2012), but these approaches are arguably considered top-down based on wider issues facing people in emerging economies. Coakley and Souza (2013, p. 587) add "creating specific legacies and developmental outcomes is a matter of power relations," and FIFA and the IOC manage and control the events.

There are often spurious claims that sports produce social change rather than the organisations that govern and manage them. Castles (2001) argues for us to understand change we need to consider development from the bottom-up. One major challenge is countries host mega-events to showcase their power and presence in the world, but some recognition of social benefits is necessary to address wider intangible impacts beyond the tangible impacts (Smith, 2012). Horne and Manzenreiter (2006) further add that it is assumed mega-events will bring positive social and economic impacts, but questions arise (locally, regionally and nationally) shortly after the spectacle wears off. Therefore, the need to focus on local communities and associated intangible conditions is necessary to understand the full impact of an event. This requires different epistemological and methodological rationales that cannot always be analysed deductively through quantitative statistical analysis. Wise (2017) reinforces Castles' (2001) argument that more inductive research is needed, but scholars must get more involved in communities to help express local voices and inform public policy. To understand regeneration and social transformation holistically, it is especially important to observe communities before, during and after sporting mega-events are held in a particular locale – this is especially important in the more peripheral cases in remote regions of Brazil. Thus, sport for development initiatives are movements towards establishing sustainable inclusive futures, but still support (especially funding) is needed and wellbeing initiatives need to be stressed in public policy agendas and among those delivering programmes (see Kidd, 2008; Levermore

& Beacom, 2009). The same is true as destinations promote tourism regeneration alongside event-led change where social sustainability is overshadowed by discussions of (intended) economic impacts (Wise, 2016). Bottom-up initiatives are concerned with grassroots development, and critical scholars point out that (perceived) social impacts are difficult to manage in emerging economies (Alegi, 2007). Each of the addressed points relates to critical notions of sustainable regeneration and social transformation in support of addressing wider impacts linked to sport, events and tourism.

More research is needed in Brazil so that future impacts are achieved and investments are sustainable over the longer term. There is a need to develop further interdisciplinary and international research using innovative methodologies in new and emergent research areas of global importance – especially in emerging economy countries following mega-events because rapid increases and a vulnerable society are at risk of struggle. There are important scalar relations to consider as well and the need to address local, national and global issues within the context of examining how and why sporting mega-events, leisure opportunities and tourism produce economic, political, social and cultural transformation in a country. Impacts concerning economic, political, social and cultural transformation will be influenced differently in the core and peripheral cities. For instance, Rio de Janeiro and São Paulo, the established core mega-cities in Brazil, have a long history of hosting events and handling high volumes of tourists, but in the mega-event hosting periphery identified in this study, destinations such as Natal or Cuiabá may struggle and issues concerning exclusion may negatively impact these places and their populations if they see sharp increases in tourism. Other challenges facing the building of new venues in destinations such as Manaus and Cuiabá is local competitions do not attract large enough crowds to fill these venues – despite Manaus hosting six football matches for the 2016 Summer Olympics.

A final point is future research needs to focus on emergent research that addresses economic development, social impacts and policy agendas at various scales, including: what types of transformation in society do sporting events, tourism and leisure cultures produce? How do sporting events, tourism and leisure cultures produce social transformation in society? How might sporting events, tourism and leisure cultures need to be revised or adapted in order to address social issues at the local, regional and global levels? Finally, specific to the points of sport, events, tourism and regeneration in Brazil, we need to ask if sporting mega-events will see increased opportunities in more peripheral cities/ regions of the country, and what is being done to manage, spread or introduce tourism and subsequent events into new markets across the country.

References

Agnew, J. & Duncan, J. (Eds.). (1989). *The power of place*. Boston, MA: Unwin Hyman.
Alegi, P. (2007). The political economy of mega-stadiums and the underdevelopment of grassroots football in South Africa. *Politikon, 34*, 315–331.

Bale, J. (2003). *Sports geography.* London, England: Routledge.
Barton, J., Gwynne, R. & Murray, W. (2007). Competition and co-operation in the semiperiphery: Closer economic partnership and sectoral transformations in Chile and New Zealand. *The geographical journal, 173,* 224–241.
Castles, S. (2001). Studying social transformation. *International political science review, 22,* 13–32.
Chalip, L. (2006). Towards social leverage of sport events. *Journal of sport & tourism, 11,* 109–127.
Clawson, D.L. (2011). *Latin America and the Caribbean: Lands and peoples.* Oxford, England: Oxford University Press.
Coakley, J. & Souza, D.L. (2013). Sport mega-events: Can legacies and development be equitable and sustainable? *Motriz: Revista de educação física, 19,* 580–589.
Curi, M., Knijnik, J. & Mascarenhas, G. (2011). The Pan American Games in Rio de Janeiro 2007: Consequences of a sport mega-event on a BRIC country. *International review for the sociology of Sport, 46,* 140–156.
Conner, N. (2014). Global cultural flows and the routes of identity: The imagined worlds of Celtic FC. *Social & cultural geography, 15,* 525–546.
Cresswell, T. (2004). *Place: A short introduction.* Oxford, England: Blackwell.
Darnell, S.C. (2012). Olympism in action, Olympic hosting and the politics of 'Sport for Development and Peace': Investigating the development discourses of Rio 2016. *Sport in society, 15,* 869–887.
de Menezes, T.R. & de Souza, J.F. (2014). Transportation and urban mobility in mega-events: The case of Recife. *Procedia-social and behavioral sciences, 162,* 218–227.
Delaney, D. & Leitner, H. (1997). The political construction of scale. *Political geography, 16,* 93–97.
Farias, E. (2014). The Carnival of Rio de Janeiro: A social ritual of enjoyment. *Re-Vista: Harvard review of Latin America,* http://revista.drclas.harvard.edu/book/carnival-rio-de-janeiro.
Gaffney, C. (2008). *Temples of the earthbound gods: Stadiums in the cultural landscapes of Rio de Janeiro and Buenos Aires.* Austin, TX: University of Texas Press.
Gaffney, C. (2010). Mega-events and socio-spatial dynamics in Rio de Janeiro, 1919–2016. *Journal of Latin American geography, 9,* 7–29.
Gaffney, C. (2016). The urban impacts of the 2014 World Cup in Brazil. In: R. Gruneau & J. Horne (Eds.). *Mega-events and globalization: Capital and spectacle in a changing world order.* Abingdon, England: Routledge (pp. 167–185).
Getz, D. (2013). *Event tourism.* Putnam Valley, NY: Cognizant Communication Corporation.
Gibson-Graham, J.K. (2002). Beyond global vs. local: Economic politics outside the binary frame. In A. Herod & M. Wright (Eds.). *Geographies of power: Placing scale.* Oxford, England: Blackwell (pp. 25–60).
Harris, J. & Wise, N. (2011). Geographies of scale in international rugby union: The case of Argentina. *Geographical research, 49,* 375–383.
Henry, I. & Gratton, C. (2001). *Sport in the city: The role of sport in economic and social regeneration.* London, England: Routledge.
Herod, A. (2011). *Scale.* London, England: Routledge.
Herod, A. & Wright, M. (Eds.). (2002). *Geographies of power: Placing scale.* Malden, MA: Blackwell.
Horne, J. & Manzenreiter, W. (Eds.). (2006). *Sports mega-events: Social scientific analyses of a global phenomenon.* Malden, MA: Blackwell Publishing.

International Olympic Committee (2013). Olympic Charter. https://stillmed.olympic.org/Documents/olympic_charter_en.pdf.

Kidd, B. (2008). A new social movement: Sport for development and peace. *Sport in society, 11,* 370–380.

Koch, N. (2013). Sport and soft authoritarian nation-building. *Political geography, 32,* 42–51.

Lawrence, S. (2016). 'We are the boys from the Black Country'! (Re)Imagining local, regional and spectator identities through fandom at Walsall Football Club. *Social & cultural geography, 17,* 282–299.

Levermore, R. & Beacom, A. (Eds.). (2009). *Sport and international development.* New York, NY: Palgrave MacMillan.

Maharaj, B. (2015). The turn of the south? Social and economic impacts of mega-events in India, Brazil and South Africa. *Local economy, 30,* 983–999.

Maiello, A. & Pasquinelli, C. (2015). Destruction or construction? A (counter) branding analysis of sport mega-events in Rio de Janeiro. *Cities, 46,* 116–124.

MacKinnon, D. (2011). Reconstructing scale: Towards a new scalar politics. *Progress in human geography, 35,* 21–36.

Millington, R. & Darnell, S.C. (2014). Constructing and contesting the Olympics online: The internet, Rio 2016 and the politics of Brazilian development. *International review for the sociology of sport, 49,* 190–210.

Reis, A.C., Sousa-Mast, F.R. & Vieira, M.C. (2013). Public policies and sports in marginalised communities: The case of Cidade de Deus, Rio de Janeiro, Brazil. *World leisure journal, 55,* 229–251.

Roche, M. (2000). *Mega-events and modernity.* London, England: Routledge.

Schelling, V. (1998). Globalisation, ethnic identity and popular culture in Latin America. In R. Kiely & P. Marfleet (Eds.). *Globalisation and the third world.* London, England: Routledge (pp. 141–162).

Shears, A. & Fekete, E. (2014). Re-constructing the map: NBC's geographic imagination and the opening ceremony for the 2012 London Olympics. *Sociological research online, 19,* http://www.socresonline.org.uk/19/1/7.html.

Smith, A. (2012). *Events and urban regeneration: The strategic use of events to revitalise cities.* London, England: Routledge.

Smith, N. (1990). *Uneven development: Nature, capital and the production of space.* Oxford, England: Blackwell.

Smith, N. (2000). Scale. In R. Johnston, D. Gregory, G. Pratt & M. Watts (Eds.). *The dictionary of human geography.* Oxford, England: Blackwell (pp. 724–727).

Stevenson, N. (2013). The complexities of tourism and regeneration: The case of the 2012 Olympic Games. *Tourism planning & development, 10,* 1–16.

Storper, M. (1997). Territories, flows, and hierarchies in the global economy. In K. Cox (Ed.). *Spaces of globalization.* New York, NY: The Guilford Press (pp. 19–44).

Swyngedouw, E. (1997). Excluding the other: The production of scale and scaled politics. In R. Lee & J. Wills (Eds.). *Geographies of economies.* London, England: Arnold (pp. 167–176).

Taylor, P. & Flint, C. (2000). *Political geography.* New York, NY: Prentice Hall.

Turner, R.S. & Rosentraub, M.S. (2002). Tourism, sports and the centrality of cities, *Journal of urban affairs, 24,* 487–492.

Wallerstein, I. (1974). *The modern world system,* Vol. 1. New York, NY: Academic Press.

Wise, N. (2015a). Geographical approaches and the sociology of sport. In R. Giulianotti (Ed.) *Routledge handbook of the sociology of sport*. London, England: Routledge (pp. 142–152).

Wise, N. (2015b). Maintaining Dominican identity in the Dominican Republic: Forging a baseball landscape in Villa Ascension. *International review for the sociology of sport*, *50*, 161–178.

Wise, N. (2016). Outlining triple bottom line contexts in urban tourism regeneration. *Cities, 53*, 30–34.

Wise, N. (2017). In the shadow of mega-events: The value of ethnography in sports geography. In N. Koch (Ed.) *Critical geographies of sport: Space, power, and sport in global perspective*. London, England: Routledge.

Wise, N. (in press). Rugby World Cup: New directions or more of the same? *Sport in society*, (online first) DOI: 10.1080/17430437.2015.1088717.

3   Durban's FIFA 2010 beachfront 'beautification'

Brij Maharaj

Introduction

Tourism is a major economic activity in the city of Durban. Durban has long earned its prime position as one of South Africa's most popular year-round tourist destinations due to its expansive beaches, warm ocean, sunny climate and diverse cultural heritage. The recent upgrading, or beautification, of Durban's beachfront was one of the major infrastructure developments in the city linked to the 2010 Fédération Internationale de Football Association (FIFA) World Cup. More specifically, the '2010 and Beyond Strategy' intended to promote Durban as Africa's premier sport and tourism destination. The beachfront regeneration serves as a legacy project for residents and tourists who visit the city. Evaluations of event-led urban regeneration concepts such as partnerships, spatial targeting, integration, competition, empowerment and sustainability are areas of importance (see Jones & Gripaios, 2000).

This chapter critically assesses Durban's FIFA 2010 beachfront beautification regeneration project, especially in terms of its implications for the poor. A major concern was that the Durban beachfront project would displace informal traders and thousands of subsistence fishermen from the area, depriving people of their livelihoods. The informal traders were not offered any compensation or guarantee that they would be allowed to move back to their spaces after construction work was completed (Maharaj, 2015). Paradoxically, beachfront restaurants remained vacant during the duration of the event, and three years after, the World Cup had taken place in the city. A positive outcome of the revamp was increased investments in the hotel sector along the beachfront. Ironically, during the preparation for FIFIA 2010, Durban lost its 'Blue Flag' status due to ineffective water management procedures, as well as weak environmental monitoring strategies. The failure to maintain the beachfront in terms of crime and grime has been a major concern.

Historical background of the Durban beachfront

The city of Durban, often cited as, 'the warmest place to be' and 'Africa's playground' is one of South Africa's premier tourist destinations. Tourism in Durban is a major economic contributor to the area, resulting in the city investing in the industry to enhance its various tourist facilities and services over the years. As a result, regeneration has taken place in the coastal areas, as the city is well known for its beautiful beaches (Table 3.1). However, due to South Africa's apartheid regime, the city was unable to fully realise its full tourism potential in years gone by. During the apartheid era, the Group Areas Act of 1950 and Separate Amenities Act of 1953 resulted in the best beaches, hotels and tourist attractions around Durban's Golden Mile being reserved solely for the use by the white minority. This ensured that tourism activity within this area was entirely a white phenomenon. The black majority was denied access to these facilities, and were allocated substandard amenities (Maharaj *et al.*, 2008).

In 1989, the city opened up its beaches to all races despite the opposition from white conservatives. Since then, the white tourist population decreased and the black tourist population increased on the Durban beaches. By the end of 1994, about 80% of all rented accommodations in Durban were occupied by Africans, coloureds and Indians. The beachfront remained a catalyst for tourism, attracting about 4.5 million visitors annually, generating about R6.4 billion (all monetary figures in South African Rand) for the local economy (eThekwini Municipality, 2003, p. 7), and providing around 65,000 jobs directly (Maharaj *et al.*, 2008). Since the historic 1994 democratic elections, numerous policies were used to promote the city as a tourism mecca – with variable results. The city still faces considerable challenges of unemployment, poverty, inequality, as well as the ongoing battle against crime and grime.

Table 3.1 eThekwini Coastal Swot Analysis (eThekwini Municipality, 2003, p. 5–6)

Strengths	Weaknesses
• Climate & long seasons • Beach & sea • High level of interest in beach tourism and associated activities • High market awareness • High volumes • Investment in current infrastructure and new facilities like uShaka, Point Development and the Casino • Good MICE facilities • Emerging international MICE and cruise tourism destination	• Crime • Poor quality of public facilities • Neglect / deterioration of tourism assets • Single primary attraction of the Beach • Lack of diversity & quality of tourism secondary attractions • High volume budget / emerging tourists • Low tourism revenue yield • Decrease in 'length of stay' in Durban • Loss of market share of higher spend tourists
Opportunities	**Threats**
• Product regeneration and diversification; • Retain, develop and regain mid to upper-income tourism markets; • Linkages with TKZN for marketing and branding opportunities	• Strong competitors in beach tourism markets • Lack of unique selling features • Negative market perceptions • Lack of holistic approach to destination management • Procrastination • Limitations of current product assets • Limited Tourism 'Primary and Secondary Attractions' compared with competitive destinations

Durban is a hub of activity due to the golden mile on the beachfront, various tourist attractions, and the different sporting venues. The city's golden mile illustrated in Figure 3.1 shows all the beaches and most of the place names and hotels, comprises of a "6 km long strip of beachfront lined with beaches, lawns, promenades, luxury hotels and restaurants" between Blue Lagoon and the uShaka Marine World (Oliver, 2001, p. 92). However, the beachfront remained

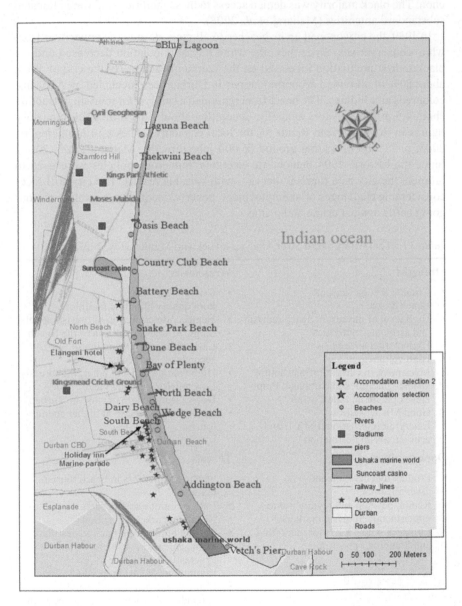

Figure 3.1 Map of the Durban beachfront.

chronically neglected in terms of aesthetic appeal, amenities, safety and security. This state of affairs persisted into the early 2000s as is evident from the SWOT analysis presented in Table 3.1. Planning for FIFA 2010 provided an opportunity to address some of the threats and challenges facing the beachfront (Table 3.1), and to rebrand Durban as a 'world class' tourist destination. The beachfront was to be upgraded through two phases. Phase I of the upgrade was completed in time for the 2010 FIFA World Cup.

Upgrading the Durban beachfront

Phase I: Durban central

The upgrade to the beachfront in Durban was one of the major infrastructural developments initiated as part of FIFA 2010 preparations. The entire area was remodelled and modified, and facilities redeveloped at various nodes. In 2005 the city manager, Mike Sutcliffe, stated that the intention was to cater to a variety of visitors, ranging from rich international and local tourists; those interested in water sports; local residents; the large crowd on New Year; and self-catering family leisure outings (Robbins, 2005). The head of Durban's strategic projects unit, Julie-May Ellingson, emphasised that the beaches were Durban's main attraction, "and if we don't get them right, we cannot talk about growing tourism" (Cole, 2008, p. 2). The development objectives of the beachfront upgrade included: integrating the central beachfront, providing new amenities for a diverse range of beach users, greening (including increasing safety through environmental design and landscaping), developing key nodes along the promenade (Addington Beach Node, the New Beach Node, and the Dairy Beach Node), and promoting a healthy lifestyle (Ellingson, 2013). The 'big vision' was to use FIFA 2010 as a catalyst to change the face of Durban.

The long-term goal of construction to the promenade was geared toward extending it from the Port's northern breakwater to the mouth of the Umgeni River. However, a more immediate goal was extending the Promenade from the uShaka Marine World beach to the Country Club Beach (Phase I). Also included in the construction plan were walkways leading to the Moses Mabhida Stadium, hence integrating the beachfront with the sports precinct. Notwithstanding the inconvenience and some delays, the revamped beachfront was widely welcomed by the public: "Everyone was commenting favourably about the scope of the project and the general user friendliness of this brilliant new amenity. Also impressive was the high police visibility, including mounted metro police for crowd control and general lack of litter" (Master Builders Association, 2010, p. 10).

According to city manager Mike Sutcliffe, the beach revamp also eliminated the last vestiges of apartheid:

> At the beachfront you see every race, class and ethnicity, with no one really being hassled [...] the integration of all the different beaches – from South

Beach up to North Beach and then going right up past Suncoast – has allowed us to start appreciating this magnificent area.

(Zakas, 2010, p. 2)

However, writing in February 2012, journalist Paddy Harper argued that the 'apartheid hangover' was still evident on the beachfront, noting that 'the new beachfront is magnificent, but Suncoast beach – out of choice by those who use it – is predominantly an Indian beach. Vetch's is white and South Beach is black' (Harper, 2012, p. 29).

Phase II: Blue Lagoon

Phase II of the upgrade project started on 26 March 2012 and included a 2.2 km stretch extending from the Country Club Beach 1 in the South, to Blue Lagoon in the North. The upgrade was put forward because the 2.2 km stretch was considered to be in urgent need of a facelift due to its neglected state (the last upgrade in the area was in 1985). The upgrade would also seamlessly link the 'Golden Mile' to uShaka, Moses Mabida and Blue Lagoon. The aim of the upgrade is to provide beach visitors with more parking, picnic sites, new paving, street lights, street furniture, braai facilities, bus drop-and-go services, bus holding areas, and improved jet skiing and kite surfing facilities (SSI, 2011). The basic principles influencing Phase II upgrade included recognising the beach as an economic asset; providing public spaces and recreational facilities; and sensitivity to environmental issues, safety and security (SSI, 2011). The eThekwini Municipality believed that these proposals would please a wide range of users and interest groups as it would provide them with a safe and healthy environment with exercise and recreational space to support a healthy lifestyle (Breetzke, 2011).

When the Municipality announced the proposed Phase II upgrade in early 2011, many members of the public were unhappy with the decision to embark on another multi-million Rand beach upgrade. This criticism was due to the conditions in the Phase I upgrade slipping in terms of policing, cleaning and general maintenance soon after the hosting of the 2010 FIFA World Cup. There was a public view that it would be prudent for the municipality to spend the money on upkeep and maintenance of that area rather than embarking on a new beach upgrade. Despite these concerns, the municipality proceeded with the upgrade of Phase II of the Durban 'Golden Mile,' claiming that it involved a smaller section of beach area and therefore would cost much less than Phase I which cost the city R250 million. At the beginning of the project it was estimated to cost R80 million and would be completed by March 2013 (Savides, 2011).

However, by April 2013 the construction for the Phase II upgrade in Blue Lagoon was still not completed. Mike Andrews, the project executive of the Strategic Projects Unit (SPU), claimed that it would be ready by 26 May 2013 in time for the East Coast Radio Big Walk, but this did not materialise. The delays were attributed to the excessive summer rains and minor modifications to the original plans, and this resulted in a R2.3 million increase in costs, and the completion

date of the upgrade was moved to October 2013 (*Mercury*, 15 July 2013). However, in late 2013 the construction site in Blue Lagoon was minimised to allow
for the opening of the Blue Lagoon Promenade so the locals and festive season
tourists could walk the entire length of the promenade.

Displacing the poor

The displacement of Durban's poorer urban residents emphasises how regeneration strategies lead to exclusion and limited benefits for all. This section outlines
how the beautification of Durban's beachfront has impacted Blue Lagoon traders
and fisherfolk. There were about 20 informal traders at Blue Lagoon who operated with permits who sold food products, and scores who did not have author-
ization to be based in the area. Most traders with permits have been located in
the Blue Lagoon area for over 10 years, and were sole income earners for their
families (Moodley, 2014). The eThekwini Municipal officials from the Business
Support Unit (BSU) and SPU held a public meeting with the informal traders
with permits whose jobs and livelihoods were based in Blue Lagoon area. They
were told that they would be temporarily moved to Coconut Grove, adjacent to
the Blue Lagoon, for the duration of the upgrade (Mntuyedwa, 2012). Mike
Andrews informed the traders that the plan was to have a proper food court for
traders at Blue Lagoon from different race and cultural backgrounds in order
to promote diversity in the area. Also, traders would be provided with formal
shelters which would be divided into sections, based on the nature of their economic activity (Masikane & Ntumbu, 2012).

Mike Andrews said that the Blue Lagoon informal traders would be let back in
the area to trade by the December 2013 festive season, but this did not materialise as only the public were allowed back in the revamped zone, while the traders
remained in Coconut Grove. The traders with permits were finally allowed to
return to Blue Lagoon in November 2015. However, the much vaunted promise
of improved facilities for traders did not materialise. They were promised brick
buildings, but were allocated to shipping containers, and worked under hazard-
ous conditions, without running water or electricity. Traders complained about
the small space and high temperatures, and they were limited to two people per
container (see Akoob, 2016). Another trader noted that they now needed to prepare food differently, changing how they operate their businesses (Akoob, 2016).
Traders believed that notwithstanding the expensive upgrades to the area, Blue
Lagoon would never return to its former glory when they initially moved to
Coconut Grove, mentioning at first: 'business was very quiet, but slowly increased
over time; however, it never matched the business of Blue Lagoon. We are back
but it is not the same' (Akoob, 2016, p. 2). Tozi Mthethwa, a spokeswoman for
the Municipality, responded that 'a business model for the area was still being
formalised. In the interim, a short-term solution was developed and services were
still being installed' (Akoob, 2016, p. 2).

In an attempt to make the beachfront attractive to international tourists during the FIFA World Cup, fishing was banned from the beachfront, adversely

affecting the livelihoods of about 2000 subsistence fishermen. This decision was made without any consultation with the fishermen. City officials did not link the ban directly to the World Cup, but argued that it was part of the beach-front upgrade project. Several fishermen were upset, and expressed their concerns regarding how fishing affected the World Cup because they were unable to earn a living and provide for their families if they were unable to fish in this accessible area (see Fihlani, 2010, p. 1). The fishers were being excluded from what was once public space which they used for decades and were losing their livelihoods:

> We were born 5 kilometres away from the beachfront. God gave us the beach to have a good time, like the surfers are having a good time. Now we must spend hundreds of Rands to go the South and North to do fishing. It's very unjustified. Even during the apartheid era it was not like this.
>
> (van Grootheest, 2011, p. 2)

Hence, according to Dray (2009, p. iii) 'the fishers are losing a way of life, and experiencing a loss of identity and a communal subsistence economy.'

The fishers established the KwaZulu-Natal Subsistence Fishermen Forum in May 2010, and initiated some public protest action, which received sympathetic media coverage. Many fishers changed their modus operandi by operating in the evenings, when security was less stringent. Others began to take more risks by moving into illegal zones like the harbour where fishing was not permitted (Gray, 2009).

Private sector confidence

An important, positive outcome of the beachfront regeneration was increased confidence and private investment in the area. Since 2013, the Tsogo Sun Group invested R320 million in upgrading its hotels on the beachfront. The first project focused on merging the Maharani and Elangeni hotels on the North Beach into one complex (R220 million), and the refurbishment of the Garden Court Marine Parade (R110 million). According to Samantha Croft, the hotel's general manager, initially the intention was to invest R52 million in the Elangeni project, and then a more ambitious plan was adopted with the merger of both hotels to undertake an extensive upgrade of all rooms, add conferencing facilities and new amenities with views of the beachfront (see Naidoo, 2013). Tsogo Sun chief executive, Marcel von Aulock, emphasised that this expansion was in response to the upgrading of the beachfront:

> Our group's investment into the Southern Sun Elangeni and Maharani hotel complex is a direct response to the substantial investment into the revival of the Durban beachfront promenade by the eThekwini municipality. Durban has been upgraded as a destination and we are proud to be a part of it.
>
> (Naidoo, 2013, p. 1)

James Nxumalo, mayor of eThekwini said that the Tsogo Sun investment was a vote of confidence in Durban. Then, in February 2014 the Tsogo Sun Hotel Group announced a further R1.8 billion investment over three years in the north beach area. Mike Dowsley, the executive director of Suncoast Casino, Hotels and Entertainment said:

> To improve our hospitality infrastructure [...] There is now going to be a 2,000-seat multi-purpose venue, a 22,000 m² retail mall, as well as additional restaurants and a new entertainment area and banqueting facilities [...] We have got to get the right mix – how many shops and restaurants [... and] there will also be resort-style rooftop swimming pools.
>
> (Cole, 2014, p. 1)

City manager S'bu Sithole welcomed the Tsogo Sun investment decision, which fit in with the integrated development plan for the promenade. He argued that this was an affirmation of the decision to revamp the beachfront as part of the 2010 project, which was now bearing fruit. The city manager said that he was:

> delighted with the continued faith shown in the Durban city [...] by Tsogo Sun and that a development of this scale would be a significant catalyst for the continued rejuvenation of the Durban beach front, which has been strongly supported by the City through then redevelopment of the promenade and its subsequent extension.
>
> (Moneyweb, 2014, p. 1)

Tsogo CEO Marcel von Aulock, subsequently announced in November 2015 that 'following an assessment of the Durban retail market, the investment in the Suncoast expansion had increased to R3.5 billion. The revamp will include a 49,500 m² retail mall and additional restaurants' (Hasenfuss, 2015, p. 1). He reaffirmed that since the upgrading of the beachfront, the economic growth potential of the area was being realised: 'Word appears to be getting out as people realise what is happening in Durban and the city is rapidly growing its reputation as a superb conference and event destination' (*Sunday Tribune*, 14 September 2014).

Beach reinvention or contradiction?

In the process of reinventing and beautifying the beaches, several contradictions emerged, including vacant restaurants, loss of Blue Flag status, and crime and grime, which basically undermined the goals of the regeneration project. This section looks specifically at a number of key themes and contradictions facing beachfront regeneration in Durban, focusing on: vacant restaurants, the loss of the Blue Flag status and a look at grime and crime.

Vacant restaurants

The beachfront redevelopment plans included accommodation for 12 fast food and upmarket restaurants. However, these premises were not leased out to businesses during the 2010 FIFA World Cup, apparently for logistical reasons. However, these premises remained vacant for the next three years, ostensibly because the city did not get the right 'mix' of applicants, and have been described as 'a big nasty wart on the pretty beachfront's comely face' (Scott, 2013, p. 1). Waren Ozard, regional manager of the Federated Hospitality Association of South Africa (Fedhasa) complained that the empty beach restaurants were bad for the city's tourism image: 'We have a fantastic new beachfront, but other than the new Circus Beach Café and the eateries around Joe Cools in North Beach there are few other eating places' (Naidoo, 2012, p. 1). The former deputy mayor, and speaker in the eThekwini Municipality, Logie Naidoo replied that the city was looking for higher quality, specialised, restaurants. However, by October 2013 the restaurants were still not operational and were viewed as 'white elephants.' The reason for the lack of interest was attributed to the complex tender procedures with which established restaurateurs were not familiar. Councillor Rick Crouch of the Democratic Alliance argued that award of contracts for the restaurants was being delayed in order to favour business people who were politically connected:

> As with the new stadium, the restaurant and hospitality industries were not consulted or involved in the planning of these restaurants and now they are surprised when the industry is not interested [...] and the city officials tell us that they did not receive any tenders from qualified professional restauranteurs. This is absolute nonsense.
>
> (Crouch, 2012, p. 1)

The Councillor also referred to most of these projects as white elephants, and that ratepayer monies were wasted in the process of developing and planning.

Prime property lying vacant for more than three years meant that the public coffer was losing out. Based on a rental of R90 m^2 (total 2058 m^2) property agents estimated that the monthly loss in rentals was R185,220. This amounted to a loss of more than R7 million over three and half years (Bowman, 2012). Furthermore, R64,000 per month was paid by the city for security and maintenance. The problem was compounded because the empty facilities had deteriorated because of a lack of maintenance and vandalism, and expenses for repairs and renovations would be necessary (Scott, 2013). The restaurants were finally operational in early 2014.

Loss of Blue Flag status

Beach awards such as the Blue Flag status play an important role in promoting tourism (Lucrezi et al., 2015). The loss of an award is viewed 'as such a major and demoralising blow that not applying for an award is sometimes deemed preferable to risking the adverse publicity which results from losing one' (McKenna *et al.*, 2011, p. 576). Blue Flag status is the 'the international eco-stamp of approval for pristine beach management' (Tolsi, 2008, p. 1). Blue Flag certification is determined by the Foundation for Environmental Education (n.d.), an independent NGO, and it describes itself as follows on its website:

> A world-renowned eco-label trusted by millions around the globe for the coastal environment, water quality, safety and access for all: the Blue Flag represents a serious and profound commitment to both people and the environment.

South Africa was the first country outside Europe to receive this accreditation. In order to qualify for Blue Flag status, beaches have to demonstrate excellence in terms of cleanliness, good sanitary facilities, pollution controls, safety, security, amenities and environmental management (Bisetty, 2004). Between 2001 and 2008 many of Durban's beaches had Blue Flag status. For example, in 2004 South Beach was awarded Blue Flag status. According to Mayor Obed Mlaba, this was confirmation 'that our beaches are great [...] this is just one of the reasons why, year after year, South Africans come to this city for their holidays, not just in summer but all year round' (Metro Reporter, 2004, p. 1). Mike Sutcliffe welcomed this 'great accolade,' mentioning: 'Our approach to our natural heritage is to create world class facilities for the enjoyment of all and to do this within strict parameters [...] and meeting international standards on issues such as environmental protection' (Metro Reporter, 2004, p. 1).

However, in 2008 as preparations were well underway for FIFA 2010, four of Durban's main beaches (North Beach, South Beach, Bay of Plenty and Addington Beach) lost their Blue Flag status because of poor water quality, especially the presence of *E. coli* (in sewage), and high levels of pollution. Rather than address the problems, city manager Mike Sutcliffe chose to withdraw from the Blue Flag accreditation process, and accused those who oversee the process of political bias. Elena von Sperber, international coordinator stated that cities and countries are not forced to participate in the programme: 'We will not beg, and cannot force, a municipality to stay in the programme [...] If the municipality wants its flags back, it would have to work towards ensuring that those beaches fulfil the criteria again' (Nair, 2008, p. 6). In a scathing editorial comment, the *Daily News* (29 April 2008) described Durban's beaches as a 'playground of filth':

> The golden beaches and warm surf are fetid with pollution – so much so that the city has lost the internationally recognized Blue Flag on four of its five beaches, but the city administration does not seem to give a damn!

Five years later, largely as a result of pressure from the tourism industry, business sector, and provincial government, Mayor James Nxumalo announced that Durban would rejoin the Blue Flag accreditation programme (Aberdeen, 2013).

Grime and crime

The eThekwini Municipality began the Phase I upgrade promising the public that the improved conditions on the beach would remain even after the World Cup was over to sustain an influx of international and national tourists and locals in the city. However, the dying palm trees, lack of policing, crime, litter, and the smell of urine and defecation on the piers returned in the revamped area. After the accolades of FIFA 2010, it would appear that the city authorities failed to maintain the revamped beachfront. Six months after the 2010 FIFA World Cup, the beachfront was described as a mess, because 'maintenance and upkeep has slipped' since the 2010 FIFA World Cup (Savides, 2011, p. 5). In a letter to the *Sunday Tribune* newspaper, Lisa Guastella stated:

> eThekwini filled us with promises of how wonderful it would be. However, these promises appear to lie in tatters [...] The litter and pieces of glass have returned [...] and the smell of urine and defecation has also returned.
>
> (Savides, 2011, p. 5)

Julie-May Ellingson conceded that 'there were issues around litter and these have to be addressed, but we have to get to the point when the public is responsible as well' (Cole, 2011, p. 2). However, problems related to litter, vagrancy and anti-social behavior continued and reached crisis levels in 2015.

In October 2015, Anne Batchelder, Director of the Amashova Cycle Race, which had about 12,000 entrants, stated that if the regular mess in the beachfront was not sorted out, this prestigious event would no longer be held in Durban. City Councilor for the area, Martin Meyer, said: 'It was absolutely terrible: an eyesore. There was vomit, urine, faeces, pieces of glass. This is the worst I have ever seen. I spoke to the cleaners who were overwhelmed. The mess was too much for them' (Cole, 2015, p. 1).

The Durban Chamber of Commerce and Industry (2013) called for the appointment of a dedicated precinct manager for the beachfront in order to address the various problems, and it would appear that the city management was considering this proposal seriously. Perhaps the last word on the Durban beachfront should be from photographer Matt Kay explaining the concept text for his solo exhibition 'The Front', where he explains Durban's beachfront in the upcoming years:

> Will either be an arcade for tourists, or lost to the degradation and squalor that thrives just behind the promenade [...] at present it is a truly distinctive place in Durban, outside the determination of class, race or wealth restrictions, the beachfront is free to all who want to use it.
>
> (Kay, 2015, p. 1)

The author goes on to explain that the nature is continually changing as a result of more visitors. Some of the main concerns that exist are while the promenade seems integrated, segregation and exclusion persist (see Kay, 2015).

There were several indications that the beachfront beautification regeneration project was not sustainable beyond 2010. The empty restaurants three years after the World Cup represented a wasted opportunity to benefit from, and to promote, urban regeneration and increase tourism, much of this mirrored in allegations of political interference. Another damning indictment was the failure to consult with experts and assess market demands when the restaurants were planned. The loss of the Blue Flag status was another blow, largely due to high levels of *E. coli* and pollution. The failure or inability to deal with crime and grime further compounded the problems on the beachfront. This can be contrasted with the actual FIFA 2010 tournament period as being regarded as impressive, with high police visibility and general lack of litter (Master Builders Association, 2010). It would appear that the city did not have the capacity, resources or political will to sustain the beachfront beautification regeneration project. Mega-event projects are seldom sustainable beyond the event, and often have adverse social consequences for the poor and disadvantaged.

Conclusion

A legacy of FIFA 2010 in Durban was the regeneration of the beachfront and its surroundings. Phase I was completed in time for the event, and Phase II commenced soon thereafter. The beach upgrade was widely welcomed by locals, visitors and the business sector. It also served as a catalyst for major investment along the beachfront, particularly in the upgrading of hotels and associated facilities. The Blue Flag fiasco certainly did not help the cause of the city as it attempted to promote itself as a global destination, and was almost a reckless decision. Buildings designated for restaurants were vacant for more than three years resulting in loss of revenue. This raised questions about public accountability. The inability to maintain the beachfront reflects a failure of the municipal leadership and administration. The downside was the displacement and marginalisation of informal traders and fisher folk who were dependent on the beachfront for their livelihoods. Hence, 'existing forms of employment (were) overlooked and undervalued' (Raco, 2004, p. 35). The revitalised beachfront was deemed to be a restricted public space. In aspiring for global, world class status, poverty was an embarrassment. Hence, FIFA 2010 in Durban served as a smokescreen for the purging of fisher folk, informal traders, and other visible signs of poverty. It also served as a catalyst for the diversion of public spending priorities from more urgent social priorities such as the provision of basic services for the poor, including water, sanitation and housing. Given the challenges observed above concerning the 2010 FIFA World Cup in Durban, the city needs to consider a number of measures as the city will host the 2022 Commonwealth Games. A number of plans already exist ahead of 2022. The city plans to get rid of the Stables flea market in the beachfront precinct and a high-rise building is planned next to the casino. Once more the last bits of public spaces are regenerated through private investments, a city that was once the incubator of apartheid ideals is now the pioneer of class-apartheid.

References

Aberdeen, Z. (2013). Praise for city's Blue Flag bid. *Daily news*, 14 June, 3.

Akoob, R. (2016). Traders at Blue Lagoon claim neglect. *Post*, 28 January, 2.

Bisetty, V. (2004). Blue Flag for city beaches. *Daily news*, 8 July, 4.

Bowman, C. (2012). Empty shops turn golden mile to ghost town. *Sunday tribune*, 11 March, 11.

Cole, B. (2008). R100m shine for Golden Mile. *Daily news*, 10 December, 2.

Cole, B. (2011). Plans to extend beachfront upgrade. *Daily news*, 25 January, 2.

Cole, B. (2014). R1.8bn expansion for Durban casino. http://www.iol.co.za/business/companies/r18bn-expansion-for-durban-casino-1752405.

Cole, B. (2015). Clean beaches or we go. *The independent on Saturday*, 10 October, 1–2.

Crouch, R. (2012). Beachfront restaurants white elephants. http://www.famouspublishing.co.za/crest/beachfront-restaurants-white-elephants/.

Daily News. (2008). Playground of filth. *Daily news*, 29 April, 14.

eThekwini Municipality. (2003). Coastal Tourism Initiative, market segmentation and product identification study. Final Report 14 August 2003. Prepared by Haley Sharpe Southern Africa (Pty) Ltd, Kloof.

Dawood, Z. (2015). Row over city's false publicity gloss. *Daily news*, 10 April.

Dray, A. (2009). The politics of the privatisation of public space: The subsistence fishers of Durban, KwaZulu-Natal (Unpublished Master's Thesis) University of KwaZulu-Natal.

Durban Chamber of Commerce and Industry. (2013). A business vision for the economic development of Durban. http://durbanchamber.co.za/profiles/blogs/a-business-vision-for-the-economic-development-of-durban.

Ellingson, J. (2013). MILE strategic planning master class from vision to implementation. http://www.mile.org.za/Come_Learn/Capacity%20Enhancement/Master%20Class/Multimedia%20Library/Strategic%20Planning%20Master%20Class%202014/Day%203.2-Julie-May%20Ellingson.pdf.

Fihlani, P. (2010). Durban fishermen cry foul over 'World Cup ban.' http://www.bbc.com/news/10555317.

Foundation for Environmental Education (n.d.). Pure water, clean coasts, safety and access for all. http://www.fee.global/blue-flag.

Harper, P. (2012). The madness that is Durban's disease. *City press*, 5 February, 29.

Hasenfuss, M. (2015). Hopes for uptick in spending drive Tsogo Sun. http://www.bdlive.co.za/business/transport/2015/11/20/hopes-for-uptick-in-spending-drive-tsogo-sun.

Jones, P. & Gripaios, P. (2000). A review of the BURA awards for best practice in urban regeneration. *Property management*, *18*, 218–229.

Kay, M. (2015). "The Front": A solo exhibition by Tierney Fellow Matt Kay – Concept note. http://www.marketphotoworkshop.co.za/exhibitions/entry/the-front-a-solo-exhibition-by-tierney-fellow-matt-kay1.

Lucrezi, S., Melville Saayman, M. & Peet Van der Merwe, P. (2015). Managing beaches and beachgoers: Lessons from and for the Blue Flag Award. *Tourism management*, *48*, 211–230.

Maharaj, B. (2015). The turn of the South? Social and economic impacts of mega events in India, Brazil and South Africa. *Local economy*, *39*, 983–999.

Maharaj, B., Pillay, V. & Sucheran, R. (2006). Durban – A tourism Mecca? Challenges of the post-apartheid era. *Urban forum*, *16*, 262–281.

Masikane, Z. and Ntumbu, A. (2012). Consultation for Blue Lagoon informal traders. *Metro ezasegagazini*, 11 May. http://showme.co.za/durban/news/consultation-for-blue-lagoon-informal-traders/.

Master Builders Association. (2010). A visit to the new revamped Durban beachfront. http://www.masterbuilders.co.za/news/2010/June/a_visit_to_the_new_revamped_durban_beachfront.htm.

McKenna, J., Williams, A., Andrew, J. & Cooper, G. (2011). Blue Flag or red herring: Do beach awards encourage the public to visit beaches? *Tourism management, 32,* 576–588.

Metro Reporter. (2004). We've got the Blues: Durban beaches win awards. *Natal witness,* 29 October, 1.

Mntuyedwa, N. (2012). Blue Lagoon area in EThekwini under construction. http://thenetworks.co.za/2012/05/blue-lagoon-area-in-ethekwini-municipality-under-construction/.

Moneyweb. (2014). Tsogo Sun announces the granting of regulatory approvals for the expansion of the Suncoast Casino http://www.moneyweb.co.za/mny_sens/tsogo-sun-holdings-limited-tsogo-sun-announces-the-granting-of-regulatory-approvals-for-the-expansion-of-the-suncoast-casino/.

Moodley, L. 2014. Public spaces, livelihoods and displacement: A case study of the Durban Blue Lagoon upgrade (unpublished honours project). University of KwaZulu-Natal.

Naidoo, S. (2012). 18 months and beach restaurants still empty. http://www.iol.co.za/mercury/18-months-and-beach-restaurants-still-empty-1207160.

Naidoo, S. (2013). Maharani to return to Durban with 220m hotel upgrade. http://www.iol.co.za/business/companies/maharani-to-return-to-durban-with-r220m-hotel-upgrade-1496107n.

Nair, N. (2008). Durban told to clean up its beaches. *The times,* 27 March, 6.

Raco, M. (2004). Whose gold rush? The social legacy of a London Olympics. In A. Vigor, M. Mean & C. Tims (Eds.). *After the gold rush: A sustainabe Olympics for London.* London, England: DEMOS/IPPR (pp. 31–50).

Robbins, T. (2005). Durban's beachfront modified to capture target market. http://www.engineeringnews.co.za/article/durbans-beachfront-modified-to-capture-target-markets-2005-03-25.

Savides, M. (2011). On a slippery slope: A take on Durban's proposed beachfront upgrade expansion. *Sunday tribune,* 16 January, 5.

Scott, C.M. (2013). Durban beach front restaurant facilities remain vacant. https://hearonearth.wordpress.com/2013/06/10/durban-beach-front-restaurant-facilities-remain-vacant/.

SSI. (2011). Basic assessment process: Durban central beachfront upgrade (Phase II). SSI Engineers and Environmental Consultants, Pinetown.

Sunday Tribune. (2014). Hotel group invests in Durban beachfront properties. http://yourproperty.co.za/hotel-group-invests-in-durban-beachfront-properties.

Tolsi, N. (2008). The big stink over Durban beachfronts. http://mg.co.za/article/2008-03-30-the-big-stink-over-durban-beachfronts.

van Grootheest, S. (2011). Resistance and representation: The organization of protest by subsistence and recreational fishermen during the FIFA World Cup 2010 (Masters Thesis). University of KwaZulu-Natal.

Walford, L. (2015). Beachfront louts are bad for business. http://bereamail.co.za/65470/beachfront-louts-are-bad-for-business/. Zakas, L. (2010). Durban wows the world, wins world acclaim. *Star,* 16 July, 2.

4   Mega-event scepticism in South Korea

Lessons from the 2014 Incheon Asian Games

Jung Woo Lee

Introduction

The Incheon Asian Games in 2014 is arguably the most controversial sporting event that South Korea has ever hosted. In terms of sporting performances, it was certainly an occasion through which the South Korean team was able to display its sporting prowess. Also, the President of the Olympic Council of Asia praised a safe and effective delivery of the Asian Games at the closing ceremony. When considering non-sporting issues related to this continental sporting festival, however, a different mood can be detected. Staging a sports mega-event is often closely connected to a social and economic policy of the host country or city (Horne, 2016). The Incheon Asian Games was no exception. Yet, unlike the organising committee's claim that the Games would boost the local economy before the event, Incheon is now suffering from a huge deficit (Kim, 2014). Also, a number of newly built sporting facilities, including the new Asian Games stadium, are now on the verge of turning into white elephants (Choi, 2014). It appears that the major legacy of the Asian Games is a heavy financial burden.

Over the last two decades, South Korea displayed a strong desire to bid for and host a diverse range of sports mega-events (Lee, 2015). For instance, this small peninsula country has staged the Fédération Internationale de Football Association (FIFA) World Cup Finals, Formula 1 Grand Prix and the International Association of Athletics Federations (IAAF) World Championships, and in 2018 will host the Winter Olympic Games. It appears that South Korea, especially the local governments in host cities, firmly believes that large-scale events will bring positive implications. Yet, the Incheon Asian Games makes policy makers and the public reconsider this belief. After observing the financial burden that this sporting mega-event engendered, a sceptical view of hosting a sports mega-event is gradually on the rise. In this respect, the Incheon Asian Games marks a significant turning point – although an overly optimistic view has not yet completely disappeared. This chapter provides a critical overview of the social, economic and cultural issues concerning the Incheon Asian Games. Particular attention will be paid to the construction project, the sporting legacy programme and the cultural relations activity associated with the 17th Summer Asiad. By examining a series of unfortunate incidents, this work aims to offer an exemplary case of a not-so-successful sports mega-event so that these negative practices will not be repeated. Before investigating them, however, this chapter will briefly discuss key agendas and claimed legacies of hosting a sports mega-event in South Korea.

Hosting sporting mega-events: Key agendas

There is no need to highlight that a sports mega-event is not simply a sporting contest but an occasion with socio-political and economic implications. In South Korea, at least three specific rationales for hosting such an event can be identified. These include: (1) sport mega-event driven development and regeneration, (2) the improvement of its international reputation and (3) the demonstration of South Korean culture to the world. Referring to the rationales, first, hosting a sports mega-event offers a useful economic opportunity for the government of the host city to implement an urban regeneration programme (Yamawaki & Duarte, 2014). The host city can enhance the quality of urban environment since the preparation process entails the construction of amenities and physical infrastructures, such as upgraded or new transportation networks, communication systems, and other convenient facilities (Horne, in press). More importantly, the large amount of public funds, which are not normally available to be spent on such major civil engineering projects if an international sporting competition is not to be held in the city, are often given to the local authority to facilitate the redevelopment works associated with a sports mega-event (Preuss, 2015).

Because of the effect of sports mega-event driven development, a number of South Korean cities intend to host a major sporting event. In fact, various types of competitions from the international rowing championship to the Winter Olympic Games have been awarded to South Korean cities. Regarding this, one commentator notes that when a local government wins the rights to host a sporting event, its major interest does not lie in sporting contests themselves but actually in an urban regeneration project that hosting initiates (Chung, 2014). In Korea, once its city is chosen to host a sports mega-event, the central government subsidises various construction works directly related to the event (Choi *et al.*, 2013). In addition, as staging a major international sporting event creates useful business opportunities, commercial corporations also invest in associated facility development projects. The financial supports and investments from public and private sectors enable the local government to implement and eventually materialise costly urban regeneration without entirely relying on the local budget. Therefore, in South Korea, hosting a sports mega-event is often viewed as one of the most effective strategies to upgrade an urban environment.

The second rationale, hosting a sports mega-event works as a diplomatic instrument to improve international reputation of the host country (see also Henderson, Chapter 1, this collection). South Korea observed that by staging the Olympic Games and the Asian Games in the 1980s, it could display its remarkable industrial development – rapidly transitioning from one of the poorest to one of the fast developing economies in the world (see Koh, 2005; Bridges, 2008). In the twenty-first century, South Korea has strived for recognition as an influential power state in global politics. Concerning international relations today, it is important to secure both hard (i.e. economic prosperity and military power) and soft power (i.e. morally correct government policy and attractive cultural resources) to become a leading advanced nation (Nye, 2008). For South Korea, it is this soft power that needs to be developed in order to realise its aspiration. While hosting a sport mega-event does not automatically bring the soft power resources to the country, the implementation and management of socio-cultural programmes associated with sport mega-events can help accumulate this soft power capital.

International development through sport is one of such activities that can accrue the nation's soft power. Sport as a development tool is used to assist the development of emerging economies around the world (Levermore & Aaron, 2009; Maharaj, Chapter 3, this collection; Wise and Hall, Chapter 2, this collection). The United Nations (2009) recognises the usefulness of sport in improving social conditions in poorer developing nations, and international sport governing bodies such as the International Olympic Committee (IOC) and FIFA along with non-governmental organisations such as the right to play actively, participate in international development through sport initiatives (Darnell, 2012). The host cities and the organising committees often set an international sport development programme as a key component of social legacy. Such assistance initiatives can be seen as ethical and responsible sport policy, as the successful implementation of international development programme can contribute to boosting the host nation's soft power. Because of this reason, as will be discussed later, mega-events awarded to South Korean cities also involve elements of sport and international development.

Finally, a host country and city intends to display cultural heritage to international audiences. This can be seen as the nation's cultural relations strategy, which is also closely connected to a campaign for enhancing a nation's soft power (Grix & Lee, 2013). As indicated earlier, the domain of culture, including those related to sport, becomes increasingly important in securing international political hegemony (Johnson & Cester, 2015). Staging an event with the capacity to attract global attention deems to be regarded as an effective tool for promoting cultural prowess of the host nation. Both the established core nation and an emerging state through international promotion therefore attempts to harness the tactic of hosting a major global sporting competition as a means to cultivate their own cultural relations (Grix & Lee, 2013; Grix & Houlihan, 2014). South Korea is a country which actively utilises this tactic (Lee, 2016). It should be noted that while its economy is one of the strongest in the world, South Korea is still located in a relatively marginalised position in the realm of cultural politics and diplomacy (Lee, 2009). In other words, there has been the unbalanced development between hard and soft power in the county. Because South Korea is eager to change this situation and thereby improve its international standing, it is important for the country to adapt the way it represents, communicates and delivers its cultural products effectively to the wider global community. To do this, it comes as no surprise that South Korea is aggressively aiming to bid for and host mega-events to display its cultural merit alongside its economic prowess.

Asian Games driven development in Incheon

In 2007, the South Korean port city of Incheon was selected to host the 2014 Summer Asian Games. A brief explanation of Incheon's geographical location in South Korea and in Asia will help in understanding this port city's intention to host the continental sporting spectacle. Incheon is located 30 km west of Seoul, but because most of the economic and cultural capital in the country tends to be heavily concentrated in Seoul, the port city had witnessed the problem of comparative underdevelopment despite (or because of) close proximity to the capitol (Kim & Jung, 2014). Due to this unbalanced development, the port city is merely regarded as Seoul's satellite that its economic and social environments were relatively neglected within the wider capital zone even though Incheon is the third largest city in the country in terms of population. Therefore, increasing the visibility of the city given its cultural and economic geography in South Korea has long been a major task of the local politicians.

In addition, Incheon is a port city where the major trade seaport and the main gateway airport into the country are positioned. The fact that the city has such international transportation infrastructures indicates that the city has a potential to develop into a regional and global hub. As Sino-South Korean economic ties continue to strengthen, Incheon is expected to play an important role in Northeast Asian trade in the coming years because of its logistically important geographical location. Nevertheless, the international transportation infrastructure in Incheon merely offers a highway to the capital city where most business meetings take place. It appears that Incheon's public facilities yet again mainly serve the interests of Seoul. In an attempt to attract more international capital and resources to Incheon to augment its capacity to become a Northeast Asian business hub, the Incheon metropolitan government have been recently investing in extensive urban regeneration. This includes the opening of a free trade zone and the installation of convenient facilities for foreign visitors in their wider municipal area. In spite of these efforts, the port city's potential has not yet materialised.

Incheon's willingness to host the Asian Games must be understood in relation to its relative underdevelopment and its desire to develop into a Northeast Asian economic exchange and trade hub. A few rationales can be identified in this respect. First, the metropolitan government of Incheon expected that the central government would allocate more development funds to the port city so that it could improve the condition of its urban environment if Incheon won the rights for hosting the Asian Games. Second, by staging this continental sporting event, the city would be able to re-establish and promote its new geographical identity as a multicultural business hub in Northeast Asia. Moreover, hosting the Asian Games was perceived to not only help facilitate the city's urban development endeavours to reclaim its underestimated potential domestically, but also disseminate its rebranded urban image across Asia and further afar. The project of staging the sports mega-event was, therefore, an attractive option for the metropolitan government in achieving a much delayed urban regeneration initiative.

When the metropolitan government prepared for its Asian Game bid in 2007 they encountered an unexpected problem. As part of a bidding campaign, it is important for the candidate city to show the Olympic Council of Asia a message that the central government is fully supportive of the bid. Then South Korean President, Roh Moo-hyun, was lukewarm about Incheon's Asian Games bid. This was because of Pyeongchang's simultaneous efforts in trying to host the Winter Olympic Games. Considering this winter sporting competition as a more significant national project, the central government was in favour of supporting Pyeongchang's bid – worrying that undertaking two separate bidding campaigns might negatively affect Pyeongchang's effort to win the Winter Olympics (Kim, 2012). In addition, Incheon was financially in deficit from overspending the city's budget on urban redevelopment projects. Hosting a mega sporting event would require more public funding and the central government rightfully expected that staging the Asian Games would worsen Incheon's economic circumstances.

Despite a lack of support from the central government, Incheon carried out its aggressive bidding campaign and was successfully selected to host the 17th Asian Games. The Incheon city justified the rationale for hosting this sporting event with reference to its own financial survey which anticipated that the Asian Games would bring economic benefits to the port city by promoting tourism in the destination during the sports events and attracting more foreign direct investment after the Games (see KIEP, 2007). Based on this survey, the metropolitan government believed that it could resolve the current financial deficit by marketing the city through the sporting event. During the preparation period, tensions arose again between the municipal and central governments over the provision of public funds. No issue exemplifies this conflict better than building sporting facilities, particularly the construction of the main Asian Games Stadium.

Initially, in 2008, Incheon proposed to build 21 new sporting facilities (including the main Asian Games Stadium) out of 39 sporting fields necessitated to stage the Asian Games. Yet, given the huge amount of money needed to construct these venues, the central government did not approve this Asian Games development plan. The metropolitan government resubmitted its Asian Games development proposal and this time only 12 of 40 essential sporting facilities would be new constructions. This proposal still included the construction of the main stadium – the most expensive venue. The central government recommended using the underused, but still functional, World Cup stadium built for the FIFA World Finals in 2002 instead because it was a more sustainable option particularly considering the amount of taxpayers' money used simply to maintain it. Nevertheless, in response to this, Incheon promised that no public funds would be spent on building this most expensive facility and it would seek a funder from the private sector to complete the main stadium construction project. This would reduce almost 40% of financial supply from the central government. On this condition, the South Korean government approved Incheon's Asian Games development plan in 2009.

In 2010, amidst Incheon's serious financial deficit, Song Young-gil (the newly elected mayor) proclaimed that improving the city's economic condition was his most urgent monetary policy. Incheon's new mayor said that the municipal government should renovate the World Cup stadium for the purpose of the Asian Games because it was simply unable to secure sufficient private funds to construct the new main stadium. This plan seemed fair and acceptable given the city's financial difficulties. Yet citizens and local developers from the west Incheon area (where the proposed construction site was to be located) protested against the new mayor's idea. West Incheon was a comparatively underdeveloped part of the city and people here considered the venue construction a valuable opportunity to upgrade their living conditions. Local politicians representing west Incheon also joined this protest. In the end, the new mayor, unable to persuade its citizens, dropped his idea and returned to the original plan.

Given that no organisations from the private sector were willing to invest in the main stadium construction project, the metropolitan government again sought financial support from the central government – who initially refused this request outright. In response, millions of Incheon citizens signed a petition for the publicly funded Asian Games Stadium while politicians representing Incheon city put further pressure on the government. Subsequently, the central government agreed that it would subsidise one-quarter of the total cost needed, and the rest of the money would be deducted from the budget to be allocated to the municipal government in the years following.

After these incidents, the municipal government managed to deliver the Asian Games as planned in 2014. Given the sheer cost to build the new sporting facilities, Incheon's debts increased following the Asian Games. Measuring the long-term economic impact of hosting the Asian Games at this stage is a difficult task, but it is clear that Incheon city is suffering from a heavy economic burden – a significant portion of which is accumulated from the construction and maintenance of the sporting facilities. It seems that a large amount of taxpayers' monies was wasted, given that the Asian Games main stadium (the most costly facility to build) is currently of very little use and on the verge of becoming a white elephant. It seems that claimed economic benefits and development opportunities associated with hosting the Asian Games are unlikely to materialise in the feasible future.

The Asian Games and international sport development

Sport has been increasingly used as a tool for international development and for sporting mega-events today (Levermore & Aaron, 2009), and the South Korean government also takes this sport for international development initiative seriously. The government set Official Development Assistance (ODA) to be one of the nation's major foreign policy agendas, with a number of sport governing bodies in South Korea actively engaged in various international sport development activities (Na & Dallaire, 2015). The Incheon Asian Games was no exception. When Incheon was elected to be a host of the 17th Summer Asiad, the metropolitan government of Incheon claimed that this sporting occasion would make a valuable contribution to the development of sport in Asia. In order to achieve this goal, Incheon city introduced the Vision 2014 programme.

The Vision 2014 programme refers to an international sport development campaign associated with the Incheon Asian Games. The Incheon metropolitan government in collaboration with the Olympic Council of Asia (OCA) initiated this sport assistance programme with the aim of supporting the development of sport in less well-off nations in Asia. The Vision 2014 consists of three major activities: (1) inviting young athletes from developing countries to training camps in Incheon, (2) dispatching qualified sports coaches to marginalised regions in Asia and (3) providing sport equipment for athletes in underdeveloped nations in the continent (Incheon Metropolitan Government, 2015). Given South Korea has recently emerged as an international sporting power, this sport development opportunity has potential to identify and foster sporting talents in peripheral countries in the continent. Through this, the Incheon Asian Games also potentially contributes to reducing the development gap between Northeast and Southeast Asia.

The metropolitan government of Incheon undertook this international sport development initiative for eight years from 2007 to 2014, costing around $20 million (all monetary figures in US dollars). By implementing the Vision 2014, Incheon city could establish close international partnerships with those 30 Asian nations. From over 30 Asian countries, 696 athletes benefited from this Vision 2014 campaign which included 155 sport development programmes. As part of the Vision 2014, Incheon also assisted sport development in North Korea. Given the escalating political tension between the two Koreas, the South Korean port city's attempt to help its northern neighbour signalled messages of peace – showing how sport can transcend ideological conflicts and political differences. More importantly, this initiative enabled 97 participants from developing Asian nations to take part in the 2014 Asian Games. This can be seen as a visible impact of this international sport development programme.

This international development programme can be understood as the South Korean port city's cultural relations strategy which potentially fosters Incheon's and South Korea's soft power in the relations between Asian states. Nye (2008) notes the nation-state whose foreign policy is concerned primarily with universal humanitarian values is more likely to shape a favourable international circumstance to the state so that it can fulfil its diplomatic aims more smoothly. In effect, a country's effort to keep global social justice constitutes one of the key factors that increase a destinations attractiveness – which eventually contributes to enhancing its soft power. International sport development, particularly those activities designed to improve sporting skills and opportunities in the less developed world, is a way of providing material and technical support – and is of paramount importance in this respect. Such efforts are certainly seen as a diplomatic, or related to sport diplomacy, to increase an influence of a specific country within the system of international sport governance. The Vision 2014 programme appears to be one such tactic to enhance Incheon's merit.

Without underestimating the valuable contribution that Incheon made by implementing this Vision 2014, it should also be pointed out whether this international assistance campaign is genuinely related to the principle of universal humanitarianism. A close examination of the context in which this international sport development programme took place reveals a slightly different picture. As noted earlier, the central government did not wholeheartedly advocate for Incheon's intention to host the Asian Games. Given the competitive nature of the event bidding campaigns between New Delhi and Incheon, strong government support turned out to be crucial in order to win the Games. The lack of governmental endorsement was a severe disadvantage to Incheon. In an attempt to outweigh this shortcoming, the metropolitan government pledged the implementation of Vision 2014 which would offer technical and material resources for sport development to developing Asian countries if the Asian Games was awarded to Incheon. It is difficult to claim that Incheon won the continental sporting event because of this pledged assistance programme. Nevertheless, given many member states of the Olympic Council of Asia would benefit from Incheon's promise, it is no exaggeration to argue that the potential beneficiaries voted for the South Korean port city. Therefore, Incheon's international sport development programme seems to be merely a tactic to win the bid. Hence, it appears that the ethos of humanitarian development was simply a façade and that the self-interest of Incheon came first when the city offered the Vision 2014 programme. The fact that this sporting aid ceased soon after the mega-event finished also suggests this was merely a short-term and goal-oriented plan that focused only on winning the Asian Games bid.

Vision 2014 initiative exasperated Incheon's financial crisis after the Asian Games. As mentioned earlier, the city suffered from huge debts preparing for the sporting event. This was, in fact, one of the main reasons for the lack of political support from the central government. Yet, Incheon was persistent with its desire to host the Games at any costs without carefully considering the economic implications. The port city even pledged the delivery of this expensive aid project to outbid its competitors. Without entirely dismissing the ethos of Vision 2014, Incheon's agreement to deliver the international sport development project cost the port city almost $20 million – viewed as an insensible offer considering its economic situation.

The Asian Games and the 'Korean Wave'

The representation of contemporary South Korean popular culture was one of the main cultural events associated with the 2014 Asian Games. South Korea's popular cultural industry (such as music, films and television shows) has attracted much attention in Asia recently (Chua & Iwabuchi, 2008), and in the past 10 years this industry has become one stimulator of the country's economy (KOTRA, 2015). This growing popularity of Korean pop culture abroad is called the 'Korean Wave.' Currently, Korean cultural commodities are extensively circulated and consumed in a number of different Asian countries, and many South Korean film stars and pop musicians have become household names in those nations. Reflecting their popularity a large number of tourists from Asia, notably from China and Japan, regularly visit South Korea to pay homage to their pop idols. This Korean Wave focused tourism has significantly contributed to boosting the nation's image and economy (Koh, 2012). In effect, the Korean Wave is a branding technique that symbolises the Korean pop culture industry today.

The extensive circulation and consumption of South Korean cultural products in East Asian region is, to some extent, the outcome of the government's effort to foster its culture industry as part of the nation's soft power strategy (Kwon & Kim, 2014). As indicated earlier, having an attractive cultural heritage that includes contemporary mass culture constitutes an important component of cultural relations in global politics today (Nye, 2008). In this respect, the South Korean government invests in the development of culture because it considers this industry a dominant domain of creativity that helps further improve the nation's reputation (Kwon & Kim, 2014). Moreover, it is especially expected that the dissemination of Korean cultural commodities to neighbouring Asian states can cultivate a social environment in those countries wherein positive attitudes towards Korea emerge – thus regenerating the nation's image as an appealing popular destination. With these in mind, the South Korean government regards nurturing the popular culture industry a core policy agenda, and this political choice further enables the demanding market for the Korean Wave to expand continually both in the country and abroad.

Given the increasing influence of the Korean Wave in Asia, it is no surprise that the South Korean pop culture accounts for one of the major themes at the Asian Games related cultural events. In fact, the exploitation of Korean cultural commodities during the continental sporting competition seems to be Incheon's strategic choice to effectively attract the attention of people across the region to the Games, and subsequently to the host city. It was also expected that more Asian tourists would visit the port city not only for sport, but also to meet the Korean Wave stars during cultural programmes and at mini-concerts. In addition, famous South Korean film directors, Jang Jin and Im Kwon-taek, arranged the opening and closing ceremonies wherein the performances of Korean celebrities played a significant role. Also, a South Korean actress, Lee Young-Ae, was chosen to be the final torchbearer who lit the Asian Games cauldron. The finale of the opening ceremony was performed by a South Korean pop star PSY. After all, it seems that the Asian Games functioned as a theatre to display the country's sought-after cultural icons.

The use of Korean popular culture itself is not necessarily problematic. However, it appears that the opening and closing ceremonies relied too much on the cultural commodities in making the shows more spectacular. So much so that the representation of sporting tradition and historical legacies of the host city were comparatively neglected. Given that the Korean entertainment industry displayed throughout the events ceremonies has no meaningfully historical and cultural connection with Korean sports and local tradition, the abundance of the Korean pop culture failed to explain the values of the sporting competition, namely 'Diversity Shine Here,' and the narrative of Incheon's long history sufficiently. For instance, while many South Korean celebrities were invited to the ceremonies, many key sport personalities, particularly a former Manchester United midfielder Ji-sung Park and an Olympic champion Yuna Kim, arguably the most famous international sport stars who the country has ever produced, were not asked to attend the events. The selection of the final Asian Games torchbearer triggered some controversy. Conventionally, an individual who lit the cauldron was chosen from athletes whose characters and achievements suitably symbolise the values of the sporting competition. At the Incheon Asian Games, as mentioned earlier, a popular film star undertook this role simply because the actress was a well-known figure. This indicates that the central message disseminated through the ceremonies concerns the promotion of South Korean cultural commodities. The fundamental value of the Asian Games was overshadowed by superficial entertainment. Reflecting this, one commentator aptly points out that the opening ceremony of this continental sporting event turned out to be an occasion to simply promote products associated with the Korean Wave (Han, 2014).

Additionally, the ceremonies paid only scarce attention to the social and cultural history of Incheon. The opening and closing ceremonies conventionally include a section which is devoted to displaying the legacy and heritage of local traditions. Incheon was the first international seaport in the country and as the main gateway port, Incheon observed the influx of the large volume of modern cultural products and foreign goods from Europe to the country for the first time in its history. This implies that Incheon played an important role in the modernisation of Korea. The direct inter-cultural encounter that Incheon experienced in the late nineteenth century also built the circumstance that the port city easily embraces multiculturalism later. These historical narratives potentially offer useful concepts that fit the main theme of the Asian Games, yet these elements were not sufficiently utilised in the opening and closing ceremonies.

Overall, the Incheon Asian Games, particularly the opening and closing ceremonies, simply offered an extravaganza of South Korean pop culture. This may have entertained the athletes, guests, and tourists from neighbouring Asian countries, yet the essence of the Asian Games, which includes the ethos of the continental sporting festival which celebrates cultural diversity through sports and the heritage of the South Korean port city, was largely omitted from the ceremonies and other cultural events associated with this sporting competition. Given Incheon attempted to establish its new urban identity as a hub of Northeast Asian economy and transportation, the lack of demonstration acknowledging the city's local history as a traditional port city that embraced multiculturalism was arguably a major shortcoming of the event. The spectacle of Korean pop culture alone simply does not fulfil Incheon's desire to construct its new identity.

Conclusion

Incheon's metropolitan government has been undertaking a massive urban regeneration project in order to develop the port city into a node of Northeast Asian transportation and economic networks. The delivery of the Summer Asian Games, which is the largest continental sporting competition, must be understood as part of this redevelopment plan. The metropolitan government anticipated that the Asian Games would have positive implications for this new urban policy – and therefore attempted to use this sporting occasion as a vehicle to facilitate a redevelopment process aimed at rebranding Incheon as a centre of Northeast Asian industry. Boosting the local economy was also an important consideration.

This optimism disappeared once the event finished. As long as cultural, economic and political implications are concerned, the Incheon Asian Games is arguably the least successful event South Korea has ever hosted. The preparation for and delivery of the two weeks of sporting competition left a huge economic deficit, and the newly built Asian Games stadium is hardly used in the post-event period. Rather than stimulating the local economy, Incheon has become the most indebted city in the country after the event (Kim, 2014). Of course, the citizens of Incheon are mainly responsible for the repayment of this debt that hosting the Asian Games caused (Green Korea, 2015). Moreover, Incheon's international sport development programme created an additional financial burden. Surely this campaign had merit in terms of helping less well-off neighbouring nations. Nevertheless, Vision 2014 was certainly an irresponsible project, especially in consideration of the worsening economic situation that Incheon faced. Furthermore, cultural contents displayed through the opening and closing ceremonies were rather frustrating. These occasions mainly showed a series of Korean pop culture performances that did not sufficiently represent Incheon's historical legacy alongside its new urban identity that the city attempted to establish. Hence, in contrast to the optimism before the event, the 17th Asian Games appeared in some ways to influence the development of Incheon negatively.

Ironically, the Incheon Asian Games was also an important incident because of the negative impact. After witnessing the Incheon metropolitan government's financial mismanagement approach along with the inadequate orchestration of the Asian Games ceremonies, a number of civic organisations, academics and the media keep requesting that an independent and transparent post-event investigation into the preparation and delivery of the Asian Games be conducted (Choi, 2014). Incheon's fiasco also triggers mega-event scepticism within South Korea's civic society. It may be an exaggeration to state that this critical view on hosting a mega sporting event is extensively accepted by the establishment. However, it is also difficult to deny that a number of people who join this anti-mega sporting event campaign is continually increasing, especially after the Incheon Asian Games. Incheon's huge financial deficits and the city's now almost neglected sporting facilities influence Korean people and policy makers alike are challenged to objectively re-evaluate the hosting of a mega-event in their municipalities. This may be indicative of the belief of economic development and urban regeneration through hosting a mega sporting event being dismantled. If this is the case, emerging sporting mega-event scepticism and debunking myths of sporting mega-event driven development are unintended but unignorable legacies of the Incheon Asian Games—which render this sporting occasion rather significant.

References

Bridges, B. (2008). The Seoul Olympics: Economic miracle meet the world. *The international journal of the history of sport, 25*, 1939–1952.

Choi, J.W., Lee, J.M., Shin, Y.K. & Jeon, M.R. (2013). *Kuk-je-kyung-ki-dae-hui Yoo-chi mit Jee-won-ae Dae-han Bup-jae-do Jung-bi-bang-an Yeon-koo [Research into the law and regulation on hosting and supporting international sporting events].* Seoul: Minstry of Culture, Sport and Tourism.

Choi, J.Y. (2014). *Incheon Aisan Game ae Dae-han Pyoung-ga-rul huh-ha-ra [Let us evaluate the impact of the Incheon Asian Games objectivily].* Cultural action, 21 October, http://www.culturalaction.org/xe/1122161?l=ko.

Chua, B.H. & Iwabuchi, K. (2008). *East Asian pop culture analysing the Korean wave.* Hong Kong: Hong Kong University Press.

Chung, H. (2014). Pyeongchang Olympics Muck-tui nun bae-boo-re-go Jee-yeok-min en bit-du-mee [the local people suffer from huge debt caused by the Pyeongchang Olympics]. *Sisa jockey.* 5 December, (K. Chung, Interviewer) CBS. Seoul.

Darnell, S. (2012). *Sport for development and peace: Critical sociology.* London, England: Bloomsbury.

Green Korea. (2015). *Dae-kyu-mo Kook-jea-sport-dae-hui-eu Yoo-chi-was Woon-young-ei Mun-jae [The problems of hosting and managing sports mega-events].* Seoul: Green Korea.

Grix, J. & Houlihan, B. (2014). Sports mega-events as part of a nation's soft power strategy: The cases of Germany (2006) and the UK (2012). *The British journal of politics and international relations, 16*, 572–596.

Grix, J. & Lee, D. (2013). Soft power, sports mega-events and emerging states: The lure of the politics of attraction. *Global society, 27*(4), 521–536.

Han, Y.H. (2014). Han-ryu-ei Han-ryu-ae-ei-han, Han-ryu-gae-pye-mak-sik…Mun-hwa Jang-sa-koon-ei Yok-mang [The desire of the Korean Wave enterprise: Of the Korean Wave, for the Korean Wave, Korean Wave ceremonies]. *Midiaus*, 5 October, http://www.mediaus.co.kr/news/articleView.html?idxno=44595.

Horne, J. (in press). Sports mega-events – three sites of contemporary political contestation. *Sport in society*, (online first) DOI: 10.1080/17430437.2015.1088721.

Horne, J. (2016). The contemporary politics of sports mega events. In A. Bairner, J. Kelly & J.W. Lee (Eds.). *Routledge handbook of sport and politics.* Abingdon, England: Routledge (pp. 238–250).

Incheon Metropolitan Government. (2015). *White paper on OCA-Incehon Vision 2014 programme.* Incheon: Dowcom.

Johnson, M.A. & Cester, X. (2015). Communicating Catalan culture in a global society. *Public relations review, 41*, 809–815.

KIEP. (2007). *2014 Incheon Asia Kyungki-daehui-ei kyungjaejuk Paguphyogwa-wa ta-dangsung Bunsuk [The research report on economic effect of the 2014 Incheon Asian Games].* Seoul: Korea Institute for International Economic Policy.

Kim, B.S. (2012). Roh Moo Hyun Daetongryong Yonseolee Jojak-datdani eerul-sooga! [Alas! The President Roh Moo Hyun's speech was not a real]. *Asia Kyungjae*, 22 January, http://www.asiae.co.kr/news/view.htm?idxno=2012012119124686299.

Kim, C.K. & Jung, J.W. (2014). Airport and urban development: A trial research on the Incheon aerotropolis development in a global age. *Journal of the Korean urban geographical society, 43*, 65–84.

Kim, D.K. (2014). Asia Kyung-ki-dae-hui-ei Sung-gwa-wa Hyang-hoo-choo-jin-bang-an [The legacies of the Asian Games and its future development]. *Sport science, 129,* 20–27.

Koh, E. (2005). South Korea and the Asian Games: The first step to the world. *Sport in society, 8,* 468–478.

Koh, J.M. (2012). The Korean Wave culture and tourism. *Korea tourism policy, 49,* 33–40.

KOTRA. (2015). *Hanryu-ei Kyung-jae-juk Hyo-gwa-ae Dae-han Yun-ku [Research into economic effect of the Korean Wave].* Seoul: KOTRA.

Kwon, S-H. & Kim, J. (2014). The cultural industry policies of the Korean government and the Korean Wave. *International journal of cultural policy, 20,* 422–439.

Lee, G. (2009). A theory of soft power and Korea's soft power strategy. *Korean journal of defense analysis, 21,* 205–218.

Lee, J.W. (2015). Assessing the sociology of sport: On globalisation, communication and sport research in Korea. *International review for the sociology of sport, 50,* 507–511.

Lee, J.W. (2016). The politics of sports mega events in South Korea: a diachronic approach. In A. Bairner, J. Kelly & J.W. Lee (Eds.). *Routledge handbook of sport and politics.* Abingdon, England: Routledge (pp. 471–482).

Levermore, R. & Aaron, B. (2009). Sport and development: Mapping the field. In R. Levermore & B. Aaron (Eds.). *Sport and international development.* London, England: Palgrave Macmillan (pp. 1–25).

Na, D. & Dallaire, C. (2015). Korean sport for international development initiatives: exploring new research avenues. *Asia Pacific journal of sport and Social Science, 4,* 251–264.

Nye, J.S. (2008). Public diplomacy and soft power. *Annals of the American academy of political and social science, 616,* 94–109.

Preuss, H. (2015). A framework for identifying the legacies of a mega sport event. *Leisure studies, 34,* 643–664.

The United Nations. (2003). *Sport for development and peace: Towards archiving the millennium development goals.* Geneva, Switzerland: The United Nations.

Yamawaki, Y. & Duarte, F. (2014). Olympics and urban legacy in Sydney: Urban transformations and real estate a decade after the games. *Journal of urban design, 19,* 511–540.

5 A city beyond the nation

Sport, tourism and events in the remaking of Cardiff

John Harris

Cardiff is the capital city of Wales. It was only granted city status in 1905 and did not become the capital of Wales until 1955. Once a thriving seaport, it witnessed serious economic decline as a result of the deindustrialisation of the nearby south Wales valleys before emerging to reap the benefits of widespread regeneration from the mid-1990s onwards in particular (see Hooper & Punter, 2006). This changing cityscape demonstrates the shift from a seaport built upon production to an events city focused on consumption. Now Cardiff is celebrated as the shiny metropolitan core of tourism in Wales and has been at the heart of an ongoing shift in marketing promotion as the nation attempts to achieve a better position on the international stage and increasingly distances itself from images of Wales as a remote, tribal backwater (Pitchford, 1998; Pritchard & Morgan, 2003).

With significant investment in the cultural and creative industries and further inroads into the sport and tourism business, the landscape of the city has changed markedly in the past 20 years. Cardiff is now a popular destination for tourists from outside of Wales. The Cardiff Bay regeneration project (based on the waterfront development in Baltimore, Maryland), and the ultra-modern Millennium Stadium, have appeared front and centre in a range of tourism brochures and policy documentation projecting images of (post)modernity and a new urbanity that promises progress and something for the future. Yet alongside this, in some ways it could be argued that Cardiff is also increasingly moving further away from the nation of Wales itself. A stated attempt to distance the city from the (national) stereotypes of dragons and daffodils in 2008, joining the Core Cities group in 2014, and the announcement that it would work with Bristol (in England) and Newport to form the Great Western Cities alliance, all point to the ways in which Cardiff is in some ways becoming further separate and distanced from Wales. Cardiff is also omnipresent within major English and British sporting events, which although undoubtedly successful in bringing in tourism and at times generating a significant economic impact for the city, evidences the blurred and contested boundaries of national imaging and imagining.

Through reference to the cultural theorist Raymond Williams, and with a focus on two international sporting events in particular, this chapter will look at what appears to be a rather unique case – a capital city that is increasingly associated with a neighbouring nation to position and promote international events. Whilst there is a rapidly developing academic literature on event image and destination fit, there has been little recognition or analysis to date of the coupling of *EnglandandWales* or this emerging configuration of *EnglandandCardiff.* This chapter will attempt to provide a framework to better understand some of the complexities of how and where this particular city sits in relation to sport and tourism at the national level and where this fits within wider policy initiatives.

Cardiff's growth and development

Cardiff is one of the youngest capital cities in Europe having been granted city status during the first decade of the twentieth century but only belatedly being recognised as the capital of Wales in 1955. Weight (2002, p. 279) suggests that up until this time it was still regarded by most Britons as a provincial city 'with the same status as Bristol, Manchester or Glasgow.' Cardiff's claim to be the capital city of Wales rested largely on its positioning as the largest settlement in the country, for it had no specific role and little particular religious or cultural significance in the history of Wales. For many years there was little about Cardiff that really defined it as a capital city although international rugby matches provided a means of putting the country on something of an 'international' stage. Johnes (2012a) has discussed this aspect and pointed to the ways in which the days that Five Nations matches took place in the city, particularly during the halcyon days of the 1970s, provided a collective focus point for the nation. Prescott's (2015) work shows how rugby came to assume a very important place in Cardiff during the mid-1880s and provided a means of celebrating their civic pride. This of course was important in developing and reinforcing a sense of place during a period of significant inward migration into the town. During this time, and for some years thereafter, Cardiff was like many other towns and cities affected by a rapidly changing and expanding population. Cardiff experienced its most intense phase of urbanisation at a later time than many other urban areas of Britain. In the early 1800s it was not even the largest settlement in south Wales with nearby Merthyr and Swansea both comprising larger populations (Hooper, 2006). Cardiff underwent exponential growth in the second half of the nineteenth century, influenced in part by the construction of the first dock there in 1839, so that before the end of the century it was the coal metropolis of the world. One of the most populous and deprived parts of Cardiff was Butetown, an area that became known more widely as Tiger Bay. The Cardiff Bay Development Corporation was set up in 1987 and the mission statement of the Cardiff Bay regeneration project outlined its aims as follows:

> To put Cardiff on the International map as a superlative maritime city which will stand comparison with any such city in the world, thereby enhancing the image and economic well-being of Cardiff and Wales as a whole.
>
> (Cardiff Bay, 2016)

As Cardiff had grown over the years, various city leaders also sought recognition for it as the important political and administrative centre of Wales. The creation of a National Assembly, following devolution in 1999, with its shiny headquarters located in the regenerated Bay area was an important landmark here. Prior to this, the quest for capital city status was not a smooth or linear process and it was to take some time until Cardiff was recognised as being a suitable place to carry such a title. Johnes (2012b, p. 510) notes how the conquest of Wales by England preceded the urbanisation of Cardiff and the surrounding areas, so by the time urban areas began to emerge in Wales 'London was already well established as the centre of political power for the Welsh.' This is an important point that shows the place of the city and the nation within and around wider English/British institutions and public discourse. I will look at what this means in relation to sport later in the chapter when focusing specifically on the role played by Cardiff in two sporting mega-events that took place in 2012 and 2015. Before this, I will first consider the role of sport in regeneration initiatives in a broader context. The work will then also consider aspects of the wider development of the creative and cultural industries in a specific local context that have served to reposition Cardiff as an 'events city' in the twenty-first century.

Sport and regeneration

Using sport and sporting events as a focus for growth and development is a strategy that has been employed by a number of cities as a tool for regeneration across the world (Smith, 2005). Cardiff is just like many of the other cities it is often positioned alongside here (e.g. Manchester, Glasgow and Birmingham) in discussions of the role of major sporting events as a catalyst for wider urban change and to promote tourism growth. Thomas (2008, p. 240) points to the boosterist planning and development strategies used by Cardiff Council and suggested that:

> Cardiff is not distinctive in the ways that its boosters claim and its economic and physical development is in many ways very similar to that of other British cities of comparable size.

Boland's (2007) insightful work on Cardiff and Liverpool would offer some support to such a claim. Despite claims to the contrary, there is actually very little that marks the city of Cardiff as particularly distinctive from its competitors (Lovering, 2006). The move from a managerialist to a boosterist and entrepreneurial form of governance (Harvey, 1989) has been central to the place marketing strategies of numerous cities (see also Evans, 2003). Evans (2003) notes how a shift in the branding of many similar sized cities resulted in a variety of 'copycat' urban design strategies.

Yet, although acknowledging that Cardiff has become very similar to other places in the United Kingdom, it is also different to many of these cities as it is a capital city and a place that is increasingly visible not just in its national (Welsh) context but as part of a wider national (British) collective in the world of

mega-events. An early report commissioned by the Local Authority was influential in promoting a 'pro-growth strategy' and also suggested that Cardiff would
best promote itself in a regional context rather than just a city-based one (Cooke,
1992). This discussed Cardiff's place within the wider south Wales region and
in particular its role as an engine for growth in the wider 'Valleys' region. Space
does not allow a detailed discussion of this important aspect here, but the wider
role and perceived responsibility of Cardiff as a driver for regional and national
development has been discussed at some length elsewhere (see, for example,
Hooper & Punter, 2006; Lovering, 2006; Boland, 2007; Johnes, 2012b). In this
chapter I will focus more on Cardiff's position in an even wider context and
briefly consider its quest to be an 'aspiring European capital' (Cardiff Council,
2005) or even a 'world-becoming' city (see Gonçalves, 2017). More specifically,
I then focus on how and where the staging of two mega-events in Cardiff as part
of wider British and/or English configurations has impacted upon the positioning
of the city in an international perspective.

Cardiff is the only capital city in the Core Cities collective. It is also one of
only two cities from outside of England that are currently part of this group of
ten. This collective originally comprised the eight largest English city economies outside of London. Glasgow, the other city from outside of England in the
ten, has also undergone a period of extensive regeneration and used culture-led
initiatives to reposition itself as an 'events city' in the past 30 years (Garcia,
2005). Although these two cities both joined the group in 2014, Cardiff is different in that it has been an integral part of sporting events affiliated, hosted, or
staged by another nation (England). Before moving on and considering the case
of two specific mega-events that Cardiff was involved in, I will first attempt to
look at Cardiff's position in a wider context both in geographical terms and in
relation to the wider creative and cultural industries.

Where's your city? Cardiff and the world

In contemporary times, cities like London, New York, Tokyo and Paris compete
with each other for the right to stage the biggest and most prestigious events such
as the Olympic Games. Florida (2008) pointed to the growing importance of such
places and we see that these cities are not only competitors with each other, but
also function as collaborators in wider globalisation networks as they become
increasingly connected. In some ways then national borders can become less important than at any time in recent history although the suggestion that accelerated
globalisation would signal the end of the nation-state was somewhat premature.
The nation retains an important role in contemporary times and sport remains a
key site for the promotion and celebration of national identities. Friedman (2007)
suggested that 'the word is flat,' but Florida (2008) notes that it is perhaps rather
more 'spiky.' Many cities increasingly seem to be disconnected and separate from
their immediate hinterland and from the nation within which they are a part.

The stated ambition of various city leaders in Cardiff was to follow the likes
of Barcelona and Amsterdam in becoming more progressive and entrepreneurial

(see Cooke, 1992). Boland (2006) has analysed much of the policy literature produced by Cardiff Council and notes that an overtly boosterist and highly aspirational discourse dominates. Gonçalves (2017) has also looked closely at the ways in which Cardiff has presented itself as a renewed city with a focus on becoming a more visible and desirable location in European and global markets. The waterfront development was the key driver in the broader reshaping of Cardiff that attempted to improve some of the most deprived areas of the city and also better regenerate areas beyond the city centre. In some ways though this was one of the main failings of the Cardiff Bay redevelopment, for it was clearly disconnected from the city centre and traffic issues remained an unresolved aspect of this into the new millennium (see Yewlett, 2006). Whilst travelling to the Bay from the city centre may not have always been straightforward, an unlikely figure emerged to help reposition Cardiff in an international context.

Cardiff, Cymru and culture

Although the focus of this chapter is on the inter-relationship of sport, events, tourism and regeneration, it is important to also briefly position this case-study within and around the wider creative and cultural industries. Evans (2003) has capably highlighted the ways in which culture-led regeneration has reshaped a whole host of cities. Griffiths (2006, p. 495) notes that 'in the current era of globalisation, manufacturing decline and place marketing, many cities have turned to culture as a favoured means of gaining competitive advantage.' Filming the popular television shows *Doctor Who* and *Torchwood* in Cardiff has introduced the city to markets where images of Wales may not have been seen before. An article in *The Guardian* (31 December, 2009) noted: 'He can travel across time and the universe and has an unlikely ability to regenerate himself, but there is one place to which Doctor Who will always return: Cardiff.'

Whilst living in the United States, I had conversations with individuals who had no reference points at all to Wales but had seen *Doctor Who* or *Torchwood* and so finally had something they could finally associate with me (given the invisibility of Wales in a variety of other spheres). People became familiar with particular landmarks and the wider cityscape that promoted a dynamic urbanism and made good use of some of the new and easily recognisable buildings. The creative and cultural industries have long been recognised as central to the regeneration of post-industrial cities. Media accounts of a launch party to celebrate the reborn *Doctor Who* being made in Cardiff with a budget of around 1 million pounds an episode noted:

> The party was held at the swanky St David's Hotel in Cardiff Bay, which has had a rebirth just as dramatic as that of the Doctor. Cardiff's 19th-century docks have, in the space of a decade, become a prime piece of 21st-century Euro-waterfront.
>
> (*The Observer*, 13 March 2005)

That this article featured in a 'British' newspaper in a text that was also celebrating the resurgence of the Welsh rugby team (who days later would claim a
first Grand Slam title for almost 30 years) is also important to note. This was
reflective of an increasing visibility of the city in wider cultural and creative
industry spheres beyond the relatively narrow confines of a south Wales media.
Kompotis (2006, p. 186) suggests that administrators and marketers in Cardiff
have attempted to 'reimagine the city as a consumption centre whose physical
and social attributes have become aesthetic commodities to be sold and consumed by a number of target audiences.' This is true of many other cities where
a type of 'civic peacockery' leads to a significant gap between the glossy images
presented to an external audience and the everyday lived experiences of many
people within and around these cities (Boland, 2006, 2007). I have previously
commented on some of the issues relating to this with specific reference to the
hegemonic place of rugby union in the nation and the atmosphere in Cardiff on
international match days (Harris, 2008).

   In terms of developing Wales as a tourist destination, the regeneration of the
capital city has been central to a shift that has moved Wales to a more visible
place as a competitive tourist destination. One of the biggest challenges facing
key stakeholders in Welsh tourism has been the challenge in highlighting that it
is a separate country and not a region of England. Cardiff is, perhaps, the most
English of all Welsh cities (Harris, 2008) and this has been a factor influencing
some of the indifference towards Cardiff from citizens in other parts of Wales for
many years. Johnes (2012b) notes how at the beginning of the twentieth century
there were doubts about Cardiff's 'Welshness' as less than 10% of its population
spoke Welsh (compared to almost 50% in Wales as a whole). Today, around one
fifth of the population of Wales speak some Welsh and there has been a significant growth in Welsh language learning in some of the more affluent suburbs of
Cardiff.

   The increased focus on tourism and the emergence of events in the policy
discourse around the mid-1990s is central here (see Lovering, 2006). Lovering
(2006) has commented upon the cultural shift in development policy and also
highlights that in many ways the city had become less culturally distinctive
and contributed little to the cultural industries. To further explore some of the
cultural aspects of sport, events and tourism in relation to the regeneration of
Cardiff, I use the work of the cultural theorist Raymond Williams as a lens to
look at some of the key issues shaping this domain.

Putting Cardiff in its place: Locating the city in Wales, England and Britain

Bidding for and hosting large-scale sporting events have been central to the regeneration of Cardiff, not only in a physical sense through the development of
the Millennium Stadium, but also as a contributor to a wider social regeneration
that has reshaped the city in many other ways. The 1999 Rugby World Cup was
an important moment here. At the centre of this bid was the creation of a new

national stadium but the actual economic impact of this event was much lower than anticipated (Jones, 2001). The sheer size of the debt that the Welsh Rugby Union (WRU) took on to develop the Millennium Stadium was heavily criticised at the time where there was a real fear that the stadium would be another of those white elephant projects. In some ways, those governing Welsh rugby were saved by their counterparts involved in the administration of football in England as the protracted redevelopment of Wembley Stadium meant that Cardiff benefited from staging the play-off finals for the English league clubs for six years. The Millennium Stadium also hosted the FA Cup final in the same period. This most English of sporting institutions, and an iconic event in the sporting calendar, provided significant economic benefits for the city and would have showcased the stadium to a wider audience beyond that of the somewhat narrow confines of the international rugby world.

Although the sport does not have the international reach and profile of football, international rugby matches played at the Millennium Stadium are special, not just because of the established hegemonic place of rugby union as the national sport of Wales, but also due to the fact that the stadium sits right in the centre of the city and dominates the skyline (see Williams, 2000). No other international rugby stadium has such a central place in the cityscape and few sporting stadiums are as celebrated or as revered by fans and players of a particular sport across the world. The Millennium Stadium, renamed the Principality Stadium at the beginning of 2016, has become an iconic venue that in the rugby world has followed on from the equally fabled Cardiff Arms Park, which for many fans, players and coaches was one of the places they most wanted to experience a game.

Holden (2011, p. 278) highlighted that the opening of the Millennium Stadium was evidence of Wales branding itself 'as a nation of sport, not one entirely based on rugby union.' This was very much a postmodern stadium that offered a visible sign of the city's progressiveness and changing landscape (Williams, 2000). Paramio *et al.* (2008) suggest that the era of the postmodern stadium (1990s to present) is characterised by the incorporation of the latest technological solutions (such as the Millennium Stadium's retractable roof), the need to increase revenue on non-match days (through staging rock concerts and other non-sporting events), and the further development of stadiums as sites of tourism and consumption. Visitors to Cardiff can now undertake stadium tours of the Principality Stadium where its many uses as a site for various events (e.g. boxing, music, speedway) are celebrated. Images from inside and outside the stadium adorn both the front and back pages of the national events strategy (Welsh Assembly Government, 2008). This stadium is clearly the centrepiece of a reimagining of Cardiff (and Wales) as an events destination.

Something that has rarely been addressed though is where Cardiff sits when it is integrated within wider English and/or British events. It is important to recognise and highlight here that England and Britain are two different things but the common interchangeable usage between the two in some contexts has long been a source of much angst and frustration amongst the Celtic fringe. The often cited example of the encyclopaedia entry for Wales that simply said 'See England' is also a source of some angst. Wales is an English name for the land of foreigners and came into existence in the ninth and tenth centuries 'as a junior partner in a Britain run by England' (Williams, 1985/2003, p. 67). The challenge of locating Wales within and around England and/or Britain remains a somewhat problematic part of the international sports world.

In association football, the world's most popular team sport (see Giulianotti & Robertson, 2009), Cardiff City plays in the English professional league system. For a brief period it even joined its fierce rivals, and near Welsh neighbours, Swansea City in the top flight of English football. The English Premier League (EPL) is one of the most popular sporting competitions in the world and is watched by television audiences across the globe (Giulianotti & Robertson, 2009). In some ways then the presence of these teams in a league that is screened in so many markets represents a good advertisement opportunity. Television viewers can clearly see this with *Visit Wales* signage at some matches and games screened throughout the world and viewed by audiences across a number of continents. Yet the other side of this is that by having Welsh teams in an English league this may also reinforce the widely held perception that Wales is a region of England.

Cardiff has also made significant inroads in other areas of sport. The SSE SWALEC Stadium in Sophia Gardens is now a venue for international test-match cricket. This investment in the stadium, the home of Glamorgan County Cricket Club, and the only county outside of England to compete in the first-class cricket competition, has been the source of some controversy when city councillors agreed to write off almost 4.5 million pounds of debt to enable the club to safeguard its future. When Cardiff is the host city for test-matches, the home team is England. This is a different England to the one that we see on the rugby pitch but Welshmen such as Robert Croft, Greg Thomas and Hugh Morris have all represented the England team. Croft once suggested that playing for Glamorgan was like playing for Wales whilst being picked for England was akin to being selected for the British Lions. The British and Irish Lions are a rugby team that tours the southern hemisphere every four years and brings together players from the four home nations. Despite many ongoing changes to the place of Britain and British identities (whilst not forgetting the complex identity of Ireland here also), and suggestions of their demise in the age of open professionalism in rugby union (since 1995), the Lions have gone from strength to strength and are recognised as a powerful 'brand.'

Raymond Williams (1960, 1985/2003) reflected upon some of the advantages of being born in an area where there were a range of different identities. For anyone looking for an official status he concluded that it was something of a nightmare, but it was a blessing for anyone thinking about communities and societies. Communities in a wider national context have often been described as 'imagined' (Anderson, 1983). To further consider regeneration of the city of Cardiff with specific reference to sport, events and tourism, I will now focus on two mega-events that took place in Great Britain in 2012 and 2015. These events formed part of a broader portfolio of large-scale sporting events taking place across the country in a period where sport moved ever more to the forefront of wider policy rhetoric.

London 2012 and England 2015

Raymond Williams offered some interesting reflections on his experiences as a Welshman living in England:

> You don't speak to people in London, he remembered; in fact you don't speak to people anywhere in England; there is plenty of time for that sort of thing on the appointed occasions – in an office, in a seminar, at a party.
>
> (Williams, 1960, p. 3)

> A last word about these English. They are much more various than the myths allow.
>
> (Williams, 1975/2003, p. 10)

Thirteen years after the creation of a National Assembly and Wales was still very much situated firmly within the British state, and Cardiff was one of the sites for the biggest sporting event ever to be staged in Britain. Many Welsh people are comfortable with, and often very proud of, this dual identity (see Johnes, 2012a; Harris & Vincent, 2015). The policy discourse of London 2012 emphasised that these were to be a British games that would benefit the whole nation and all of its constituent parts (see Coe, 2012; Wagg, 2015). A year after a very popular Royal Wedding and during the year of Queen Elizabeth II's Diamond Jubilee, a celebration of Britishness permeated at numerous levels.

Despite the escalating costs of staging the event, and much negative press in the days immediately prior to the start of the games, London 2012 turned out to be a remarkable success. The British Prime Minister David Cameron suggested that 'it was the summer that patriotism came out of the shadows' (*The Spectator*, 7 February 2014). That it was such a success in offering a temporary 'feel-good factor' cannot be disputed but the jury is still out when considering other substantial and longer-term impacts central to the bid (see Wagg, 2015). In wider terms the whole 'legacy' agenda is often little more than an empty rhetoric that hones in on a particular buzzword and becomes a necessary part of contemporary mega-event discussion. There are similarities here to the city-branding policies discussed earlier in the chapter where we see an obvious disconnect between the glossy brochures and glitzy websites, with the everyday lived realities of local communities.

The nervously anticipated opening ceremony, which had the unenviable task of following the spectacular and very expensive showcase in Beijing four years previously, was screened to popular acclaim. From her majesty Queen Elizabeth II appearing in a sketch with James Bond, to the celebration of Britain's contribution to popular culture, there was much for people to discuss. The rapid development of social media is shown by the fact that there were more tweets about the Olympics during the opening ceremony of London 2012 than there were across the whole duration of the games in Beijing. *The Western Mail*, self-styled national newspaper of Wales (papur cenedlaethol Cymru), had much positive coverage of the event and suggested that the opening ceremony 'may also have changed ideas of what British identity – with all its cultural complexities and contradictions – actually is' (*The Western Mail*, 30 July 2012).

It is customary for the opening ceremony to end with a call to 'Let the games begin,' yet the 2012 games had in fact already begun. Two days earlier in Cardiff the Millennium Stadium staged a women's football match between the hosts Great Britain & Northern Ireland and New Zealand. On the day of the match, the front page of the *Western Mail* (25 July 2012) had a banner headline stating simply, 'Welcome to Wales.' Lord Sebastian Coe was quoted as saying 'This is a Games for the whole of the UK and we are delighted the first sporting event is in Wales' (The *Western Mail*, 25 July 2012, p. 1). The actual impact of the above event as something for the whole of Britain was much over-stated and so was never likely to really make much of an impact on places around the periphery (although the popular Olympic torch relay did take the Olympics to communities across the nation). Tickets for women's football matches had to be given away in some locations as there just wasn't the demand to watch many of these, de-spite the fact that numerous other events were sold out. Staging football matches in Cardiff and Glasgow linked well to the narrative of an inclusive Britishness which highlighted that this was an event for the whole country (something highlighted on numerous occasions during the course of bidding for the event). Of course all speculative talk of major nations having their holding and training camps in Wales never really materialised and the 2012 event did not get any-where close to matching the hype and unrealistic expectations of what this could possibly offer to cities and towns further outside of London and its immediate geographic surrounds.

As part of the Great Britain and Northern Ireland team, or as now more com-monly referred to as Team GB, Welsh athletes played a part in ensuring that the host nation was successful in performance terms and surpassed the medal target it had been set. Sport Wales (2013), like all other stakeholders, celebrated the success of 'home' athletes and noted that as a sporting nation, Wales continues to punch well above its weight. Many of these athletes are lottery-funded and supported by UK Sport. Dependent on the particular sport, some of these most successful Welsh athletes live and train in England and benefit from the facilities and expert coaching to be found in that part of the wider British nation. The role of Cardiff as a British city then is important to note. It had always been more subsumed under London, England and Britain than the major Scottish cities. The fact that Wales had never been a unitary kingdom meant that its union with England, formalised during the Tudor period, made the integration of the two a smoother process than the subsequent union with Scotland at the beginning of the 1700s.

Harris and Vincent's (2015) analysis of the *Western Mail's* coverage of London 2012 noted the different ways in which the local/national remained important and the presentation of 'our' (British) accomplishments were shared and framed within the umbrella of an identity that is subsumed as part of a bigger and wider collective. So whilst celebrating the successes of athletes from all parts of Great

Britain and Northern Ireland, the focus of the *Western Mail's* coverage of London 2012 was almost always on sites where there was some Welsh aspect/angle present. England 2015 offered a very different scenario though for the English would no longer be part of 'our' team, even though Cardiff was one of the host cities, but would now be the opponents on the field of play as Wales and England got ready to face off in an eagerly anticipated Rugby World Cup (RWC) competition.

The 2015 RWC was hosted by England although Cardiff also featured in the RFU's bid for this event and was to be chosen as one of the host cities. This type of decision in international rugby is not that unusual, for Wales had hosted the 1999 RWC although only one fifth of all matches actually took place in the country. Cardiff had also hosted matches in 1991 (United Kingdom) and 2007 (France) tournaments and so has now been a host city for every RWC ever staged in the northern hemisphere. The Visit England promotional campaign used the words of Jerusalem to highlight images of 'England's green and pleasant land.' Jerusalem has been put forward as a potential anthem for England's sporting teams who mostly still use 'God Save the Queen.' This, of course, is also the British national anthem and had attracted some controversy in London 2012 when the Welsh players in the GB&NI football team had not joined in the singing (see Harris & Vincent, 2015).

The politics of international rugby governance are also clearly visible here when looking at how and where the matches were played. The Wales matches against two of the other core nations (England and Australia) both took place at Twickenham in London, the home of English rugby. The matches against Fiji and Uruguay were allowed to take place at the Millennium Stadium as these are two nations that do not have the voting rights of the big eight (see Richards, 2007; Harris, 2010; Wise, in press) and so despite this tournament being titled 'England 2015,' Uruguay and Fiji had to face Wales in Cardiff in front of a partisan crowd.

The so-called 'group of death' would mean that one of the hegemonic powers of international rugby would not make it to the knockout stages and the match between the two 'host' nations would prove crucial. Australia topped the group and so, as many would have predicted before the tournament began, it was the match between England and Wales that would prove to be the decisive one in deciding the fate of these two teams. The Chief Executive of World Rugby, Australian Brett Gosper, had not endeared himself to many Welsh rugby fans when he tweeted, 'England fail to exit pool in World Cup? [...] Not the words we want to hear during #RWC2015' after the England cricket team had been knocked out of the Cricket World Cup. Gosper's tweet turned out to be a prophetic one and England became the first host nation in the history of the RWC to exit the tournament before the knockout stages of a tournament.

The Welsh victory over England in London became *the* news story in Wales across all media with front page-headlines in newspapers such as 'Our greatest win ever!' (*Wales on Sunday*, 27 September 2015) and 'Anthem of the brave: How tale of sporting heroism unfolded to unleash euphoria' (*The Western Mail*, 28 September 2015) evidencing the importance of this victory to wider national imaging and imagining. Wales was to exit the competition at the quarter-finals though, when it was defeated by South Africa, and the four leading southern hemisphere teams made up the list of semi-finalists to further reinforce the dominance of leading nations from that part of the rugby world. Yet whilst there was obvious disappointment at not making it past this stage, there was still much celebration and reflection on the fact that Wales had defeated the hosts and the team that Wales wants to beat more than any other.

Concluding remarks: From *EnglandandWales* to *EnglandandCardiff*

After more than a century as a city, and over 60 years as the capital city of Wales, Cardiff has developed into a city that finally resembled the place it had long-strived to become. This is visibly shown in the following extract from the novel *Cardiff Dead*:

> The old stadium, the Arms Park, was almost invisible from the centre of town. You were only really aware of it when you looked at it from over the river in Riverside. The new stadium dominated the centre and you could see it from almost anywhere in Cardiff. And, like pretty much everyone else, Tyra found it surprisingly inspiring. It suddenly made you aware that Cardiff was changing, that all the bollocks you heard people spit on the TV about being a European capital for the new century was really true.
>
> (Williams, 2000, p. 231)

The significant investment in sport and the long-standing importance of sporting events has certainly played a key role in this (Holden, 2011; Harris, 2008, 2015). Johnes (2012b, p. 523) described it well when noting that the transformation of Cardiff is remarkable 'when the point of comparison is Cardiff itself in the past rather than other cities in the present.' Yet, as noted at various points in the edited collection of Hooper and Punter (2006), Cardiff is neither as unique nor as distinctive as the policy rhetoric and marketing literature often claims. Hughson *et al.* (2005, p. 180, *emphasis added*) reflected upon the ways in which sport has become an increasingly important part of wider cultural representations of place and note how 'sport featured in the bids by *English cities* for the title European City of Culture. The title, to be invested in 2008, was keenly sought by the finalists Birmingham, Bristol, Cardiff, Liverpool, Newcastle/Gateshead and Oxford.' Cardiff failed in its bid to be crowned European Capital of Culture for 2008, but the Europe of regions seemed to offer much to a country such as Wales that has been marginalised in many spheres. However, the country found itself wiped off the map of Europe in 2004 when the front cover of the Eurostat Yearbook somehow managed to sink Wales into the Irish Sea. Cardiff had undoubtedly benefited from various government initiatives aimed at moving some things beyond London but now, in the Welsh context, it was clearly the hegemonic core and so would itself increasingly attract criticism and jealous comments from other cities and towns on the periphery (see Harris, 2015).

Holden (2011, p. 279) has commented on the significance of the Millennium Stadium as central to this regeneration of the city and how for the City Council 'it marked a key step in the effort to regenerate the city, an ideal that lay behind the unsuccessful bid to host the Commonwealth Games in 1986.' Yet in some ways whilst this case provides yet another example of a city using international sporting events as a central part of regeneration strategies, it also represents a case of a city moving further away from the nation within which it is a part. Cardiff is not just located within a particular national boundary but is the capital city of that country and often seen as the driving force of a wider city-region or as a Welsh metropolis (see Hooper & Punter, 2006; Johnes, 2012b). Its close proximity to England and the strong road and rail links means that Cardiff is in many ways more connected with the west of England and key places down the M4 corridor to London than it is to many other places within a national (Welsh) border. Joining the Core Cities group in 2014 and promoting it as 'the closest capital city to London' evidences this. *The Western Mail* (12 February 2016) noted how the triumvirate of Bristol, Cardiff and Newport are trying to work closer together and had officially formed the Great Western Cities region early in 2015, but the same newspaper had a feature about the rivalry and competition between Bristol and Cardiff just three days later (15 February 2016). Neither Bristol nor Bath (a city with a passion for rugby and a place featured in the Visit England marketing materials for the event) were chosen as host cities for England 2015 but Cardiff was awarded eight matches and so hosted more games than any other city outside of London in this English tournament.

A final word

The Welsh Assembly Government (2008, p. 3) noted that 'Major international events influence the way we see Wales and the world, and how the world sees Wales.' This is an important point to consider when we reflect upon the position of Cardiff in relation to the mega-events discussed in this chapter. An emerging area of research in the event management literature concerns the synergies between event image and destination fit (e.g. Chalip & Costa, 2005). The hegemonic status of rugby union within Wales means that the RWC can be seen as a good fit for selling the city and the nation. Yet having Cardiff as a host city for England 2015 also points to the continued challenges involved in recognising and promoting Wales as a distinct and separate entity. Cardiff was both present and absent from the study commissioned to gauge the economic impact of the 2015 RWC, where some of the text focused on the legacy agenda of the Rugby Football Union (RFU) and the tourism benefits to England, but also had to occasionally make reference to the *EnglandandCardiff* coupling (Ernst & Young, 2015). Developing the SSE SWALEC stadium as a venue for test-match cricket where the home team compete as England is also important to note here. No research to date has attempted to tackle this complex and multi-layered intersection of identities within and around these fuzzy frontiers. Wales is indeed a part of Britain, and the Welsh may claim to be the first Britons, but Wales is not a part of England.

England and Britain are two different things but they are words that are often used interchangeably with little recognition of the important differences.

In becoming a European capital for the new century, Cardiff had changed markedly from the place it was as recently as the mid-1990s. In some ways it now finally resembles a capital city. Cardiff is clearly the preeminent signifier of Wales in much of the national tourism promotion, although Pritchard and Morgan (2003) suggested that this may in turn have led to the marginalization of alternative imagined communities of Wales. I have previously noted that using the city as a symbol of 'Welshness' and using sport (especially rugby union) as a way of promoting and selling the city seemed to be an effective strategy to promote images of a new and vibrant Wales centred upon enterprise, leisure and consumerism (Harris, 2008). Such an approach is not unique to Cardiff but it is evident that this city seems to move ever further away from the nation of Wales even though the special place of rugby offers a form of synergy between the two. The capital city, just like the nation within it sits, is to borrow from the words of Gwyn A. Williams (1985) something that has been made and remade over time. Writing more broadly about Wales he suggested that the nation is 'an artefact' and that this has often been remade in a British context. Raymond Williams (1975/2003) observed that the making of myths involves inventing and tolerating many illusions. He knew much better than most the ways in which 'selective traditions' of a nation are central to the tales we tell (see Williams, 1960, 1983). Those involved in the regeneration of cities also craft a particular narrative that tells a story of post-industrial change and draws upon selected elements of the past to point a path for the future. Williams (1975/2003, p. 6) noted that the feeling for the past is more than just a fancy, 'but it's how past and present relate that tells in a culture.'

References

Anderson, B. (1983). *Imagined communities: Reflections on the origins and spread of nationalism*. London, England: Verso.
Boland, P. (2006). Competitive cities: unpacking the theoretical debates. In A. Hooper & J. Punter (Eds.). *Capital Cardiff 1975–2020: Regeneration, competitiveness and the urban environment*. Cardiff, Wales: University of Wales Press.
Boland, P. (2007). Unpacking the theory-policy interface of local economic development: An analysis of Cardiff and Liverpool. *Urban studies, 44*, 1019–1039.
Cardiff Bay. (2016). Regeneration project. http://cardiffbay.co.uk/index.php/the-regeneration-project.
Cardiff Council (2005). *Cardiff beyond 2005*. Cardiff, Wales: Cardiff City Council.
Chalip, L. & Costa, C. (2005). Sport event tourism and the destination brand: Towards a general theory. *Sport in society, 8*, 218–237.
Coe, S. (2012). *Running my life: The autobiography*. London, England: Hodder & Stoughton.
Cooke, P. (1992). *Cardiff: Making a European city of the future*. Report commissioned by South Glamorgan County Council, Regional industrial research. Cardiff, Wales: University of Wales.

Ernst & Young. (2015). *The economic impact of Rugby World Cup 2015*. London, England: Ernst & Young.

Evans, G. (2003). Hard-branding the cultural city: From Prado to Prada. *International journal of urban and regional research, 27*, 417–440.

Florida, R. (2008). *Who's your city?* New York, NY: Basic Books.

Friedman, T. (2007). *The world is flat 3.0*. New York, NY: Picador.

Garcia, B. (2005). Deconstructing the city of culture: The long-term cultural legacies of Glasgow 1990. *Urban studies, 42*, 841–868.

Giulianotti, R. & Robertson, R. (2009). *Globalization and football*. London, England: Sage.

Gonçalves, A. (2017). *Reinventing a small, worldly city: The cultural and social reinvention of Cardiff*. London, England: Routledge.

Griffiths, R. (2006). City/culture discourses: Evidence from the competition to select the European Capital of Culture 2008. *European planning studies, 14*, 415–430.

Harris, J. (2008). Match day in Cardiff: (Re)imaging and (re)imagining the nation. *Journal of sport & tourism, 13*, 297–313.

Harris J (2010). *Rugby union and globalization: An odd-shaped world*. Basingstoke, England: Palgrave Macmillan.

Harris, J. (2015). Keeping up with the Joneses: Hosting mega-events as a regenerative strategy in nation imaging, imagining and branding. *Local economy, 30*, 961–974.

Harris, J. & Vincent, J. (2015). Narratives of Britishness and Team GB in the national newspaper of Wales. *International journal of sport communication, 8*, 1–17.

Harvey, D. (1989). From managerialism to entrepreneurialism: The transformation in urban governance in late capitalism. *Geografiska annaler B, 71*, 3–17.

Holden, R. (2011). Never forget you're Welsh: The role of sport as a political device in post devolution Wales. *Sport in society, 14*, 272–288.

Hooper, A. (2006). Introduction: from "Coal Metropolis" to "Capital Cardiff". In A. Hooper & J. Punter (Eds.). *Capital Cardiff 1975–2020: Regeneration, competitiveness and the urban environment*. Cardiff, Wales: University of Wales Press.

Hooper, A. & Punter, J. (2006). (Eds.). *Capital Cardiff 1975–2020: Regeneration, competitiveness and the urban environment*. Cardiff, Wales: University of Wales Press.

Hughson, J., Inglis, D. & Free, M. (2005). *The uses of sport: A critical study*. London, England: Routledge.

Johnes, M. (2012a). *Wales since 1939*. Manchester, England: Manchester University Press.

Johnes, M. (2012b). Cardiff: The making and development of the capital city of Wales. *Contemporary British history, 26*, 509–528.

Jones, C. (2001). Mega-events and host-region impacts: Determining the true worth of the 1999 Rugby World Cup. *International journal of tourism research, 3*, 241–251.

Kompotis, P. (2006). Marketing the city of Cardiff: Is the red dragon white and middle class? *Contemporary Wales, 18*, 167–190.

Lovering, J. (2006). The cultural transformation of Cardiff. In A. Hooper & J. Punter (Eds.). *Capital Cardiff 1975–2020: Regeneration, competitiveness and the urban environment*. Cardiff, Wales: University of Wales Press.

Paramio, J., Buraimo, B. & Campos, C. (2008). From modern to postmodern: The development of football stadia in Europe. *Sport in society, 11*, 517–534.

Pitchford, S. (1998). *Identity tourism: Imaging and imagining the nation*. London, England: Elsevier.

Prescott, G. (2015). *'This Rugby Spellbound People': The birth of rugby in Cardiff and Wales*. Cardiff, Wales: St David's Press.

Pritchard, A. & Morgan, N. (2003). Mythic geographies of representation and identity: Contemporary postcards of Wales. *Tourism and cultural change, 1,* 111–130.

Richards, H. (2007). *A game for Hooligans? A history of Rugby union.* Edinburgh, Scotland: Mainstream.

Smith, A. (2005). Reimaging the city: The value of sport initiatives. *Annals of tourism research, 32,* 217–236.

Thomas, H. (2008). Book review: Hooper A and Punter J (Eds.). Capital Cardiff 1975–2020. *Urban Studies, 45,* 239–241.

Wagg, S. (2015). *The London Olympics of 2012: Politics, promises and legacy.* Basingstoke, England: Palgrave Macmillan.

Weight, R. (2002). *Patriots: National identity in Britain, 1940–2000.* London, England: Macmillan.

Welsh Assembly Government. (2008). *Event Wales: A major events strategy for Wales 2010–2020.* Cardiff, Wales: Welsh Assembly Government.

Williams, G. (1985). *When was Wales? A history of the Welsh.* London, England: Penguin.

Williams, J. (2000). *Cardiff dead.* London, England: Bloomsbury.

Williams, R. (1960). *Border country.* London, England: Chatto & Windus.

Williams, R. (1975/2003). Welsh culture. In. D. Williams (Ed.). *Who speaks for Wales? Nation, culture, identity: Raymond Williams.* Cardiff, Wales: University of Wales Press.

Williams, R. (1983). *Towards 2000.* London, England: Chatto & Windus.

Williams, R. (1985/2003). The shadow of the dragon. In. D. Williams (Ed.). *Who speaks for Wales? Nation, culture, identity: Raymond Williams.* Cardiff, Wales: University of Wales Press.

Wise, N. (in press). Rugby World Cup: New directions or more of the same? *Sport in society,* (online first) DOI: 10.1080/17430437.2015.1088717.

Yewlett, C. (2006). Cardiff transport. In A. Hooper & J. Punter (Eds.). *Capital Cardiff 1975–2020: Regeneration, competitiveness and the urban environment.* Cardiff, Wales: University of Wales Press.

6 Using the Event-Scorecard and the Event Management System as powerful strategic tools for destinations

Examples from Switzerland

Jürg Stettler, Christine Herzer, Anna Wallebohr and Heinz Rütter

The importance of events for tourism destinations

Due to the increasing importance of events, their impacts in recent years have been recorded systematically. In particular, the economic effects have been analyzed and evaluated in numerous scientific and practice studies since the 1980s (Davidson & Schaffer, 1980; Burns *et al.*, 1986). There are various reasons for this development. On one hand, there is a general trend in society towards experiential orientation (Opaschowski, 2001), whereas participation in an event shall remain a unique experience in the memory of the event visitors. On the other hand, events offer a communication platform for companies, regions, cities and more specific tourist locations. Extensive reporting from media can have significant multiplier effects in terms of branding and reputation of company or destination brands (Schulze, 2005). Therefore, events (especially sport events) play an increasingly important role in destinations today (Preuß & Weiss, 2003). In addition to the listed opportunities to use events as a tool for regional economic regeneration, development and tourism promotion, they also cause a variety of negative impacts in different areas. Most of the time only the economic impacts are analysed – the crowding of regular tourists – and therefore the related 'missing' overnight stays are rarely considered or evaluated (Müller, 2001). Due to restriction in quality of life (for example, traffic restrictions or noise pollution) the population is increasingly critical towards events (Small *et al.*, 2005). The impact of events on the environment plays an important role and must be documented transparently (Boykoff, 2014). Because of the number of opportunities and increased competitiveness among tourism destinations, the public sector, organisers and economic partners are challenged to offer a diverse and coordinated events portfolio, which contributes to the strategic positioning of the destination.

Event impact research

Events have various positive and negative impacts. When delivering an event, it is important for a destination to build on the positive impacts while minimizing the negative ones. The impacts of events are usually divided into the three dimensions of sustainable regeneration (economic, ecological and social). Positive impacts are often mentioned in the context of economy, especially when considering monetary effects, the construction and expansion of infrastructures, or increased employment raise the attractiveness and reputation of the host destination. Positive impacts are often also noticed in the social sector. Events can mobilise people and provide for involved groups of people, such as viewers, volunteers, athletes or artists, as well as provide the young talent and the region an opportunity to share positive experiences and strengthen the community. These are achieved in particular by honorary engagement or volunteering (Wagenseil *et al.*, 2014). Additionally, the improved surroundings through modernised infrastructure make a place more attractive for the local population. Given positive impacts, negative impacts are becoming more and more important. The careful use of natural resources and an elaborate plan regarding waste management are needed because of increased CO_2 emissions or energy consumption during events (Death, 2011). Some cities have strict pollution limits, which are often associated with noise disturbance, (traffic) limitations on site or cost-intensive investments by the public sector.

The increased commercialisation and demands of mega-events resulted in major investments in destinations over the past several decades. Since the 1990s, the analysis of Olympic Games as well as World and European Championships were a major point of focus in Europe (Késenne, 1999; Preuß, 1999). Globalisation and social development as well as increased competitiveness and pressures on the event sector led to the conceptual development of several economics focused event analysis frameworks (tools) to identify the event induced monetary effects such as value-added income and employment for the host region (see Faulkner *et al.*, 2003; Jones, 2005; Lee & Taylor, 2005). This chapter focuses on the procedure as well as the analysis and use of economic impact analyses. Though, economic impact analyses are considered valid in the social sciences, they have been criticised for inconsistencies and a lack of transparency (e.g. Delpy & Li, 1998; Lee & Taylor, 2005; Crompton, 2006). Disputes link to possible sources of error (e.g. Köhler & Drengner, 2012; Raybould & Fredline, 2012; Davies *et al.*, 2013), which led to more developed and approved methodological approaches recognised to this day (e.g. Bramwell, 1997; Fredline *et al.*, 2005).

Measuring intangible effects as well as negative impacts was at first largely neglected in research and practice. However, debates concerning issues pertinent to sustainability and regeneration required more holistic analyses to move forward studies focusing on the impact of events. Several holistic measuring instruments to assess event impacts have been developed (e.g. Rütter *et al.*, 2002; Gans *et al.*, 2003; Fredline *et al.*, 2005; Stettler *et al.*, 2005). These authors not only cover the tangible economic effects, but also evaluate intangible economic as well as ecological and social effects of events (Köhler, 2013). Since the 1990s political shifts developed around more sustainable approachs based on the Brundtland report, which led to various international institutions shaping criteria, policies and guidelines applicable to events.

Mules and Faulkner (1996) previously pointed out that events which were carried out without support by public institutions were rarely profitable. Often it would lead to resistance among the population, which is why the impact research became increasingly important for practical support in recent years. Thereby, it is mainly about the national and regional economic impacts of events. They are used up to this day as an important political decision-making basis for the advancement of events by the public sector (Köhler & Drengner, 2012). This is evidenced among diverse studies which were executed with the aid of the Event-Scorecard, an instrument developed by Rütter *et al.* (2002) and further revised in 2005 (see Stettler *et al.*, 2005).

Measuring sustainable effects of events with the Event-Scorecard

To evaluate economic, ecological and social impacts of major events, appropriate methods and instruments are needed. Generally it can be noted that the economic effects of events have been widely examined. This is primarily due to the fact that the necessary data is comparatively easy to collect and organisers, stakeholders and customers are interested in precise economic evaluations. More and more often researchers have attempted to investigate external market effects and non-monetary costs and benefits. But such research is difficult and available methods for quantification are still lacking. With the developed and tested analysis-instrument, the Event-Scorecard, which was elaborated within the framework of three research projects (see Rütter *et al.*, 2002; Stettler *et al.*, 2005; Stettler *et al.*, 2010), meaningful data of economic, ecological and social impacts of all kinds of events can be identified and effectively calculated. Therefore, sport, cultural and other events can be analyzed and compared, regardless of their duration and size.

Figure 6.1 gives an overview of the overall model of the Event-Scorecard. The Event-Scorecard is divided based on areas of data collection, evaluations, calculations, projections and results. The three areas are coordinated systematically and as far as possible standardised (particularly in terms of data import and export interfaces). The overall concept of this study covers the effects in the three traditional dimensions of sustainability economics, ecological and social responsibility, for which separate relevant indicators have been developed. The basis for the data collection is preliminary talks with event organisers. Then event data is collected with specific questionnaires (organiser, player and visitor survey) and by a tally sheet the visitor frequency of the event is determined. Calculation models have been developed for each dimension and results differ by destination. The economy model is, compared to the ecology and social model, more complex and consists of an estimation model, a person model and an overall model.

Determining the economic impact of sports events occurs in the context of an overall system for the collection of the economic importance. The framework forms an added value network, which is oriented at the national accounts (focusing on Switzerland). This added value network represents the entire sports sector, including the operation of sports facilities, school sports, sports education and sporting events. Based on this overall system, the events are examined in terms of the different sectors (private households, companies, government, foreign countries) (see Figure 6.2).

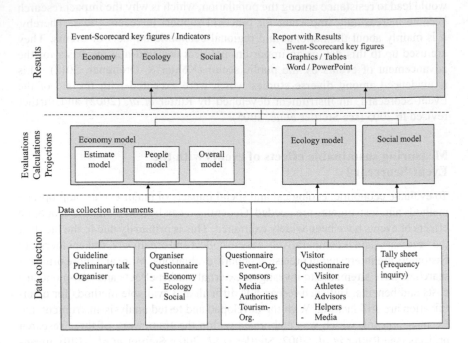

Figure 6.1 Schematic overview of the model Event-Scorecard.

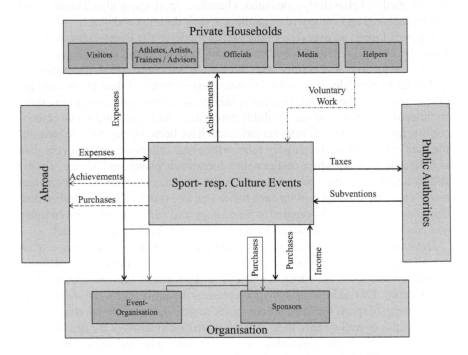

Figure 6.2 The event in the overall economic model (Stettler *et al.*, 2005).

Given this approach, both direct and indirect effects can be detected. Central to the analysis are the turnovers: the gross value added and the resulting impact on employment. The methodology of the Event-Scorecard differs between effects on the region of the event and effects on the entire country (not including the effects on foreign countries). As far as possible, the effects are shown according to the different economic sectors. In doing so, the input indicators from the production accounts of the Federal Statistical Office of Switzerland are used. In addition, tax revenues and subsidies from the government are recorded and displayed.

Two important areas of investigation include ecological impacts and social impacts of sustainability and regeneration. The ecology part covers the analysis of the ecological impacts of the event. It examines traffic and four ecological areas: energy, air, climate and waste. In addition to a quantitative analysis of the five areas, the realised actions from the organiser for the reduction of impacts on the environment are recorded and evaluated. Ecological impacts of events can be recorded, for example, through indicators such as transportation routes, passenger-kilometers, means of transportation choice, emissions, energy, water or waste. In the area of the social impacts, the organiser, visitors, helpers and possibly also the population judge the image of the event. In addition, aspects of benefit such as the identity-forming function with the region or the enabeling of social contacts as well as social damage aspects such as doping problems or health hazards are appraised. For the area of society, among other things, the satisfaction, the image, and the acceptance as well as the participation of the population are recorded structually.

Comparison of Event-Scorecard key indicators of selected major sport events

The Event-Scorecard has been applied, in different levels of detail, at 23 sport and cultural events since the year 2000 and has proven itself in practice as an appropriate tool for an impact analysis. Six major sport events are discussed based on results and indicators of an economic analysis. All were analyzed with the same methodology of the Event-Scorecard. The data from these three one-time and three recurring major sport events allow drawing a comparison and conclusions from the different impacts of large sport events.

Evaluation of one-time major sport events

Regeneration efforts can be extremely costly for one-time events, but can play a role in generating a positive image. One-time major sport events contribute to an increased awareness and a positive image of a region. If these effects are sustainable and if guests return in a region after the event is being questioned. However, the evaluated data of the three analysed events confirm that tourism at least temporarily benefited greatly from the major sports events. The three events discussed in this section include: the UEFA Football European Championship 2008, the IIHF Ice Hockey Championship 2009 and the IAAF European Athletics Championship in 2014. Also conclusions are drawn from a comparison of the key indicators of the three one-time major sport events.

UEFA Football European Championship 2008 Switzerland (UEFA EURO 2008)

UEFA EURO 2008, co-hosted by Switzerland and Austria, was regarded as the top sporting event that year in Europe. In Switzerland the UEFA EURO 2008 generated an economically relevant turnover of CHF 1.7 billion and a gross value added of around CHF 1 billion. The added value impact of the UEFA EURO 2008 corresponded (based on the whole year 2008) to a contribution of the Swiss GDP of 0.18%. Given the size of the Swiss economy and the fact that it was a three-week event, its contribution was deemed remarkable. Regarding accommodation a significant increase of 70% was achieved compared to the previous year in the host regions in the months before the UEFA EURO 2008. Despite the increase, strong crowding-out effects caused an overall decrease in overnight stays in the host regions of Geneva, Berne and Zurich. All of Switzerland was faced with declining numbers of overnight stays in hotels but the sales increased significantly in the hospitality industry in the second quarter of 2008 due to the higher prices for hotel stays. The public authorities spent approximately CHF 150 million for the UEFA EURO 2008. At the same time, the state benefited from tax revenue of approximately CHF 140 million.

IIHF Ice Hockey World Championship 2009 Zurich/Berne (IIHF WC 2009)

From 24 April to 10 May 2009 the IIHF Ice Hockey World Championships were held in Switzerland (the host regions were Berne and Zurich-Kloten). The different groups (visitors, coaches/athletes, staff) generated more than 300,000 days of (visitor) stay, setting off 112,500 overnight stays in the host cantons of Berne and Zurich-Kloten (RP & ITW, 2009a). On average a visitor spent 249 CHF per day. Total revenues in Switzerland add up to CHF 175 million, where CHF 118 million was generated in the host cantons of Berne and Zurich-Kloten. This corresponds to a gross value added for Switzerland of CHF 76 million and CHF 48 million, respectively, in the cantons of Berne and Zurich.

IAAF European Athletics Championship 2014 Zurich (IAAF EC 2014)

In addition to the annual athletics top event 'World Class Zurich' in 2014, IAAF EC 2014 was held in Zurich and with the Event-Scorecard. The caused sales by all players who were part of the IAAF EC 2014 throughout Switzerland amounted to CHF 146 million (cf. RP & ITW, 2014a). Of which approximately CHF 95 million (65%) emerged in the canton of Zurich (one of the total 26 cantons of Switzerland). The IAAF EC 2014 generated a total gross value added of CHF 66 million in all of Switzerland, of which approximately CHF 40 million (61%) incurred in the canton of Zurich. These economic effects generated a tax volume of a total of CHF 8 million.

To realise the described economic effects, a working volume in all of Switzerland of about 680 full-time equivalents (FTE) was needed. More than 60,000 overnights were generated by all groups of visitors of the event for tourism. Around 47,000 (78%) of them were attributable to the hotel industry. Altogether, the hotel industry of the canton of Zurich listed around 400,000 overnight stays in August 2014. So the IAAF EC was responsible for around one-seventh of the overnight stays in the canton of Zurich in August 2014 and was therefore important for Zurich's tourism and hospitality industry.

Evaluation of recurring major sport events

Compared to single major events, recurring major sporting events can be a long-term location factor for the host regions and help to increase awareness and tourist revenue. Building on the above section of one-time major events, this section looks at the Ski World Cup race 2009 in Adelboden, the Swiss Federal Wrestling and Alpine Festival 2013 in Burgdorf (FWAF) and the football games of the Raiffeisen Super League season 2013/2014. Conclusions are drawn on the evaluation of recurring major sport events.

FIS Ski World Cup Adelboden 2009 (Ski WC 2009)

Since 1967 the Ski World Cup Adelboden is an inherent part in the calendar of the FIS Ski World Cup Tour. The men's event attracts more than 30,000 visitors to the vacation region. In 2009 a total of 33,000 guests visited the FIS Ski WC in Adelboden, of which approximately 28,000 were actual spectators. More than 80% of the audience came from outside the vacation region of Adelboden, thereof 79% from Switzerland and about 4% from abroad, which in total caused 18,100 overnight stays (RP & ITW, 2009b). The total turnover caused by the Ski WC in all of Switzerland was CHF 13 million, of which CHF 7.5 million can be assigned to the holiday region Adelboden and 5.7 million CHF to the rest of Switzerland. CHF 5.5 million was generated as gross value added in all of Switzerland. Thereby it was the largest value accrued by the tourism and hospitality industry based on wholesale and retail trade.

Swiss Federal Wrestling and Alpine Festival Burgdorf 2013 (FWAF 2013)

FWAF is a national event and the biggest recurring sporting event in Switzerland. The event is carried out every three years, most recently held in Burgdorf (Emmental). Due to the increasing popularity of the FWAF the visitor numbers have been rising strongly in recent years. In particular the number of visitors to the festival site, which is accessible without a ticket, has almost doubled between 2001 (100,000 visitors) and 2013 (approximately 174,000 visitors). The analysis with the Event-Scorecard (RP & ITW, 2013) showed that the average spending of one visitor during the entire stay at the event in 2013 totalled 160 CHF per day per guest and 400 CHF for overnight guests. With that the FWAF 2013 generated a total turnover in Switzerland of approximately CHF 128 million. This resulted, including the indirect effects, in a total of CHF 63 million gross value added in Switzerland. Considering only the direct value (30 million CHF in Switzerland), one can assign approximately 63% (approximately CHF 19 million) to the region. This is a high value for events of this size and shows that the regional roots of the event have worked very well in economic terms.

Raiffeisen Super League Championship 2013/2014 (RSL 2013/2014)

Football, with more than 315,000 active football players and 2 million spectators in the season 2013/14, is the most common sport in Switzerland. Many professional football clubs are a significant economic factor in their regions and are comparable to medium-sized businesses relating to added value and employment. The total activities of the 10 RSL clubs triggered a turnover of about CHF 800 million and a gross value added of about CHF 453 million (RP & ITW, 2014b). This corresponds to almost half of the value generated by the UEFA EURO 2008 in Switzerland or about six times the value of the IIHF WC of 2009. At the same time, the activities of the RSL clubs managed a working volume of 3300 FTEs throughout Switzerland. The economic activities of the clubs also led to tax revenues in the amount of CHF 42 million in Switzerland.

Comparisons of one-time and recurring major sport events

One-time major sport events can contribute to an increased awareness and a positive image of the host region. The image factor plays a significant role in the economic regeneration of the host destinations across Switzerland as observed above. Regular recurring events create strain on physical regeneration efforts to upgrade infrastructures. These events also support tourism when there is a regular flow of visitors, which in turn supports the image of the destination. How sustainable these effects are, however, and if guests will return to a region again after the event is questionable. The data evaluation of the three one-time events confirms though that tourism at least benefits in the short term from the major sport events. That way the UEFA EURO 2008 triggered 50,000 overnight stays per match day. Tourism in Zurich and Berne benefited from approximately 7000 additional overnight stays per day of the Ice Hockey World Championships and the IAAF EC generated 10,000 overnight stays per event day. Although these three exemplary events are one-time major sport events, a wide range is seen in the comparison of the results. The EURO 2008 is in terms of all indicators by far the largest sport event in Switzerland. However, the size advantage relativises itself in perspective that the EURO has only taken place in Switzerland (and Austria) on one occasion and may not be staged there again for some time. One-time events need to have a critical size to induce a perceptible legacy. The event size is a relative indicator, depending on the economic viability of a region or the importance of a sport. Table 6.1 presents a comparison of economic impacts to show the difference between one-time and recurring events.

Frequently scheduled major sporting events form the foundation of this niche industry landscape. They are long-term location factors for the host regions unlike the one-time events. But also with these events there are significant differences. Big national events with rotating venues such as the Federal Wrestling and Alpine Festival or also the Federal Gymnastics Festival form, in economic terms, are among the top group. But also recurring annual events at the same locations like the alpine FIS Ski World Cup (for example, in Adelboden) or more of the 21 SwissTopSport events, which take place in Switzerland and are among the best in the world in their particular sports (swisstopsport.ch, online) such as the Swiss Indoors in Basel (tennis) or the Engadin Ski Marathon, are outstanding events for the particular sports and regions. They contribute to the increase of awareness and raise the tourist revenue of a destination. Often major sport events integrate the destination's name in the designation of the event so that the venue provides additional awareness. Recurring events can be smaller than one-time events to induce changes. This is often the case with event-led projects (Smith, 2012) like upgrading or renewing infrastructure in the operational realisation of the event.

The analysis using the Event-Scorecard has shown that both unique one-time and recurring sports events can have positive effects on the economy of a particular region in a country. However, concrete evidence relating to the cost-benefit ratio cannot be shown by the existing impact analysis. In practice, such analyses are missing extensively (Késenne, 2005); however, they would be very important

Table 6.1 Comparison of economic impacts of one-time major sport events

Event	Length (in days)	Visitors (per day)	Over night stays (per day)	Added value (CHF/per day)	Occupation (FTE/per day)
One-time major sport events					
UEFA EC 2008	22	309,090 (matches & public viewings)	50,000	45.8 Mio.	391
IIHF WC 2009	16	18,875 (days of stay)	7,031	4.75 Mio.	30
IAAF EC 2014	6	24,249	10,000	11 Mio.	113
Recurring major sport events					
Ski WC 2009	3	11,000	6,033	1.83 Mio.	16
RSL 13/14	36 (per Team)	6,111	41	126,000	110
FWAF 2013	3	70,000	28,333	21 Mio.	213

to make specific decisions for the promotion of events. In particular, the need for high investments by the public sector lead to the fact that valid statements about the short- and long-term cost/benefit ratio can rarely be met. For Switzerland, but also for other countries and destinations, the question is, due to the increasing demands on the orientation of a mega-event, whether co-hosting solutions can be promising examples such as the UEFA EURO 2008 (Switzerland and Austria) or the same event that followed in 2012 (Poland and Ukraine). The event in 2020 will take place in 12 European countries to celebrate the EURO's 60th jubilee. Events like the UEFA EURO are always organised in multiple locations, but not always in more than one country. The more countries that are involved as host nations, the more heterogenous and different they are – and the more complex event organisation becomes. The final total costs of organisation are higher than if the event was organised by one country as transaction costs arise. The countries of Switzerland and Austria (who hosted the UEFA EURO 2008) are alike, additional transaction costs could be kept to a minimum. Multi-country events in general induce lower costs per country (in terms of building or upgrading infrastructure), but additional costs (for transactions and tourism promotion) and the marketing, image and economic benefit for each country is lower since less games will be played. At this stage, no studies are known to have analysed and compared costs and benefits of multi-country and single-country events.

The practical experience also shows that with the use of the Event-Scorecard the economic effects are prevailing in the foreground and the ecological and social aspects are rarely analyzed. Previous research suggests this is because of the efforts and costs associated with the analysis of indicators to focus on the environment and society. Furthermore, economic impact analyses serve as an approved instrument for the eligibility of events at public institutions. In recent years the sustainable management of events has gained in importance and has generated numerous other analytical tools from science. The following section will briefly describe the instruments previously mentioned as well as present a concept for sustainable management of major events.

Sustainable realisation and long-term legacy of major events

The context of international events shows that the establishment of a sustainable event strategy is obligatory in order to survive in an increasingly diversified events landscape across Europe. The public sector on a regional and national level and other private economy players (sponsors, visitors, associations and clubs) as well as the general public are showing increasing interest in sustainable implementation of events and an appropriate reporting of those.

Indicators and key figures

Indicators and key figures are not always easy for event organisers to gather, which is why in recent years various guidelines and instruments have been developed for science and practice. The most important internationally accepted standard of sustainability reporting is the guideline of the Global Reporting Initiative (GRI). This initiative, supported by the UN, has created a specially fitted version of the GRI methodology for events in January 2012 (Event Organisers Sector Supplement and GRI-EOSS), which was updated in June 2013. This version, the so-called industry addition for event organisers, provides a basis which enables the integration of economic, ecological and social factors to be established at a management level. For this purpose, in cooperation with relevant stakeholders, which topics are the most important for the event are defined. Based on those facts, an analysis and monitoring concept was developed in which targeted improvements can be introduced in these selected areas. Here areas such as waste management or use of voluntary or regional value can be examined. This management practice already experiences wide acceptance in many other industries. For example, about 80% of the 350 world's best-performing companies and corporations report according to the GRI standards (Sustainability Update KPMG AG, 2013). Other significant international standards and guidelines are based on ISO 20121 (event sustainability management system), the Olympic Games Impact (OGI) Study developed by the International Olympic Committee (IOC) as well as the Sustainable Sport and Event Toolkit (SSET) developed by the Vancouver Organising Committee for the 2010 Olympic and Paralympic Winter Games (VANOC) and the International Academy of Sports Science and Technology (AISTS).

Sustainability management of major events

The concepts and tools developed in recent years can help event organisers and tourism stakeholders create sustainable events. However, events must not only be sustainable, they also have to serve a long-term benefit for the regions. In this context, the NIV-concept was developed for the Olympic candidacy Grisons 2022 (GR 2022) in which through the sustainability (N) a foundation was created, aimed at ensuring ecological, socially responsible and economically productive games (Lacotte *et al.*, 2013). Moreover, it should be possible, in consideration with the NIV-concept, to offer a platform for innovations (I) and by that creating a long-term legacy (V) through major events for the benefit of future generations. This is achieved through innovative projects in the three dimensions of economy, environment and society, with concrete and measurable goals in which the implementation is controlled by ensuring funding and clear responsibilities (see Figure 6.3). According to Smith (2012), projects of any dimension can result in events-led regeneration.

The NIV-concept was adapted and concretised as a pilot project for the World Ski Championship 2017. Nineteen projects in the fields of economy, ecology and society arose based on an NIV-Vision and NIV-Charter for the World Ski Championship 2017. Concerning the environment, for example, traffic will be diverted to public transport systems. Individual traffic will be kept to a minimum by means of attractive combination offers and offering a smart traffic management system for the Ski World Cup 2017. One of the projects gives guests and athletes an understanding of the history of winter sport in St. Moritz and therefore makes

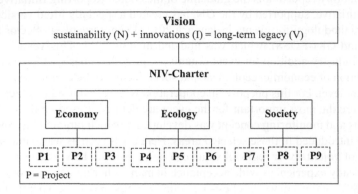

Figure 6.3 NIV concept.

skiing more exciting – an attempt to bring more people to the mountain. Media communications of the Ski World Cup in 2017 will be used to promote alpine snow sports in the area of mass sports. This way society also benefits from the event.

For the achievement of the specific project goals, a strategic and operational management is still needed, which manages suitable control and ensures the re-alisation of the projects. Only through that can the implementation of such a concept be guaranteed. The event then becomes a sustainable major sporting event and the creation of a long-term and positive legacy for the region and the population will be possible.

Strategic event management system for destinations

Numerous studies have shown that events play an important role for destinations or regions through their economic effects, taking social and ecological needs into account. Through a successful positioning and strategy of a destination via events it is possible to increase awareness, attract new customers as well as main-tain and strengthen a long-term ability to compete (Chalip, 2005; Getz, 2008). From a scientific perspective, effects of events are often only detected as a sin-gular individual entry and not the impacts of events among each other (Ziakas & Costas, 2011). In practice, therefore, the challenge for managers of cities and re-gions is to strategically coordinate and control the promotion of events. As part of an ongoing research project (Stettler *et al.*, 2012), the Event Management System has been developed using the example of the destination Engadin St. Moritz, which contributes to the targeted-strategic regulation, evaluation and support of events in tourist destinations. During implementation, the economic, social and ecological impacts of events were examined and evaluated, considering the existing framework. The Event Management System has been developed so that it can be adapted to other destinations or public and private subsidy institutions.

An overview of the entire system is imparted (see Figure 6.3) as well as the individual core modules of the Event Management System are explained closely, with the core modules outlined in Figure 6.4. The methodology and the approach of the strategic Event Management System for destinations are built modularly. The various instruments make it possible to measure, analyze and directly compare a large number of different events.

First, the overall system will be presented via a guideline and the approach and application of the instruments will be described. The event strategy of the destination serves as the basis for the event's evaluations and distribution of aid money. This is obligatory and must be worked out at the beginning with the leaders of the destination. For the data collection of the events, several specific instruments have been developed.

In a first step, the triage questionnaire allows with little effort a preselection and withdrawal of events, which clearly do not meet the requirements for support. Then with the analysis questionnaire, all the necessary information for the calculation of the evaluation and granting of funds are raised. The validation questionnaire and survey of the visitors are used to review the information of the analysis questionnaire and for the investigation of additional information about the event. The methodology of the Event-Scorecard is applied, when meaningful data on the economic, ecological and social impacts on an event have to be collected and calculated. In a final step the overall rating, the weighting of the events and the distribution of support contributions is calculated using the event evaluation and promotion tool (Excel tool).

Through the described procedure, management-decision-bases are created, which allow an objective evaluation and transparent distribution of support funds and provide an input to a clear positioning and contribute to increasing the value of the destination. The management tool is a comparatively simple and

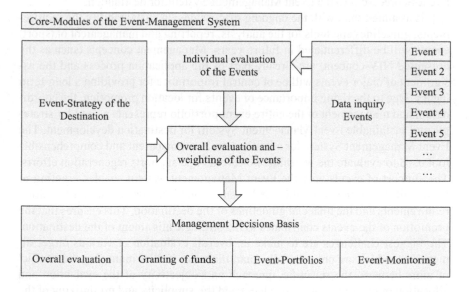

Figure 6.4 Core modules of the Event Management System.

inexpensive tool to make objective and strategic decisions. Furthermore, it serves for the optimization and further development of the event portfolio of the destination for a long-term and sustainable positioning.

Conclusion and future directions

The importance of sport events will increase for the promotion of locations through the economic regeneration of sport-related industries and also the increased visitor and media interest. The pressure of competition in the event sector will rise. The experience with the Event-Scorecard has shown that with its development a conflict of aims exists between the relevance of an indicator and the demand for it. From the perspective of demand the data interests of the players (in particular the organisers) is much greater on the economic impacts than on the social and ecological impacts. But from the perspective of sustainability all three impact areas are synonymous. Due to the demand the Event-Scorecard should be expanded primarily in the field of economics. However, from the perspective of the relevance and balance the methodological extension should take place primarily in relation to the social and ecological effects. Future developments refer amongst others to the collection and projection of the basic population and structure of visitors and visitor frequency, respectively. In addition, the focus should be on the media sector to capture media attention, the development of indicators of media coverage as well as a media effect model in coordination with international evaluation methods and standards for a sustainable development (for example, the Global Reporting Initiative [GRI]). This will contribute to destination image regeneration linked to sustainable event planning and development. Another development possibility exists, referring to the more systematic integration of the Event-Scorecard into the Event Management System for destinations.

It is assumed that, with the ongoing discussions on sustainability the requirements, guidelines and tools for the analysis, reporting and management of (sport) events will be differentiated in future years. Management concepts (such as the presented NIV-concept) are already part of the application process and the assignment of major events will be of central importance for providing a long-term legacy. Due to the rising importance of events for location promotion, the coordination and management of the entire event portfolio represents a need for strategic and sustainable Event Management System for destination development. The Event Management System for a destination is a transparent and comprehensible tool used to evaluate the worthiness of events and supports regeneration efforts. The support of events with the Event Management System enables granting of funds tailored to the destination and event strategy in consideration of location requirements and the financial guidelines of the destination. This ensures that the promotion of the events contributes to the strategic alignment of the destination. The biggest challenges are to make an overall evaluation of various target dimensions, which are only partially quantifiable as well as managing the conflict of aims between the scientific approach and objectivity of the evaluation and allocation of resources on the one hand and the simplicity and minimizing of the associated effort on the other hand. The first experiences using the example of the destination of Engadin St. Moritz showed that the Excel-based event evaluation and allocation of resources could be accomplished with relatively little effort. The effort increases only significantly when the data of the organisers should be checked with the help of various validation tools (for example, with visitor surveys). But a destination itself can decide how much effort it wants to conduct for the evaluation, rating and review of events.

References

Boykoff, M.T. (2014). Media discourse on the climate slowdown. *Nature climate change, 4*, 156–158.

Bramwell, B. (1997). Strategic planning before and after a mega-event. *Tourism management, 18*, 167–176.

Bundesumweltministerium (BMU) & Deutscher Olympischer Sportbund (DOSB) (2007). Green Champions für Sport und Umwelt. Leitfaden für umweltfreundliche Sportveranstaltungen. Berlin: BMU & DOSB.

Bundesumweltministerium (BMU) & Umweltbundesamt (UBA). (2008). Leitfaden für die umweltgerechte Organisation von Veranstaltungen. Berlin: BMU & UBA.

Burns, J., Hatch, T. & Mules, T. (Eds.). (1986). *The Adelaide Grand Prix. The impact of a special event.* Adelaide, Australia: Centre for South Australian Economic Studies.

Chalip, L. (2005). Marketing, media, and place promotion. In J. Higham (Ed.) *Sport tourism destinations: Issues, opportunities and analysis.* Oxford, England: Elsevier Butterworth-Heinemann (pp. 162–176).

Crompton, J.L. (2006). Economic impact studies: Instruments for political shenanigans. *Journal of travel research, 45*, 45–67.

Davidson, L.S. & Schaffer, W.A. (1980). A discussion of methods employed in analyzing the impact of short-term entertainment events. *Journal of travel research, 18*, 12–16.

Davies, L., Coleman, R. & Ramchandani, G. (2013). Evaluating event economic impact: Rigour versus reality? *International journal of event and festival management, 4*, 31–42.

Death, C. (2011). 'Greening' the 2010 FIFA World Cup: Environmental sustainability and the mega-event in South Africa. *Journal of environmental policy and planning, 13*, 99–117.

Delpy, L. & Li, M. (1998). The art and science of conducting economic impact studies. *Journal of vacation marketing, 4*, 230–254.

Faulkner, B., Chalip, L., Brown, G., Jago, L., March, R. & Woodside, A. (2003). Monitoring the tourism impacts of the Sydney 2000 Olympics. *Event management, 6*, 231–246.

Fredline, L., Raybould, M., Jago, L. & Deery, M. (2005). Triple bottom line event evaluation: A proposed framework for holistic event evaluation. In third international event conference: The impacts of events (pp. 2–15).

Gans, P., Horn, M. & Zemann, C. (2003). Sportgroßveranstaltungen - ökonomische, ökologische und soziale Wirkungen, ein Bewertungsverfahren zur Entscheidungsvorbereitung und Erfolgskontrolle. Schriftenreihe des Bundesinstitutes für Sportwissenschaft. Schorndorf: Hofmann.

Getz, D. (2008). Event tourism: Definition, evolution, and research. *Tourism management, 29*, 403–428.

Jones, C. (2005). Major events, networks and regional development. *Regional studies, 39*, 185–195.

Jones, M. (2009). *Sustainable event management. A practical guide*. London, England: Earthscan.

Késenne, S. (1999). Miscalculations and misinterpretations in economic impact analysis. In J. Jeanrenaud (Ed.). *The economic impact of sport events*. Neuchâtel, Switzerland: Center International d'Etude du Sport (pp. 29–40).

Késenne, S. (2005). Do we need an economic impact of sport events or a cost-benefit analysis of a sports event? *European sport management quarterly, 5*, 133–142.

Köhler, J. (2013). Events als Instrumente des Regionalmarketing. Entwicklung eines Bezugsrahmens zur regional-strategischen Eventwirkungskontrolle (dissertation), Technische Universität Chemnitz.

Köhler, J. & Drengner, J. (2012). Eine kritische Betrachtung der ökonomischen Wirkungsanalyse von Veranstaltungen–Darstellung von Fallstricken und ihren Konsequenzen am Beispiel der Bob- und Skeleton-WM 2008. In C. Zanger (Ed.) *Erfolg mit nachhaltigen Eventkonzepten*. Wiesbaden, Germany: Gabler (pp. 202–224).

Lacotte, U., Reber, D. & Schmid, V. (2013). NIV Bericht für Graubünden 2022, St. Moritz & Davos.

Lee, C.K. & Taylor, T. (2005). Critical reflections on the economic impact assessment of a mega-event: The case of 2002 FIFA World Cup. *Tourism management, 26*, 595–603.

Mules, T. & Faulkner, B. (1996). An economic perspective on special events. *Tourism economics, 2*, 314–329.

Müller, W. (2001). *Erlebnismarkt und Menschenbild. Rahmenbedingungen von Erlebnismärkten und Konsequenzen für die Führungskultur in Unternehmen*. Düsseldorf, Germany: Berneux.

Opaschowski, H.W. (2001). Deutschland 2010: Wie wir morgen arbeiten und leben-Voraussagen der Wissenschaft zur Zukunft unserer Gesellschaft, 2. Aufl., Hamburg, Germany: Germa Press Verlag.

Preuß, H. (1999). *Ökonomische Implikationen der Ausrichtung Olympischer Spiele von München 1972 bis Atlanta 1996*. Kassel, Germany: Agon Sportverlag.

Preuß, H., & Weiss, H.J. (2003). *Torchholder value added. Der ökonomische Nutzen der Olympischen Spiele 2012 in Frankfurt Rhein-Main*. Eschborn, Germany: AWV-Veri.

Raybould, M. & Fredline, L. (2012). An investigation of measurement error in visitor expenditure surveys. *International journal of event and festival management, 3*, 201–211.

Rütter, H., Stettler, J., Amstutz, M., Birrer, D., Breiter, M., Laesser, C., Landolt, M., Liebrich, A., Marti, B., Mehr, R., Müller, H.R., Scherly, F. & Schmid, F. (2002). Volkswirtschaftliche Bedeutung von Sportgrossanlässen in der Schweiz. KTI-Projekt. Schlussbericht. Luzern.

Schulze, G. (2005). *Die Erlebnisgesellschaft. Kultursoziologie der Gegenwart*. 2nd ed. Frankfurt, Germany: Campus.

Small, K., Edwards, D. & Sheridan, L. (2005). A flexible framework for evaluating the socio-cultural impacts of a (small) festival. *International journal of event management research, 1*, 67–77.

Smith, A. (2012). *Events and urban regeneration: The strategic use of events to revitalise cities*. London, England: Routledge.

Stettler, J., Rütter, H., Linder, P., Mehr, R., Liebrich, A., de Bary, A., Beutler, S. & Laesser, C. (2005). Volkswirtschaftliche Bedeutung von Sportgrossanlässen: Indikatorenbildung und Vereinfachung der Methodik. Schlussbericht des KTI-Projekts Volkswirtschaftliche Bedeutung von Sportgrossanlässen: Indikatorenbildung und Vereinfachung der Methodik. Luzern.

Stettler, J., Caliesch, D. & Herzer, C. (2010). Methodenevaluation des Forschungsprojektes UEFA EURO 2008™ und Nachhaltigkeit und methodische Erweiterung der Event-Scorecard zur Messung der volkswirtschaftlichen Effekte von Sportgrossevents, Schlussbericht des Teilprojekts 2 des Forschungsgesuchs, Sportökonomisches Monitoring unter besonderer Berücksichtigung von Sportevents und Sportinfrastruktur-Projekten der Ressortforschung des Bundesamtes für Sport BASPO 2008–2011. Luzern.

Stettler, J., Rütter, H. & Caliesch, D. (2012). Event-Scorecard und strategisches Event-Management-System für Destination. In S.M. Hirt (Ed.). *Event-Management. Grundlagen für Studium und Praxis.* Bad Berleburg: Versus.

Sustainability Update KPMG AG (2013). Sustainability Update KPMG AG. http://www.kpmg.com/DE/de/Documents/kpmg-sustainability-update-dezember-2013.pdf.

Swissolympic (n.d.). Swissolympic. http://www.swissolympic.ch/Ethik/ecosport/Hilfsmittel/Leitfaden-Nachhaltigkeitsbericht.

Swisstopsport (n.d.). Swisstopsport. http://www.swisstopsport.ch/.

Wagenseil, U., Durrer Eggerschwiler, B., Taufer, B., Störkle, M. & Hausmann, C. (2014). Freiwilliges und ehrenamtliches Engagement im Tourismus. Ein interdisziplinäres Forschungsprojekt für Tourismusorganisationen und touristisch relevante Eventorganisationen. Luzern.

Ziakas, V. & Costa, C.A. (2011). Event portfolio and multi-purpose development: Establishing the conceptual grounds. *Sport management review, 14*, 409–423.

7 Sports and event-led regeneration strategies in post-earthquake Christchurch

Alberto Amore and C. Michael Hall

Introduction

Sports and event-led regeneration strategies have been a significant characteristic of major cities in the developed world since the 1970s and are an integral, though widely debated, component of urban redevelopment policy (Hall, 1992, 2006; Coaffee, 2013). Policies for sport-led regeneration projects are usually justified as a necessary condition for the hosting of hallmark events (Norris, 2002), or are the result of peer pressure from major sports franchises and federations (Hall & Wilson, 2016).

Such strategies usually involve the allocation of substantial urban landholdings to accommodate sports infrastructure along with associated retail, hospitality, leisure and tourism facilities. Specific sport and events-led regeneration is therefore often inseparable from broader redevelopment and growth coalition processes that seek to promote urban competitiveness, predominantly through corporatist governance modes (Hall, 2001, 2006). Nevertheless, the majority of research on sports and event-led regeneration has focussed on areas that have suffered significant deindustrialization or physical and economic decline. In contrast, the present chapter examines the role of sports and events infrastructure and event hosting as part of post-natural disaster induced regeneration (Gotham & Greenberg, 2014; Johnson & Olshansky, 2010; Amore & Hall, 2016).

This chapter is based on findings from research undertaken between April 2013 and November 2015 on the provision of new amenities for leisure and tourism in the Christchurch central business district (CBD) following the earthquakes of 2010 and 2011. These earthquakes lead to major losses of life and the destruction of over 70% of the city's CBD. Data for the analysis was collected from organizations' websites, Christchurch City Council (CCC) archives, Cabinet papers and documents retrieved from the Canterbury Earthquake Recovery Authority (CERA) and the Christchurch Central Development Unit (CCDU). A two-round series of semi-structured interviews with participants was undertaken between May and November 2015. The names of the participants indicated in this chapter are fictional and their affiliations are not reported. Using the case of the 2010 and 2011 earthquake sequence in Christchurch in New Zealand, the chapter examines the role of sport and events in post-earthquake urban regeneration and the accompanying issues it raises with respect to governance, policy process and planning practice.

In outlining a framework for post-disaster regeneration in sports and events, Table 7.1 illustrates sports and event-led regeneration strategies and compares them with regeneration practices in post-disaster contexts where regeneration strategies typically embrace the 'build back better' rhetoric of quasi-regime partnerships (Gotham & Greenberg, 2014). This is usually framed by authoritarian forms of disaster recovery governance that reprise the principles of 'disaster capitalism' (Johnson, 2011; Klein, 2007; Passavant, 2011), which requires triggering events such as natural disasters, as a necessary condition for the adoption of neoliberal-inspired redevelopment agendas. The extraordinary circumstances during the emergency phase give way to special government legislation that authorises clearance and compulsory land acquisition and eventually culminates in what Gotham and Greenberg (2014) refer to as the *tabula rasa*. This chapter primarily examines how sport, and demands for new stadium development, has been integrated into the Christchurch rebuild, though the success of the strategy, as well as the broader regeneration trajectories set by the national government and its agencies, remains significantly open to question at the time of writing. Before examining the strategy in detail, the chapter will briefly contextualise the study area.

Context: Sports facilities in Christchurch, New Zealand

Christchurch is the second largest city of New Zealand and the main urban area and gateway of the South Island. The major high profile sports venue before the earthquakes was the AMI Stadium at Lancaster Park, home to both cricket and rugby. First developed for cricket in 1880, the ground was shared with the Canterbury Rugby Football Union (CRFU) from 1911 on, which eventually became the main user of the stadium in the following decades. Notwithstanding the building of Queen Elizabeth II Park (QEII Park) for the 1974 Commonwealth Games, the AMI Stadium at Lancaster Park maintained its role as the major sports venue in Christchurch. When SANZAR (the body that coordinates two competitions of the Rugby Unions of South Africa, New Zealand and Australia) established the Super Rugby competition in 1996, the CRFU chose AMI Stadium at Lancaster Park as home stadium for their new franchise, the Crusaders. This resulted in a major upgrade of the facility to host professional rugby games and the first rebranding of the venue as Jade Stadium in 1998. In 1999, the management of the stadium passed to the newly established Jade Stadium Limited. The new management body was registered as a Local Authority Trading Enterprise under the exclusive ownership of the CCC and its main purpose was the development and management of the stadium.

Following the International Rugby Board (IRB) decision to appoint New Zealand as host for the 2011 Rugby World Cup, Jade Stadium Limited received approximately (all monetary figures in this chapter in New Zealand dollars) $40 million ($46.17 million on current value) from the CCC to redevelop the

Table 7.1 Sports, events and disaster recovery regeneration strategies (adapted from Hall, 2001, 2004; Saxena, 2013; Amore & Hall, 2016)

Type of strategy	Form of participation	Funding	Policy implications	Outcomes
Sports-led regeneration	Public sector, professional sports and associated businesses, and private owners of sports franchises	Mainly subsidised by the public sector, with property tax abatements and other incentives for sports franchises and stadia development	Requires access to large areas of valuable land May require special legislation for decision-making, compulsory land acquisition and delivery	Externalisation of socio-economic costs to local residents Venues can encourage economic return to hospitality and retail If team is successful contributes to local pride and identity
Events-led regeneration	Public sector led, Usually without an overarching policy framework that can be sustained over the long term. Establishment of specific agencies.	Varies depending on the scale of the event, type of event and pace of regeneration strategy Predominantly public-led	Highly contested by local residents, particularly when excluded from decision-making Importance of planning events through the three main timescales (pre–during–post) Selective stakeholder partnerships Suspension of normal planning regulations	Can create economically unsustainable facilities Can act as catalysts for further investments and projects
Disaster recovery regeneration	Establishment of dedicated recovery agencies Formal partnerships of mainly local authorities and investors (consortia)	Mainly public sector through temporarily convened disaster-management agencies Eventual private sector investment whereas real estate prices drop	Importance of involving the community in decision-making process Shifting of policy priorities among stakeholders accordingly to the agenda set by the disaster management agencies.	Increasing disaffection by locals, especially if excluded from the decision-making process. Likely provision of more effective infrastructure Potential to increase the resilience of communities to future disasters

stadium (CCC, 2007). Another $20 million had to be secured through other funding sources, including naming rights. This led to the rebranding of the stadium to AMI Stadium in 2008 (CCC, 2008). The project included making the stadium all-seated, the creation of new parking areas, and the construction of new stands to accommodate up to 45,000 spectators.

The earthquake on 4 September 2010 did not affect the stadium. However, when the 22 February 2011 earthquake struck the newly built stands suffered major damage and the site was subject to intense liquefaction, including the playing surface (Knowler, 2011). Despite the city and venue management hoping to still be able to host Rugby World Cup games in September 2011, it soon became clear that the games allocation to Christchurch would be rescheduled to venues in other cities. According to Vbase, the damages to the stadium were severe and 'diverting part of the rebuilding effort away from people's homes and suburbs would have been huge' (Small, 2011, p. B.5). Soon after the IRB final decision, limited demolition occurred at the AMI Stadium at Lancaster Park.

The earthquakes also affected QEII Park, which had become a suburban sports complex home to football, athletics and other indoor sports. Following the September 2010 earthquake, the venue reopened to host the Special Olympics trials in October. The whole complex was damaged beyond repair as a result of the February 2011 earthquake (Tutty, 2011). A brand-new $300 million Metro Sports Centre is going to replace QEII Park original functions in the CBD (CCDU, 2012b, 2013d, 2015; CERA, 2013a), while the original site is currently under discussion for the development of a Greenhouse Complex (CCT, 2015) similar to the Eden Project in the United Kingdom.

In order to host international test and one-day cricket (in particular the 2015 ICC Cricket World Cup), Hagley Oval, a cricket ground in Hagley Park, a major greenspace in central Christchurch, was substantially upgraded with the addition of banked terraces, a new pavilion and lighting for night games. Given that Hagley Park is a public reserve there are substantial limits on how many major games can be played on Hagley Oval. Hosting approximately 8000 people, Hagley Oval was able to provide a home for international cricket after the loss of AMI Stadium at Lancaster Park as well as provincial games that had previously been played at QEII Park. Although there was substantial public opposition to the redevelopment of Hagley Oval, the hosting of international cricket in Christchurch again was promoted as a significant indicator of post-earthquake rebuild success and the regeneration of the CBD (Marks, 2015). The following section focuses on the proposal for the development of a Stadium Precinct under the Christchurch Central Recovery Plan (CCRP) released in July 2012 (CCDU, 2012b), scheduled for 2022 at the time of writing, in the Southeast edge of the CBD.

CBD Stadium

Since the aftermath of the 22 February 2011 earthquake, the issue of a stadium has become one of the key rebuilding planning topics. On the eve of the *Share an Idea* initiative, run by the CCC in June 2011, the then Vbase Chief Executive,

Bryan Pearson, suggested that the AMI Stadium at Lancaster Park was going to partially reopen in February 2012 (Wood, 2011). The first Christchurch CBD Draft Plan released in August 2011 foresaw the retention of the existing stadium and the creation of a sports hub nearby (CCC, 2011b). The location of such a hub was at that time feasible because the CCC owned some land in proximity to the stadium and it was claimed that it would 'strengthen Christchurch's reputation as a premier international sporting destination' (CCC, 2011b, p. 69).

The project was welcomed by the local Institute of Architects as 'one of the few truly new ideas' (NZIA, 2011). However, a geotechnical report released in August 2011 found substantial damage to foundations and the stands of the AMI Stadium at Lancaster Park, to the point that the then Christchurch Mayor, Bob Parker, was doubtful about the venue's future (Greenhill, 2011). Nevertheless, the final CBD Draft forwarded to the Minister for Canterbury Earthquake Recovery, Hon. Gerry Brownlee, in December 2011 still foresaw the creation of a sports hub, with the location to be determined during the feasibility study (CCC, 2011a). Following a period of consultation with advisors, the Minister concluded that the Draft Plan did not contain sufficient information about the actual implementation of the sports hub and other projects (DPMC, 2011a). The Minister and the Cabinet therefore vested CERA with the role of targeting specific areas of the Christchurch CBD to locate key anchor projects in order to catalyse recovery (DPMC, 2011a).

The National Government identified the building of a new stadium in the CBD as one of the 12 key anchor projects to be included in the Request for Proposals (RFPs). On 18 April 2012, Hon. Brownlee and CERA's then Chief Executive, Roger Sutton, announced the establishment of the CCDU (New Zealand Government, 2012). A period of 100 days was given to the CCDU to develop a blueprint for the implementation of the Central City Plan, the stadium anchor project, in collaboration with a team of local and international architects and planners led by Boffa Miskell. Following an early phase of site identification for the sports precinct, the planners concluded that the CBD Stadium project site should be located in the southeast edge of the CBD in proximity to the projected Bus Interchange (CCDU, 2012b, 2013a, 2013e).

The first proposal in July 2012 was for a 35,000 seat covered stadium occupying three city blocks (CCDU, 2012a). On 19 March 2013, CERA and the CCDU issued a notice to take land for the CBD redevelopment and proceeded with the acquisition of the lots (CERA, 2013b). At the final date of the fieldwork (November 2015) the national authorities had purchased more than $38 million worth of land from 26 different landowners. In parallel with land acquisition, national and local authorities began negotiations to agree on the public share of the costs for the stadium. On 26 June 2013, the parties announced the basis of the Cost Sharing Agreement (CSA) for the CBD Stadium, which foresaw a joint contribution from the public sector in the range of $300 million including the land (CERA, 2013a). However, another $200 million would be sought from private investors. The Crown was chosen as the head of the project, while the CCC agreed to cover most of the public share of costs for a total of $253 million (CERA, 2013a).

However, the CBD Stadium project was not a priority for most stakeholders. The building of the CBD Stadium was originally scheduled to begin at the end of 2015 (CCDU, 2013a). However, the financial struggle of the CCC, the success of the temporary AMI stadium, and the ongoing negotiations with the insurance companies for the pay-out of the AMI Stadium at Lancaster Park (Cairns, 2014) led to a postponement to at least 2020 (CCDU, 2014a). Finally, the party responsible for the submission of the business case, the CCDU, has not yet provided such document to the CCC. According to the CSA, the CCDU had until 30 June 2016 to come up with a business case. At the time of writing, however, the CCDU still had not provided such mandatory document (Murphy, 2016).

Governance

Since the establishment of CERA in April 2011, the governance of post-earthquake Christchurch has been dynamic. Until September 2014, there was a strong hierarchical structure centred on the figure of the Minister for the Canterbury Earthquake Recovery, Hon. Gerry Brownlee (CERA, 2011), with both CERA and the CCDU reporting directly to the Minister. In some circumstances the Minister and his advisors opted for the extension of national authority, as occurred with the decision of putting the CCC to one side in the delivery of the CBD recovery plan and establishing CCDU as the responsible body (Brownlee, 2012) and the regulation for compulsory land acquisition for the anchor projects through the Crown (CCDU, 2013c). On the eve of the September 2014 General Election, Prime Minister John Key announced the repositioning of CERA and the CCDU as departmental agencies under the Department of Prime Minister and the Cabinet (DPCM) (DPMC, 2014). Six months later in March 2015, the New Zealand Government announced the establishment of Regenerate Christchurch and Ōtākaro Limited as replacements of CERA and the CCDU, respectively. While Regenerate Christchurch is a 50:50 participation between national and local authorities with a board of members appointed by both parties, Ōtākaro Limited runs the portfolio of anchor projects led by the Crown, including the CBD Stadium project.

The short-term partnership between April and July 2012 that led to the launch of the CCRP, reflected a public-private partnership (PPP) approach to governance. The $30 million project led by Boffa Miskell (Woods Bagot, 2014) involved a team of senior architects from Christchurch and Australia working with public officials from the CCDU and the CCC over a period of 80 days. The Minister for the Canterbury Earthquake Recovery and the Cabinet had the final say on the plan, with the Crown Law Office providing legal advice for the completion of the CCRP. All the planners and officials agreed not to release any information to third parties until the ultimate release of the CCRP. This proved to be quite controversial, particularly for CCC officials that had worked in drafting the recovery plans for the CBD throughout 2011:

[This was] very demoralizing for a local government. And for the level of consultation and expertise that had been brokered into that process. [...] And we were asked to do it by central government. And so to have it set aside, and then have another team created and given a hundred days to come up with a new one [...] with the provisory that they would not talk to us, and their staff had to sign, what do you call them, where you can't talk. So that was very frustrating, because essentially it meant that you'd had all that expertise and knowledge just set aside and not tapped into.

(Anna)

The CBD Stadium project included in the CCPR foresaw a PPP with the inclusion of Non-Government Organizations (NGOs) and the philanthropic sector (CCDU, 2012b). Following the release of the CSA it was decided to give the Crown the lead of the project, with the CCC contributing to most of the publish share of the costs (CERA, 2013a). The report did not specify the private actors involved in the project. Most likely, the participation of private investors is going to be in the form of consortia of local and international developers as established for the Convention Centre Precinct development (CCDU, 2014b). Post the launch of the CCRP, the CCDU and CERA organized information sessions for potential international investors. Concerns were raised about CERA and CCDU staff lacking commercial and property management experience (McCrone, 2013b; New Zealand Parliament, 2013). Their efforts were far from being successful, particularly for the anchor projects. As *Frank* stressed:

And I said [to CERA] "What are you taking them on through the city? And what are you going to show? You are going to show them absolute desolation" And of course they took them through and they never came back.

As the Government began to scale back towards the end of 2014, the CCC started a series of meetings with major investors from China (CDC, 2014). Efforts culminated with the signature of a non-binding agreement between the Council and Guoxin International in September 2015 worth $3.1 billion (Smellie, 2015). The objective is to divert the investment to "tender for large rebuild projects planned by the private sector," including the CBD Stadium (Anonymous, 2015a).

The design and delivery of the CBD Stadium has been heavily influenced by the insurance settlement between the CCC, owner *de facto* of the AMI Stadium at Lancaster Park, and Civic Assurance. The venue was insured for a sum of $143 million and the pay-out would have been invested by the CCC to cover most of its $253 million share foreseen in the CSA (CERA, 2013a). However, Civic Assurance argued that three international loss adjustment firms reported that the AMI Stadium at Lancaster Park was repairable at the cost of $50 million (Anonymous, 2015c) and concluded that they were 'most unlikely to agree to pay [...] almost three times that amount just so the council [could] demolish the current stadium and build another elsewhere' (Anonymous, 2015b). It is important to note that Civic Assurance was the insurer of Christchurch key civic assets such as the Town Hall and the Art Gallery, and that most of the CCC infrastructure was underinsured when the February 2011 earthquake struck (Anonymous, 2013) and that the then CCC CEO, Tony Marryatt, was also Chairperson of Civic Assurance. The CCC argued that the payout from Civic Assurance should be in the range of $900 million, but eventually agreed for a $635 million final settlement in December 2015, the largest insurance payout ever agreed in New Zealand (Cairns, 2015b). It is likely that part of the money will be set aside for the CBD Stadium following the release of the business case.

There was no unanimity among stakeholders that the provision of a new or refurbished stadium should be a priority. Even the Christchurch & Canterbury Tourism (CCT) Sports Tourism and Events Plan stated that the stadium 'is not a high priority from an event generation and economic benefit perspective in comparison with other sports that currently have no adequate facilities for hosting national and international events' (CCT, 2013, p. 41). Nevertheless, the Request for Proposal (RFP) developed by Boffa Miskell during the tender process in April 2012 identified the CBD Stadium being among the 12 anchor projects to include in the ultimate CCRP, *Gabriel* remarked: "there was not analysis to really support that. It was really just a political decision. The Minister [Brownlee] had a view [but] there was no analysis to say that it should be a priority over other projects in the city."

In contrast, a few months after the launch of the CCRP, the then CEO for CERA, Roger Sutton stated that there were just other things to make happen before discussing the investment over the CBD Stadium (Greenhill, 2012b). Similarly, with the election of Lianne Dalziel as CCC Mayor in November 2013, most of the newly elected Council 'didn't think a new stadium was the most important thing to get building' according to *Colin*. Although this did not prevent CERA and the CCDU to proceed with land acquisition for the CBD Stadium and the CRFU pressuring for the CBD Stadium project to start as soon as possible (McCrone, 2014).

Following the settlement with Civic Assurance at the end of 2015, the CRFU CEO, Hamish Riach reiterated that it was 'frustrating that the stadium has been so disregarded in amongst all the priorities' (Cairns, 2015b) and hoped for advanced conversations to take place for the delivery of the business case and the project itself (Murphy, 2016). Nevertheless, concerns remain about the size of the complex, the type of project designed, and the associated costs.

Policy processes

Despite some evidence of shared intents and objectives, the policy processes around stadium provisions in post-earthquake Christchurch have often put national and local authorities in opposition. Since the first draft of the CCC Central City Plan, there have been diverging visions of intents, priorities and processes between key national authorities, the Minister *in primis*, and representatives of the local council. In particular, the process of negotiations culminated with the announcement of the CSA was done behind closed doors between a narrow number of CCC executive officials led by the then CEO Tony Marryatt and the representative of the Crown and the Government led by the then CCDU Director,

Warwick Isaacs. Moreover, the authoritarian set of regulations for land purchase under the Crown turned out to be a particularly controversial issue, as landowners of anchor projects land were subject to the restricting legislation outlined in the *Canterbury Earthquake Recovery Act 2011* (hereafter CER Act 2011). Finally, it soon became clear that the involvement of the local community during the *Share an Idea* session became a mere tokenistic episode of community engagement that growth coalitions used at their advantage to justify the need for a stadium in the CBD of Christchurch.

Undoubtedly, the CCC considered the provision of a stadium among the objectives in the Central City Plan drafts (CCC, 2011b) and the CCDU followed the input of the brief outlined by the Minister for the Canterbury Earthquake Recovery and the Cabinet outlining the CBD Stadium as one of the anchor projects to include in the CCRP. However, there was no intention of retaining the AMI Stadium at Lancaster Park in any of the Cabinet Papers or documents retrieved from CERA and the CCDU. Authorities simply did not consider the recovery of the AMI Stadium at Lancaster Park at first, even though some engineers had explained that the complex could be retained at a cost far lower than the tag price foreseen for the CBD Stadium (informal conversation with *Gabriel*). Conversely, the CCC sought to repair the AMI Stadium at Lancaster Park along with other major community facilities (CCC, 2012a, 2013). Nevertheless, the CCC acknowledged that details over the AMI Stadium at Lancaster Park '[would] be dependent on the outcome of the Christchurch Central Development Unit's blueprint for the Central City' (CCC, 2012a, p. 9). The subordination of the CCC to the Minister became more evident following the release of the CSA in July 2013, as any suggested amendments or partial repeals of the agreement (Sage, 2014) were subject to ministerial veto. Inexorably the CCC had to secure the share of the CBD Stadium projects costs by approving the selling of key public assets (Cairns & Law, 2015) while struggling to find an agreement with Civic Assurance for the insurance payout for the AMI Stadium at Lancaster Park.

The Minister for the Canterbury Earthquake Recovery patently supported the building of the new CBD Stadium. For example, during a briefing with the blueprint team, he personally suggested possible locations of the CBD Stadium (informal conversation with *Gabriel*) and later welcomed the CSA for the new facility as a milestone accord (McCrone, 2013b). Similarly, the CRFU CEO, Hamish Riach, proactively supported the creation of the new CBD Stadium in several media releases (e.g. Greenhill, 2012a). In July 2013, for example, the official announcement of the Crusaders major sponsor deal took place on the site designated for the CBD Stadium (Greenhill, 2013b). The CRFU also conducted a survey, which showed that more than 90% of the Christchurch residents welcomed the building of a modern, mixed-use stadium in the city (Law, 2016). Supporters of the CBD Stadium project argue that the repeated delays in the delivery of the projects are just political ploys to avoid fierce public contestation during the phase of recovery, *Sam* mentioned: 'It is really, in my view, it is political [...] you know, it is a bad, a bad look to build a stadium when other things are not fixed.'

In contrast, representatives of the CCC expressed their criticisms of the CBD Stadium project. Among them, Councillor Yani Johanson stated that the agreement was a burden to the CCC's finances (McCrone, 2013b) and he voted against the selling of public assets to fund the building of the CBD Stadium in April 2015 (Cairns, 2015a). Concerns over the necessity of a large stadium in central Christchurch were raised among other stakeholders, including the Canterbury Employers' Chamber of Commerce Chief Executive, Peter Townsend (Gates, 2013). Criticisms also came from members of the Dunedin City Council, who supported the construction of a $222 million covered stadium for the 2011 Rugby World Cup and which did not achieve its economic promise (Hall & Wilson, 2016). One of the Dunedin Councillors, Lee Vandervis, emphatically stated that if the CCC '[wanted] to spend a lot of money and get nothing in return, a stadium would be the best way to go' (King, 2012). Finally, the New Zealand Treasury first ever report on the government-invested project released in November 2015 raised further concerns over the feasibility of the projects led by the Crown, including the CBD Stadium (New Zeland Treasury, 2014). The costs for the whole project, approximately $550 million for a 35,000 seat covered stadium and the role of the CRFU in the decision-making process has raised further criticisms:

> The problem is you can't rely on the good will of the Rugby Union. They want to make money [...] professional sports [...] they want to make as much money as possible. So the idea that we all compete and we spend more money building big elephants that just sit in for most of time.
>
> *(Adam)*

Like the CCRP, the CSA is a binding document that set the ground financial rules for the delivery of the anchor projects. The process that led to the agreement, however, 'was done in secret and it was well overdue' according to *Adam* so that the CCC Three-Year Plan 2013–2016 has no mention of it (CCC, 2013). Two participants further explained:

> With the Three-year Plan consultation, the Mayor [Bob Parker] would not let [Councillors] move amendments to give a fact to what people, the public, had said in our Three-Year Plan because he said it was contrary to the secret CSA they signed three days before.
>
> *(Adam)*

> One of the other problems was not that of CERA having all this excessive power, but that you had CERA negotiating with former Major Parker and former CEO Tony Marryatt and them not keeping the Councillors on the loop. The CSA has got the Convention Centre and the Stadium in it, thus binding the future Council when it hadn't actually been debated by our elected representatives. So it's the whole way, it's overriding democracy and shoving the people and people representatives out that is a problem.
>
> *(Debbie)*

The scheme for land purchase for the CBD Stadium was as controversial as that for the other anchor projects foreseen in the CCRP. CERA based the valuations on a non-government report on commercial properties done by Ernst & Young (CCDU, 2013c; Ernst & Young, 2012). The report highlighted how hospitality business stakeholders acknowledged how owners would have only invested 'the necessary capital into the central city if the Sports Stadium [was] located within walking distance from the main entertainment areas' (Ernst & Young, 2012, p. 67). The presence of extensive portions of vacant land owned by the CCC (Greenhill, 2013a) was 'a happy coincidence' according to *Thomas* and eased the process of land purchase. Some property owners and hospitality tenants publicly challenged the designation of the site (Greenhill, 2013b). However, the special legislation outlined in the CER Act allowed the Minister to use the Crown authority to override the rights of landowners and thus overcome the limited powers that the CCC had in accordance with the *Local Government Act 2002*. Without such special powers, the identification and the negotiations for the purchase of land for the CCRP CBD Stadium would have not been possible. As *Sam* stressed, 'generally, in order to build one of these mega structures, you need to control the land for these large buildings. And the CERA legislation allowed that to unlock.'

The *CER Act 2011* came along with a series of Orders in Council that suspended the ordinary legislation for Greater Christchurch Area and the Christchurch CBD. In particular, landowner contestation over land purchase could only be brought to the High Court. This proved to be quite controversial as the proposals done by CERA and the Crown were often well below the evaluations done by the landowners. While there was still scope for legal actions against CERA (Stylianou, 2013), most of the property owners accepted the offer of the Crown.

The site location for the CBD Stadium, the decisions taken and the rules set out by the leading recovery authorities to acquire the land for the project are in sharp contrast with the will of the local community of Christchurch. Over the phases that culminated with the release of the CSA, the role of the community was limited to the token of participation during the *Share an Idea* initiative run by the CCC. The decision of appointing the CCDU and the blueprint team with the delivery of the CCRP further gave the community a marginal role. The time between the Cabinet meeting vesting CERA with the authority to deliver the Central City Plan (2 April 2012) (DPMC, 2011a), the official establishment of the CCDU (18 April 2012) (Brownlee, 2012), and the submission of the proposal by the team led by Boffa Miskell (20 April 2012) gave no room for public consultation. Moreover, the government used the *Share an Idea* report to identify the anchor projects to develop in Christchurch and included the CBD Stadium project because the provision of a stadium was among the findings that emerged during the consultation stage with CCC planners as discussed by *Martha*. In contrast, the CCDU (2013b) stated: 'the community was extensively involved in the development of the draft Central City Plan – the CCC's draft. [...] and there was further opportunity for public comment in late 2011 and early 2012 after the draft Plan was delivered to the Minister. CCDU was tasked with finalising the Recovery Plan.'

However, the community considered the CBD Stadium to be the least important anchor project to be carried out (Gates, 2013). According to CCC Councillor Yani Johanson, a big project like the CBD Stadium did not respect the feedback of the community on major community projects and it had to be put on hold while more compelling recovery issues (e.g. housing) were sorted (McCrone, 2013b). Moreover, the input from the community was for an uncovered stadium (CCC, 2012b). Nevertheless, the Minister for the Canterbury Earthquake Recovery and the National Government still believed that the CBD Stadium should be covered in order to provide Christchurch with a 'world-class' venue (Stylianou & Sachdeva, 2012). A venue to be delivered with long-established firms and sports stadia planners like Populous, which was involved in the Forsyth Barr Stadium in Dunedin, and the temporary AMI Stadium in Christchurch.

Planning practice

The planning of the CBD Stadium resembles the mainstream practices of sport-focused regeneration projects around the world. The project is considered a major community project for the new city of Christchurch (CCC, 2012a, 2013) to be carried by the public sector (DPMC, 2011a). Moreover, the scale of the venue, at least 35,000 seats, follows an established rationale among policy actors according to which Christchurch should be home to a stadium second only to Auckland's Eden Park. Similarly, the project of a covered CBD Stadium with a rectangular pitch is meant to provide a multi-purpose venue as well as an improved spectator experience. The size and type of project, finally, was developed based on a portfolio of stadiums around the world as part of the drafting of the business case for the CBD Stadium.

The Cabinet considers the CBD Stadium a project that should be carried out by the public sector (CCDU, 2012b), with an initial investment 'of circa $200m–$300m plus land and excluding any associated hotel and/or retail offerings' (DPMC, 2011a, p. 37). The argument behind this approach is that private investors are unlikely to lead such big-scale projects on their own initiative. Therefore, the public sector should consider a proactive role in designating the land and deciding the type of stadium in order to gain the interest of the private sector (DPMC, 2011b). Most importantly, the government expects the private sector to lead the redevelopment around the stadium (DPMC, 2011a), with leisure and hospitality developments being the most likely scenario. *Sam* highlighted, 'the CERA mandate really has always been a national government kind of tingled private sector investment model.'

The scale of the proposed CBD Stadium has been a major dispute among stakeholders. Those in favour of a 35,000 seat venue claim that a city with an established rugby tradition like Christchurch should be home to New Zealand's second largest stadium and would secure Christchurch the hosting of rugby test matches, mentioned by *Sam*, *Richard* and *Colin*. Nevertheless, there are stakeholders suggesting a smaller venue on the range of 20,000 to 24,000 spectators (*Roy*) as current TV rights often make big-sized stadia empty shells (*Adam*) that only get sold out for hallmark events like the *All Blacks* test matches. Again, the position of the Minister for the Canterbury Earthquake Recovery for a 35,000 seat stadium in the CBD prevails:

> The Minister has a view. He loved giving the example of the Auckland Harbour Bridge. When they originally built it had four lanes. And in a relatively short period of time it was over... it was over used, it was congested and they had to put another two lanes on it. He said "We are not going to do that! We are going to build things properly from the start!" But I don't think... I mean, the... it is a very large and expensive structure.
>
> *(Gabriel)*

Similarly, the decision for a covered stadium with a rectangular pitch is the expression of a political will, with the government and the CRFU strongly advocating for a covered stadium (Stylianou and Sachdeva, 2012; Greenhill, 2013c). Stakeholders acknowledge that a roofed stadium would skyrocket the costs of the venue (*Thomas*), a scenario which would see the national government funding half of the upgrade (Cairns, 2014). There are, however, several push and pull factors around the CBD Stadium, as draft business cases suggest that returns on the investment would be very marginal (informal conversation with *Gabriel*). The ultimate decision on the type of project will only be possible following the release of the business case.

Descriptions of the CBD Stadium project, moreover, tend to emphasise the experiential dimension of sport events as a major narrative to convey the positive outcomes of the new venue, which is expected to, according to *Richard*, 'deliver an experience where people can come along [...] and feel like they're actually a part of the event.' This point was also heralded by CRFU CEO Hamish Riach, who argued that a rectangular stadium allowed spectators 'to be closer to the game action' (McCrone, 2013a).

Finally, decisions on the CBD Stadium final project are based on a portfolio of case studies retrieved from a wide range of sports stadiums around the world. CERA officials explored options for the CBD Stadium with visits to Madrid, London, Dublin, Stockholm, Bordeaux, Nice and Singapore. A more narrowed cost per seat analysis is underway, with findings from a group of 19 stadium including Etihad Stadium in Melbourne, the City of Manchester Stadium, Forsyth Barr Stadium in Dunedin and the new Perth stadium. The findings were gathered in the Stadium Precinct Scoping Study between 2014 and 2015. This study will inform the business case planned for release by the end of June 2016. A final aspect to consider about the CBD Stadium is the idea of making it a multi-purpose centre. *Sam*:

> So, the objects of this building, I would say or guess, would be to reinvigorate tourism in the city; have events; hold major events; multipurpose events and not just rugby. And I think that's a misperception, probably, in the public when they say it is just a rugby stadium.

Undoubtedly, the CBD Stadium is a project long considered by major stakeholders as necessary for the new city of Christchurch. According to the CRFU CEO, Hamish Riach, building the new stadium will provide Christchurch with a strong legacy that 'is going to feel over the next 40 to 50 years' (McCrone, 2013a). Nevertheless there are stakeholders that question the amount of money spent and the narrow return of the investment to the community. As one participant wondered:

> How is it actually ever going able to explain to any what we got for an extra 450 million dollars? How much utility you get for another 450 million? [...]
> If you do a comparison between the Performing Arts Precinct and the Stadium, you know [...] for tenth of the price you get the same number of people.
> *(Gabriel)*

Conclusions

This chapter has examined the role of stadium development in the post-earthquake context of Christchurch in New Zealand. The chapter has emphasised that the policy and planning dimensions of the use of sport for post-disaster regeneration are characterised by the suspension of 'normal' planning processes (Baade & Matheson, 2007). This allows, if not encourages, the promotion of boosterism with respect to the role of sport in urban regeneration whereby events are utilised to not only achieve planning decisions that may previously not have been tenable but which are also used to frame new notions of 'normality' in city promotion and planning (Hall, 2004, 2006). Significantly, the developments that arise at such times may contribute to a particular economic trajectory as a result of institutional and land use 'lock-in.' In the case of the Christchurch Stadium case study discussed here, the critical dimension in determining the direction of large-scale sports regeneration were the powers available to the relevant minister responsible for earthquake recovery and the extent of their powers. These were coupled with a particular vision of how a stadium should function that were informed by specific international and domestic stadium experiences. This vision received substantial support from the major sporting beneficiary – the CRFU.

Significantly, the suspension of normal democratic planning processes by the national government froze out the local council from much of the decision-making, while still placing much of the costs for developments onto them. This also meant that much of the public opinion regarding the nature and costs of the proposed covered stadium have also been ignored as have the preferred regeneration priorities. Although implementation of the CBD Stadium project has been delayed, it has not been derailed. Despite the seeming lack of international visitors and delays in producing a business case for the stadia, it is going to be extremely difficult for the considerable political capital of the national government in their vision for Christchurch and the stadium to be overturned.

While research on sports and events in post-disaster regeneration is relatively limited, the issues raised are not exceptional. According to Gotham and Greenberg (2014), the neoliberal dynamics put in place in the recovery of cities affected by natural disasters are the seeds out of which vulnerabilities grow and eventually emerge in future crisis and disasters. This rationale can also be found in mainstream urban regeneration studies, particularly with event-led regeneration practices (Coaffee, 2013) in which the suspension of normal planning practices so as to achieve deadlines are almost the norm (Hall, 2006). As a result of an 'emergency' planning culture, demand overestimations and costs underestimations often lead to disastrous large-scale projects for mega-events that balloon implementation costs at the expense of taxpayers, while many private and political actors gain. Although such situations have been long criticised, policy change has not generally followed.

If all factors remain equal, it is likely that the CBD Stadium will be built. Events have sometimes been described as a form of 'bread and circus' that may distract people and divert funds away from more pressing issues (Hall, 1992). Similarly, in a post-disaster content the redevelopment of professional sports infrastructure and the hosting of mega-events may actually undermine longer term recovery through deflecting capital spending from where it is needed most and crowding out those workers and residents who are involved in the rebuilding process (Baade & Matheson, 2007; Gotham & Greenberg, 2014). Sports may act as a form of symbolism that a city and its people are vital and rebuilding, but to what extent should the hedonic and political values and the economic interests of a small group of stakeholders, but especially professional sports franchises, frame the notion of the greater good?

References

Amore, A. & Hall, C.M. (2016). 'Regeneration is the focus now': Anchor projects and delivering a new CBD for Christchurch. In C.M. Hall, S. Malinen, R. Vosslamber & R. Wordsworth (Eds.) *Business and post disaster management: Business, organisational and consumer resilience and the Christchurch Earthquakes*. London, England: Routledge (pp. 181–199).

Anonymous. (2013). Council orders independent review of insurance gaff. *Radio New Zealand*, 25 September, http://www.radionz.co.nz/news/regional/222773/council-orders-independent-review-of-insurance-gaff.

Anonymous. (2015a). Chinese company to inject billions into Chch. *Radio New Zealand*, 23 September, http://www.radionz.co.nz/news/regional/285047/chinese-company-to-inject-billions-into-chch.

Anonymous. (2015b). Civic Assurance enters mediation over Canterbury stadium. *Insurance news*, 14 September, http://www.insurancenews.com.au/local/civic-assurance-enters-mediation-over-canterbury-stadium.

Anonymous. (2015c). Insurers suggest earthquake-damaged Christchurch Stadium can be fixed for less than $50 million. *Australian leisure management*, 19 April.

Baade, R.A. & Matheson, V.A. (2007). Professional sports, Hurricane Katrina and the economic development of New Orleans. *Contemporary economic policy, 25*, 591–603.

Brownlee, G. (2012). *Launch of the Central Christchurch Development Unit*. Wellington, New Zealand: New Zealand Government.

Cairns, L. (2014). Stadium deal critical – Mayor. *The press*, 1 February, A.3.

Cairns, L. (2015a). Bizarre move on Council Budget. *The press*, 20 April, A.1.

Cairns, L. (2015b). Record $635 million insurance payout for Christchurch City Council. *The Press*, 18 December, http://www.stuff.co.nz/the-press/news/75073343/record-635-million-insurance-payout-for-christchurch-city-council.

Cairns, L. & Law, T. (2015). Bid to stop asset sales fails. *The press*, 25 June, A.3.

Christchurch City Council (CCC). (2007). *Jade stadium redevelopment; council support*. Christchurch, New Zealand: CCC.

CCC. (2008). *CCHL Acquisition of additional shares in Lyttelton Port Company Ltd and AMI Stadium Ltd - Name protection company*. Christchurch, New Zealand: CCC.

CCC. (2011a). *Central city plan. Draft central city recovery plan for ministerial approval - December 2011*. Christchurch, New Zealand: CCC.

CCC. (2011b). *Draft central city plan - August 2011, Volume 1*. Christchurch, New Zealand: CCC.

CCC. (2012a). *Annual plan 2012–13 Christchurch Ōtautahi*. Christchurch, New Zealand: CCC.

CCC. (2012b). *Draft annual plan 2012–13 Christchurch Ōtautahi*. Christchurch, New Zealand: CCC.

CCC. (2013). *Christchurch city three year plan 2013–16 (revised) – Christchurch Ōtautahi. Volume 1 of 2*. Christchurch, New Zealand: CCC.

Christchurch Central Development Unit (CCDU). (2012a). *The blueprint plan*. Christchurch, New Zealand: CCDU.

CCDU. (2012b). *Christchurch central recovery plan. Te Mahere 'Maraka Ōtautahi*. Christchurch, New Zealand: CCDU.

CCDU. (2013a). *Anchor projects overview as at 31–10–2013*. Christchurch, New Zealand: CCDU.

CCDU. (2013b). General. Retrieved from https://ccdu.govt.nz/faq/general.

CCDU. (2013c). Land acquisition. Retrieved from https://ccdu.govt.nz/faq/land-acquisition.

CCDU. (2013d). The projects – Metro Sports Facility. Retrieved from http://ccdu.govt.nz/projects-and-precincts/performing-arts-precinct.

CCDU. (2013e). The projects – Stadium. Retrieved from http://ccdu.govt.nz/projects-and-precincts/stadium.

CCDU. (2014a). *Anchor projects overview. November 2014*. Christchurch, New Zealand: CCDU.

CCDU. (2014b). *Convention Centre Precinct announcement*. Christchurch, New Zealand: CCDU.

CCDU. (2015). *Metro Sports funding parameters agreed*. Christchurch, New Zealand: CCDU.

Christchurch & Canterbury Tourism (CCT). (2013). *Christchurch sports tourism events plan*. Christchurch, New Zealand: CCT.

CCT. (2015). *Eden Project. A proposed destination tourism project for the recovery of Christchurch and the benefit of New Zealand*. Christchurch, New Zealand: CCT.

Canterbury Development Corporation (CDC). (2014). *Christchurch Mayor emphasises Canterburys economic strength to potential investors*. Christchurch, New Zealand: CDC.

Canterbury Earthquake Recovery Authority (CERA). (2011). *Canterbury earthquake recovery authority–Proposed governance and roles - Annex 1*. Christchurch, New Zealand: CERA.

CERA. (2013a). *Cost sharing agreement*. Christchurch, New Zealand: CERA.

CERA. (2013b). *Notice of intention to take land for the stadium*. Christchurch, New Zealand: CERA.

Coaffee, J. (2013). Policy transfer, regeneration legacy and the summer Olympic Games: lessons for London 2012 and beyond. *International journal of sport policy and politics, 5*, 295–311.

Department of Prime Minister and Cabinet (DPMC). (2011a). *Cabinet minute (12) 11/20 minute of decision on Christchurch CBD recovery*. Wellington, New Zealand: DPMC.

DPMC. (2011b). *Cabinet minute EGI (12) 11/11 minute of decision on redevelopment of Christchurch central: Work programme and outputs to 100 days*. Wellington, New Zealand: DPMC.

DPMC. (2014). *Greater Christchurch earthquake recovery: Moving forward with pace and confidence*. Wellington, New Zealand: DPMC.

Ernst & Young. (2012). *Christchurch central city commercial property market study*. Christchurch, New Zealand: Ernst & Young.

Gates, C. (2013). Stadium plan least favoured. *The press,* 10 July, A.1.

Gotham, K.F. & Greenberg, M. (2014). *Crisis cities: Disaster and redevelopment in New York and New Orleans*. Oxford, England: Oxford University Press.

Greenhill, M. (2011). Fate of ground not yet decided; AMI Stadium. *The press,* 1 August, A.3.

Greenhill, M. (2012a). City still needs 'quality stadium.' *The press,* 23 July, A.5.

Greenhill, M. (2012b). Flexibility needed in stadium plans, says recovery boss. *Waikato times,* 24 October, 5.

Greenhill, M. (2013a). Notable omissions in stadium land grab. *The press,* 20 March, http://www.stuff.co.nz/the-press/business/the-rebuild/8446697/Notable-omissions-in-stadium-land-grab.

Greenhill, M. (2013b). Protester hijacks rugby stunt. *The press,* 20 July, A.3.

Greenhill, M. (2013c). Roofed stadium to cost $506m. *The press,* 29 June.

Hall, C.M. (1992). *Hallmark tourist events*. London, England: Belhaven.

Hall, C.M. (2001). Imaging, tourism and sports event fever: The Sydney Olympics and the need for a social charter for mega-events. In C. Gratton & I. Henry (Eds.). *Sport in the city: The role of sport in economic and social regeneration*. London, England: Routledge (pp. 166–183).

Hall, C.M. (2004). Sports tourism and urban regeneration. In B. Ritchie & D. Adair (Eds.). *Sports tourism: Interrelationships, impacts and issues*, Clevedon, England: Channelview (pp. 192–206).

Hall, C.M. (2006). Urban entrepreneurship, corporate interests and sports mega-events: the thin policies of competitiveness within the hard outcomes of neoliberalism. *The sociological review, 54*(2), 59–70.

Hall, C.M. & Wilson, S. (2016). Mega-events as neoliberal projects: 'Realistic if we want Dunedin to prosper,' or 'the biggest civic disgrace… in living memory'? In J. Mosedale (Ed.). *Neoliberalism and tourism*. Abingdon, England: Routledge (pp. 37–55).

Johnson, C. (2011). *The neoliberal deluge: Hurricane Katrina, late capitalism, and the remaking of New Orleans*. Minneapolis, MN: University of Minnesota Press.

Johnson, L.A. & Olshansky, R.B. (2010). *Clear as mud: Planning for the rebuilding of New Orleans*. Chicago, IL: American Planning Association.

King, C. (2012). Councillor says learn from Dunedin. *The press,* 28 July, A.4.

Klein, N. (2007). *The shock doctrine: The rise of disaster capitalism*. New York, NY: Metropolitan Books.

Knowler, R. (2011). AMI matches in doubt. *The press,* 24 February, A.23.

Law, T. (2016). Christchurch residents want new stadium. *The press,* 17 February, http://www.stuff.co.nz/the-press/news/76987200/Christchurch-residents-want-new-stadium-survey.

Marks, V. (2015). Hagley Oval's serene success story an adornment to Christchurch and cricket. *The guardian*, 14 February. https://www.theguardian.com/sport/blog/2015/feb/14/christchurch-hagley-oval-cricket-world-cup-new-zealand-earthquake-2011.

McCrone, J. (2013a). The $100 million dollar question. *The press*, 18 May. http://www.stuff.co.nz/the-press/business/the-rebuild/8689845/The-100-million-question.

McCrone, J. (2013b). A 'sneeze away' from trouble. *The press*, 7 July, http://www.stuff.co.nz/the-press/news/christchurch-earthquake-2011/8888696/A-sneeze-away-from-trouble.

McCrone, J. (2014). Great plan, but where are the investors? In B. Bennett, J. Dann, E. Johnson & R. Reynolds (Eds.). *Once in a lifetime. City-building after disaster in Christchurch.* Christchurch, New Zealand: Freerange Press (pp. 101–108).

Murphy, S. (2016). 'No business case' for Christchurch stadium. *Radio New Zealand*, 19 March, http://www.radionz.co.nz/news/regional/299353/'no-business-case'-for-christchurch-stadium.

New Zealand Government. (2012). New unit for the rebuild of central Christchurch. Wellington, New Zealand: New Zealand Government.

New Zealand Parliament. (2013). *Briefing of Christchurch cost-sharing agreement.* Wellington, New Zealand: New Zealand Parliament.

New Zeland Treasury. (2014). *Managing government investment projects 2014/2015.* Wellington, New Zealand: New Zealand Treasury.

Norris, D.F. (2002). If we build it, they will come! Tourism-based economic development in Baltimore. In D.R. Judd (Ed.). *The infrastructure of play: Building the tourist city.* Armonk, NY: M.E. Sharpe (pp. 125–167).

New Zealand Institute of Architects (NZIA). (2011). *NZIA Submission to the Draft Central City Plan.* Christchurch, New Zealand: NZIA.

Passavant, P.A. (2011). Mega-events, the Superdome, and the return of the repressed in New Orleans. In C. Johnson (Ed.). *The neoliberal Deluge: Hurricane Katrina, late capitalism, and the remaking of New Orleans.* Minneapolis, MN: Minnesota University Press (pp. 87–129).

Sage, E. (2014). Time to review earthquake rebuild costsharing agreement. https://home.greens.org.nz/press-releases/time-review-earthquake-rebuild-cost-sharing-agreement.

Saxena, G. (2013). Cross-sector regeneration partnership strategies and tourism. *Tourism planning & development, 11*, 86–105.

Small, V. (2011). Rugby just a game to quake victims. *Dominion post*, 17 March, B.5.

Smellie, P. (2015). China's Guoxin International commits to Christchurch rebuild. *National business review*, 23 September, www.nbr.co.nz/article/chinas-guoxin-international-commits-us2-bln-christchurch-rebuild-b-179102.

Stylianou, G. (2013). Lawyer says buyout offers 'unfair'. *The press*, 23 July.

Stylianou, G. & Sachdeva, S. (2012). Key backs 'world-class' covered arena for Chch. *The press*, 14 May, 5.

Thorney, A. (2002). Urban regeneration and sports stadia. *European planning studies, 10*, 813–818.

Tutty, K. (2011). QEII and Centennial Pool worst hit of sports facilities. *The press*, 25 February, A.22.

Wood, A. (2011). 'Don't forget our city' for conferences; conference and incentives sector. *The press*, 30 May, A.7.

Woods Bagot. (2014). Christchurch blueprint 100. http://www.woodsbagot.com/project/christchurch-blueprint-100-christchurch-new-zealand.

8 Urban coalitions and the production of Atlanta's downtown

*Costas Spirou, Candace Miller
and Brandi Baker*

Introduction

The quest to advance Atlanta's global city ambitions during the 1970s and 1980s necessitated that civic and business leaders embrace a series of growth strategies. One of the extraordinary outcomes of this strategy was the city's hosting of the 1996 Summer Olympic Games. These results were made possible due to carefully cultivated relationships between politicians, civic organisations and the business community. This chapter focuses on the continued efforts to reorganise Atlanta's downtown as an integral part of an ambitious urban restructuring puzzle. Our examination concerns the ongoing role of three organisations: Atlanta Convention and Visitors Bureau (ACVB), Central Atlanta Progress (CAP) and Atlanta Downtown Improvement District (ADID). Part of broader urban coalitions, these entities have played a considerable role in reshaping the urban core and have contributed to the city's quest for a 'New Atlanta.'

CAP is a private, non-profit organisation with a long history as a leader in the revitalisation of central Atlanta since 1941. CAP is an alliance of more than 200 businesses and non-profit entities and promotes a vision to reshape the city's core. Over the years, numerous central area studies commissioned by CAP addressed housing issues, transportation and safety. These agenda items have shaped the regeneration of Atlanta's downtown and pushed for the creation and continuation of sport, tourism and cultural events/activities. ACVB was established in 1913. While its goal is to support the city's hospitality and events industry, it also aims to strengthen the city's image to attract and retain conventions and meeting activities. From 2007 to 2009, the ACVB joined *Brand Atlanta*, a public-private partnership to market the city. With the fourth largest convention centre in the United States, the ACVB has focused on furthering the marketing of downtown. Beyond existing sites, the ACVB supported more than $285 million in additional attractions including the Center of Human and Civil Rights and the College Football Hall of Fame. Finally, the ADID was formed in 1995, focusing on a 120-block area. Led by a public-private board, the area now covers 200 blocks. The organisation is primarily concerned with promoting a cleaner, safer and more hospitable environment for the downtown population. One of its larger programmes, the Ambassador Force, is administered by the ADID. Its goal is to help enforce the Anti-Panhandling Ordinance. In 2009, the Ambassador Force performed roughly 2000 interventions in downtown.

These three entities are part of a broader urban coalition that aims to reshape Atlanta's downtown. Gentrification and displacement are potential outcomes of the reimaging and renewed function of the centre as a place of entertainment, events, sport and tourism which in turn can have negative distributional consequences for the city's disadvantaged residents. This latter part is not a focus of this work but it is worth noting given similar patterns elsewhere. The purpose of this chapter is to discuss the role of CAP, ACVB and ADID in reorganising and regenerating downtown Atlanta. In this regard, formed together, these three forces formulate a set of urban coalitions that impact the physical and social landscape of this reconstituted space. We address each of these and conclude with an overview of their impact.

Globalisation, urban competition and urban regimes

Globalisation is the outcome of a worldwide integration between industries, goods and workers. The era of global integration emerged following WWII and came to impact various aspects of the human interaction. Transnational companies increased their dominance during the 1950s and 1960s as plants for machinery, chemicals and transportation equipment based in the United States began locating abroad. By the 1970s, 70% of the imports to the United States were between transnational corporations. Technological development and deregulations of markets were responsible for the growth in transnational corporations. Together these two changes made it easier to utilise labour between the United States and countries abroad (Knox 1997; Pierre, 2015; Pieterse, 2015).

The process of globalisation has had a significant impact on the economy. Former Secretary of Labour Robert Reich argued that globalisation has eradicated the idea of national industries, with all products being globally integrated there will no longer be any nation-based corporations. Reich argued that this new direction has and will continue to transform our society, in the process rearranging the politics and economics. Harvey (1989) also notes that due to the emergence of globalisation, regions are more accessible to one another, making it that much easier for integration between industries around the globe. For Harvey, 'time-space compression' results in significant labour challenges, especially when considering that spatial limitations are overtaken by economic concerns. These developments proved to also impact urban development. The evolution of international integration influences some cities into being 'global' by incorporating new forms of capital and goods circulation. While incorporating new products into their markets, cities also endeavour to grow by attracting new revenue into their economy. This logic of economic growth supports the revitalisation of urban centres that have experienced social and economic dislocation. Urban growth then becomes beneficial since it fosters revenues, an expanded tax base and additional services. This can include not only businesses, but also an influx of tourists and new residents.

Accelerated globalisation has significantly enhanced the ability to produce and market goods, ultimately increasing the competitiveness of many cities. Along with an increase in competition came an increase in a region's desire to monopolise certain industries. This has created an opportunity for regions across the globe to provide their local industries with goods and services that they were previously incapable of accessing. This makes a region's ability to monopolise a particular industry much more difficult simply because this advantage is available to all regions that engage in globalisation activities. With many cities around the world taking advantage of the ability to market new goods and products, cities can engage in competitive practices. Urban competition though injects an intense environment since being on the top is highly valued. A city's performance as far as efficiency in technological advances, innovations, health care ideas and the education a region offers to its residents all plays a major role in that city's economic success and its competitive advantage. Urban competition is a result of globalisation that sequentially results in what major cities around the world will be known as 'global cities' and which nations around the world will be top notch in the process of global integration.

Within this broader conceptual framework, regime theory, as an analytic approach focusing on regimes, has been employed to explain the relationships that may exist between public and private entities across American cities. Collaborative efforts through which local governments and private actors assemble the capacity to govern prove critical. Analysing how interests are integrated within administrative coalitions helps provide insights in urban governance practices. Power is also important since it is disintegrated. Regimes emerge as the intermediary between which local governments and private actors govern. Both parties are needed to create solid governance; the local government makes policies, while the private actors create jobs and revenue.

Stone's (1989) work in the field of political science is instructive here, noting that a regime is a group connected to institutional resources that facilitate its ability in making governing decisions. These resources may include human, technical, and financial resources as well as facilities used to achieve a mission. Regimes have created a link between government control and economic resources, controlled by private sectors. Collaboration is not automatic and has to be achieved. It varies from place to place and may not be present in all environments. Once a regime is in place it is secure and can withstand many different organisations of management. Agendas related to the association between parties can be recognised. General agreement is created on the ground between communication and arrangement of resources. Beliefs and values vary but general agreements have been made with collaboration efforts to come to a consensus (Mossberger, 2001).

Atlanta's quest for a new status

Atlanta's quest for a new status began in the 1960s when William Hartsfield, a former Atlanta Mayor, persuaded the Georgia General Assembly to pass legislation for the creation of a large airport on the south side of Atlanta. Six months after his death in 1971 the airport was renamed Berry Hartsfield International Airport. It was seen as the first major step in what would become Atlanta's 'international city' campaign of the 1970s. In 1971 when the first international flight departed from Atlanta, Mayor Sam Massel declared:

> [The airport] marks the realization of a goal, which a number of people have worked very hard for over a period of many years. Atlantans have long taken pride in the development of the city's image as one of [...] international prominence.
>
> (in Bessonette, 1971, p. 31)

By the late 1970s, coverage in the media included headlines such as 'International City – It's Becoming a Reality' (Valdes, 1979). Atlanta's international status was rapidly growing. In 1979, 38.3 million passengers travelled through Hartsfield, making it the second busiest airport in the world. The 1970s proved one of significant expansion as the passenger numbers more than doubled from the previous decade making Hartsfield Airport the largest transfer hub in the world. This success was quickly tied to the economic opportunities and as one observer noted, 'This ease of access by air to and from Atlanta is of great importance to the city's drive to attract international, national and regional headquarters of companies' (Cruishank, 1981, p. 8). Atlanta's accessibility also helped expand the city's role as one of the major business events and convention centres in the country. In 1979, approximately 810 conventions were held in Atlanta and the city's international growth was attributed to its centralised airport.

In 1990, Atlanta won the bidding contest to host the 1996 Summer Olympic Games. The city considered pursuing this mega-event during the early part of the 1970s but it would be during the 1980s that the initiative received extensive civic and business support. Controversy surrounded the final decision when Atlanta was chosen over the other bidding cities of Athens, Belgrade, Manchester, Melbourne and Toronto. Some viewed Coca-Cola, headquartered in Atlanta with a long history of involvement in the Olympic Games, to have exerted influence over the selection process (Payne, 2006). Nonetheless with the achievement came the eventual cost of a large price tag of $1.8 billion of staging the Games. Investing money into the event was an initiative that Atlanta hoped would leave positive long-term effects for the city. Mayor Jackson claimed, 'People will be coming here for 20, 30, 40, years from now because of the Olympics' (Chappel, 1996, p. 72). Initial benefits included the construction of new infrastructure and increased employment with the creation of jobs and international media attention. In addition to new sporting venues, hotels and recreational attractions were introduced. The media attention brought foreign visitors to the city, before, during and after the Games. A sense of excitement was evident as Atlanta was solidifying itself to becoming the centre of the southeastern part of the United States.

The economic effect of the Olympic Games was brought to light by Mayor Campbell when he stated, 'the financial impact of the Olympics for Blacks and the city will continue long after the flame has been extinguished and the last athlete has returned home [...] It will undoubtedly propel Atlanta to a new level [...] It's going to put us in orbit' (Chappel, 1996, p. 70). In an analysis using state-level unemployment insurance data, changes in employment were measured between areas that were exposed to the Olympic venues and those that were not. Overall employment in venue and near-venue areas increased about 17% more during and after the 1996 Summer Games than in non-venue areas. The event created a positive employment impact on the locations directly associated with and surrounding the area. For example, preparation for the Games included the creation of the Centennial Olympic Park located downtown. The park was not included in the original plan, but $75 million of private funds helped create a centrepiece space that now attracts millions to the area every year. This subsequently encouraged additional development including the opening of the Georgia Aquarium in 2005, the World of Coca-Cola Museum in 2007 and most recently the National Center for Civil and Human Rights in 2014.

The airport was the most significant driver for the 'New Atlanta.' The former international terminal constructed for the 1996 Summer Olympic Games increasingly proved insufficient for the rapidly growing international flights. This led to the construction of a new terminal under the leadership of Holder, Manhattan, Moody and Hunt (HMMH), a contractor joint venture between Holder Construction Group, Manhattan Construction Co., Moody Construction Co., and Hunt Construction Group Inc. In 2012 the Hartsfield-Jackson Atlanta International airport opened the Maynard H. Jackson Jr. International Terminal. The new terminal was viewed and marketed as a gateway to the world. The number of passengers also increased since the opening of the terminal in 2012. The impact was immediate. From December 2011 to December 2012 an increase from 7,210,376 passengers to 7,453,472 passengers was observed (Monthly Airport Traffic Report, 2012). An even greater increase took place between 2013 and 2014, from 7,527,571 in 2013 to 8,280,610 in 2014 (Monthly Airport Traffic Report, 2014).

For years Atlanta has been working towards its quest for a new status as a global city. This started in the 1960s with Mayor Hartsfield's vision for Atlanta's airport, moving into Atlanta's successful staging of the 1996 Summer Olympic Games and continuing with the grand opening of the Maynard Jackson International Terminal. Hartsfield's vision turned the airfield into the busiest airport in the world. The residual Summer Olympic Games infrastructure and associated media coverage helped positively expose Atlanta internationally. From its portrayal as an international city to the proclamation as a top convention destination, Atlanta has managed to not only expand its image as a charming southern city, but also as a centre of events, travel and business.

The Atlanta convention and visitors bureau

ACVB was established in 1913 when 'business leaders turned to the lawyers at Smith and Hammond & Smith to draw up a charter for a new organization' (SGR, 2013). Over the years, the city's status of being a transportation hub has greatly expanded and the infrastructure that followed to support growth presented some very interesting opportunities. The city's leadership saw this growth as a way to leverage their assets, which included the advancement of the tourist industry. As a private, non-profit organisation, the Bureau has been promoting Atlanta globally since its inception. The ACVB has been focusing on advancing Atlanta's economy through conventions and tourism. The ACVB has identified five business goals which include: (1) expanding the room night bookings, (2) achieving 100% attendance goal for major citywide events and conventions, (3) increasing visibility of Atlanta as one of the top United States meeting and travelling destinations, (4) maintaining *Atlanta.net* as the premier hospitality online marketing platform and (5) positioning ACVB as an industry expert nationally and as the singular voice of hospitality in Atlanta (Atlanta Marketing Plan, 2014).

By engaging with meeting planners and tour operators, ACVB has emerged as a power force in shaping the future of the city. Successive municipal leaders have relied on this organisation which has worked with its more than 1200 plus member groups to meet its goals. Aggressive sales and marketing programmes have aided meeting the goal of producing Atlanta as a leading destination for conventions and tourism. Currently, ACVB's efforts support Atlanta's $12 billion hospitality industry, sustaining 230,000 jobs for metro Atlanta and generating 42 million visitors each year (ACVB, 2015). A number of infrastructural projects have been necessary to help meet the two-prong vision of the ACVB which has been to emerge as the most hospitable event and convention city in the United States and one with which it is very easy to conduct business. A key part of that goal has been the role of Atlanta's Hartsfield-Jackson International Airport as a leading national and international hub. Over 80% of the United States population resides within a two-hour flight to Atlanta, and the airport has a global reach. This accessibility gives Atlanta an advantage over other convention cities in the United States which has consequently aided the city's event and entertainment strategy. A hotel boom and the introduction of a wide variety of attractions and related facilities also proved central to this goal. The creation of MARTA in 1965 linked a sprawling metropolitan area to the downtown, increasingly inviting locals and visitors alike to explore new attractions.

The Bureau has also strategically employed the success of the 1996 Summer Olympic Games as a way to launch one of the most competitive tourism marketing plans, costing around $4 million. The effort was centralised around the description 'progressive,' a city slogan showing Atlanta's new transformation into a vibrant city. This approach was also used in an international campaign called 'Celebration.' In these efforts the ACVB showcased the transformational contributions of the Summer Olympic Games, and collaborated with the U.S. Travel and Tourism Administration, the Georgia Department of Industry, Trade and Tourism and numerous international airlines (Vesey, 1995).

Atlanta utilised the remaining infrastructure from the Summer Olympics Games to sell a 'New Atlanta' and the ACVB played a key role in this effort by integrating in its promotional efforts the legacies of the Centennial Olympic Park, the Olympic stadium, renovated hotels, repaired and well-lit downtown streets, the 'ambassadors' who now patrol downtown streets and the more than

6000 rooms that opened in time for the Games (Vesey, 1996). With this 'New Atlanta' initiative, officials hoped to impress international visitors from select countries such as the United Kingdom, Germany and Japan. The ACVB also focused on past visitors by reaching out to journalists around the world to revisit the 'New Atlanta.' *Brand Atlanta* played a key part in advancing this initiative. The organisation was a public–private group and was started by Mayor Shirley Franklin in 2007, but when it lost funding in 2009 it was enveloped in the ACVB. The primary goal was to create and sustain a brand identity for Atlanta, which was deemed crucial for attracting business and tourists. *Brand Atlanta's* union with the ACVB placed the city's branding industries centre stage under one roof. Currently, the Georgia World Congress Center (GWCC) partners with the ACVB. Together, they create a unique environment for meetings by combining southern hospitality, a trademark of the ACVB, with world class attractions provided by the GWCC. The GWCC authority operates the Georgia Dome, the 21-acre Centennial Olympic Park and Georgia World Congress Center. These three state-owned facilities are one of the largest combined sports, events, entertainment and convention centre facilities in the world. This unique infrastructure then becomes the cornerstone to attracting convention business to the city.

Various rankings have consistently placed Atlanta in the top five conventions cities nationally. In 2014 Atlanta ranked fourth as a national meeting destination behind Chicago, Orlando and Las Vegas by Cvet, an enterprise-event management supplier and in 2015 fifth behind Orlando, Las Vegas, Chicago and San Diego (Sealover, 2015). It should be noted that marketing funds have been limited for the ACVB and well below those enjoyed in 2006 by Las Vegas ($83 million), Orlando ($14 million) and Chicago ($7 million) (Stafford, 2010). This lack of marketing funding hinders the amount of advertisement Atlanta can do nationally and internationally compared to its competitor cities. Nonetheless, the ACVB has made numerous contributions in reshaping Atlanta (most notably the downtown area) through its promotional events/activities. In 2015 hotel occupancy was close to an all-time high at 70.1% and convention attendance in 2014 saw 882,000 come to GWCC meetings held at the downtown facilities. That was considerably higher than the 813,000 in 2013. Also, according to the ACVB, 19 meetings that were booked in 2015 were for groups that had not come to the city in more than a decade. That was 4 more groups from the 15 groups that came in 2014 (Stafford, 2015).

Multiple factors contributed to the success of the ACVB in advancing its goals. The first regards the partnership between the ACVB and the Atlanta Braves (Major League Baseball), the Georgia Aquarium, Stone Mountain Park and Six Flags over Georgia. The second factor concerns the founding of events such as the Meeting Professionals International, the International Association of Exhibitions and Events, and the Atlanta Travel Writers Central States Chapter meeting. These events brought in a great influx of money and revenue to the Atlanta area. The third contributing factor was the partnership with *Brand Atlanta* that created ATL Insider, one of the first social networking destination web sites in the country. The ACVB has furthered the growth and overall visibility of downtown

Atlanta. Its contributions include marketing strategies that have produced a considerable growth of visitors to the downtown area. By taking advantage of existing infrastructure, advocating for new projects, the ACVB has helped position conventions and visitor accommodations in the centre of a strategy to transform Atlanta as a centre of tourism, leisure and entertainment. This has also set the stage for additional investments in the downtown area aimed at strengthening the local economy and reconfiguring the physical presentation of the locale.

Central Atlanta Progress

CAP was created in 1967 through the immersion of two organisations, the Central Atlanta Improvement Association (CAIA) and The Uptown Association. These two entities were focused on the overall improvement of Atlanta with an emphasis on the downtown area. The CAIA was created in 1941. Behind the formation of CAIA were 12 businessmen whose improvement projects were based in the Five Points Area. Some of the leading figures included Alex W. Smith (first president of CAP and Atlanta civic leader), Robert F. Maddox (Atlanta's 41st mayor), Ivan Allen Jr. (Atlanta's 52nd mayor) and Alfred D. Kennedy (board member of the First National Bank of Atlanta and president of CAP from 1963 to 1965). The goal of CAP was to transform Atlanta into a safe, clean and liveable city. With these plans in mind, the revitalisation of downtown Atlanta began. Prior goals of The Uptown Association were to improve Ponce De Leon Avenue and North Avenue Corridor, but the 'central' redevelopment of Atlanta quickly grew past Five Points, north and west of Peachtree and Spring Street, north by Brookwood and the Coca-Cola Company (Martin, 1987). Now operating as a private, non-profit organisation, CAP is the result of an impressive alliance that includes over 200 local businesses and other institutions. Georgia State University, Emory University, Delta Airlines, and Georgia World Congress Center are a few of these organisations that are financially invested in the vision that CAP has created for the future of downtown Atlanta.

With the vision of reshaping Atlanta's economic future, the business community of downtown Atlanta and the city's government joined forces, a relationship that has been central to the direction of CAP. For example, business communities have helped formulate policies towards the regeneration of downtown Atlanta through CAP. This partnership makes it possible to accomplish the many goals of CAP such as the reconstruction of Underground Atlanta, the Bedford-Pine urban renewal project and the revitalisation of Fairlie-Poplar (Stone, 1986).

CAP has a strong working relationship with City Hall, and has had great success in developing alliances with elected officials – thus becoming part of a broader agenda of reconstructing downtown Atlanta. Andrew Young, Atlanta's second African American mayor, was well aware of the importance of business leaders setting community policy. From the persisting idea of business leaders being totally involved in the community power structure, the alliance between Young and CAP was inevitable. Following in the footsteps of Maynard Jackson, Atlanta's first African American mayor, Young cooperated with CAP to advance their innovative ideas (Stone, 1986). CAP has been involved in many projects based around the reconstruction of transportation, human services, marketing, education, public safety, urban design and housing. These projects have been the outcome of a series of planning documents that include The Central Area Study I (1971), The Central Area Study II (1988), Central Atlanta Transportation Study (1999), Central Area Action Plan (2000) and The Better Buildings Challenge and Atlanta Streetcar (2014). It is through these initiatives that this public/private partnership produced an extensive reorganisation of the city including, most recently, the downtown area.

The Central Area Study I of 1971 was the first project of CAP, Inc. It proposed several transportation policies to benefit the community since Atlanta was becoming the capital of the Southeast. Because of growing demands, CAP found it suitable to grant functional traffic distributions by addressing the conflicts between pedestrians and vehicles as well as enhancing the quality of the downtown environment. Beyond the focus on the transportation issue, the document also proposed a Five Points Park, a Peachtree Promenade, the Broad Street Mall, additional parks and landscaping and related streetscape improvements (Central Area Study I Summary, 1971).

Seventeen years later, CAP proposed Central Area Study II (1988). This focused on creating a clean, safe environment not only for the residents of downtown Atlanta but also for tourists. Instead of solely addressing transportation regulations, this plan branched into the improvement of various arts and entertainment centres, support for events, conventions and tourism, economic development initiatives, housing improvements, additional infrastructure and the marketing of parks, recreation and open spaces. In addition, public safety, retail and maintenance as well as urban design challenges of downtown Atlanta proved another area of interest. One of the most important aspects of this study was offering a housing vision in Atlanta. The plan also called for Atlanta to be a 24-hour city and create a more liveable space. The residents that Central Area Study II hoped to attract were both middle and upper class families. Attracting these families meant more income earning opportunities and the pursuit of diverse people into the city, ultimately making Atlanta a much more vibrant place. The vision to attract new housing in the downtown area focused on creating incentives that will urge developers to build newer houses. Incentives were also to be offered for new art and entertainment facilities. Furthermore, attention was placed on organisational restructuring to implement new recommendations on when and where houses should be built, and developing strategies to preserve low-income housing that already existed in the city (Central Area Study II, 1988).

In 1999, CAP began to work on another plan known as the Central Atlanta Action Plan. The first part of this was the Central Atlanta Transportation Study. Before completing the Central Atlanta Action Plan, the members of CAP had to assess current transportation conditions in order to better evaluate what strategies would be in the best interest of Atlanta's dwellers. The purpose of the Central Atlanta Transportation Study was to focus on a specific area, roughly Interstate-75/Interstate-85 to the east, Interstate-20 to the south, Northside Drive/

Howell Mill Road to the west and Brookwood Station to the north. The ultimate purpose was to recommend plans to ease the commuting process of the citizens in downtown Atlanta (Central Atlanta Transportation Study, 1999).

Another recent innovation that CAP pursued in the transportation area was the Atlanta Streetcar. The Atlanta Streetcar is a result of a unique collaboration between the business community and CAP. The capability of higher passenger loads, fewer emissions (which ultimately improves air quality), and the fact that it appeals to visitors can attract and support more tourists to the area. While the project launched as a 2.7 mile east-west route, the long-term goals for the streetcar include a north-south as well as another east-west route that will connect the King Center to the Centennial Olympic Park (Atlanta Streetcar, 2014). More recently, CAP has been involved in The Better Buildings Challenge, a project geared towards city conservation. The Better Building Challenge was first launched in 2011. It focused on the conservation of downtown Atlanta by challenging businesses to help save water as well as conserve energy. The goal of this programme is to reduce downtown Atlanta's water and energy consumption 20% by 2020. As of 31 July 2014, more than 70 million square feet of downtown Atlanta businesses are participating in the challenge. Recent successes in this point towards the extraordinary achievement of 9% energy savings and over 33 million gallons of water since the beginning of the programme (Atlanta Better Building Challenge Reaches Milestone Savings, 2014).

Over the years, CAP has contributed to the overall improvement of downtown Atlanta in many ways due to successful project planning. CAP focused on improving downtown's infrastructure, to allow reliable and quick access to the downtown area by promoting innovative technologies such as the Atlanta Streetcar. CAP, through the Central Atlanta Area Study of 1971 and the Central Atlanta Area Study of 1988, has also strategically planned initiatives to enhance the overall quality of the downtown environment not only for downtown residents but also for tourists.

The Atlanta downtown improvement district

In 1995, the decision was made to form a new initiative-based organisation which covered a 120-block area – ADID. Parented by CAP, ADID is a public-private partnership whose mission is to create and develop a more liveable and vibrant downtown environment in Atlanta for both residents and visitors. This early organisation included institutions from corporations, small local business, civic organisations, regional leaders and property owners. ADID is currently working on many projects, including the Atlanta Streetcar, now covering an area containing 220 blocks from North Avenue, Memorial Drive, Piedmont Avenue, the Downtown Connector, and the Norfolk Southern Rail.

The most prominent initiative is the Ambassador Force. The Ambassador Force is composed of about 65 men and women trained to assist in emergency situations and can be identified by their pith helmets and Segways. Either patrolling one of their 20 beats, or located at an Ambassador Force post, the goal of this programme is to provide residents, tourists, conventioneers, employees and business owners with a variety of information and assistance such as restaurant advice and directions (Atlanta Downtown Improvement District, 2014). After being a part of ADID for 10 years, the role of the Ambassador Force has expanded and now provides more services than just assistance in emergency situations – including car towing service. According to the *Atlanta Business Chronicle*, the Ambassador Force's most important job overall is to 'entice people to visit downtown Atlanta, an area once feared by many' (Antrobus, 2006). In addition to these responsibilities, ADID is also charged with providing a measure of security in conjunction with law enforcement through the Ambassador Force. One particular security-based initiative is the Wake Up and Stay Up Program. The goal of this programme is to reduce the negative connotations of individuals sleeping on the street. The Ambassador Force achieves this by patrolling and sweeping the area for 'Urban Campers' from the early morning to late night seven days a week. These sweeps are comprised of off-duty Ambassador Force officers and social workers whose goal is to coordinate and facilitate shelter for individuals with insecure housing.

Panhandling has become a political issue in Atlanta's tourist areas. In 2005 Mayor Shirley Franklin passed an Anti-Panhandling Ordinance that banned people from verbally asking for money in much of the improvement district. CAP gave its support to the ordinance and implemented the 'Give Meters' initiative to help curb giving to panhandlers. This initiative set up two dozen yellow meters that resemble parking meters, an effort designed to deter panhandling by offering an alternative means for giving to those who want to help the precariously housed of Atlanta. The money collected in these meters is redirected to charitable organisations that help the homeless. The enforcement of the Anti-Panhandling Ordinance by the Ambassador Force in the improvement district is another key responsibility. The goal is to supplement the role of law enforcement by intervening in situations where panhandling is taking place. In 2009, the Ambassador Force performed roughly 2000 informal interventions on panhandling in conjunction with the roughly 200 formal interventions performed by law enforcement. Those who were caught panhandling by the Ambassador force were ordered to move on, or directed to a 24–7 Gateway Homeless Services Center. Along with increased law enforcement, the issue of panhandling in the improvement district is addressed by education, directed giving and various homeless services in the district. The supposed purpose of these combined efforts with CAP and ACVB are to decrease and ultimately eliminate the illegal acquisition of money by those afflicted and facilitate a legal and more secure source of assistance.

Some of the latest initiatives from the ADID are geared or under the guise of environmental preservation. The Woodruff Park Master Plan supplies the six-acre park with upkeep, programming and secure funding for future maintenance. The location of the park in downtown Atlanta makes it an ideal spot for local special events and festivals including the Daffodil Festival, the Annual German Bierfest, along with convention activities including the DragonCon Parade and other artistic or performance exhibitions. Another ADID initiative founded on the basis of environmental preservation is the 'Get Around Downtown' plan. The plan encourages alternate modes of transportation such as city busses and subways, while also promoting more efficient means of individual and vehicular transportation like car/van pooling and bike riding. The phrase 'Commute Less and Work More' corresponds with the aspect of the initiative, which is reevaluating the traditional workweek in order to maximise productivity while reducing the need and usage of environmentally detrimental modes of transportation. This is to be achieved by implementing such programmes as 'Telework, Flex-Time, and [the] Compressed Work Week.'

The future goals of the ADID include the initiative to create a North-to-South public transportation system that operates without the use of harmful fuels through the 'Atlanta Streetcar' programme. According to the ADID, the initial funding will be put towards construction of the East-to-West streetcar system in the downtown area. Some of the many potential long-term results of this initiative will be a reduced dependence on cars, increased passenger loads, as well as increased public interest in transportation provided by the city. The Atlanta Streetcar Project falls under the umbrella of the larger 'Connect Atlanta Plan' which aims to increase urban mobility and sustainable development of the city, while also increasing its liveability.

Urban coalitions and impact on downtown Atlanta

Atlanta was recently named by the *New York Times* (2014) as one of the '52 Places to Go in 2014.' Titled 'A Revitalized City Center Welcomes New Museums and Streetcars,' the publication noted the availability of extensive opportunities for visitors to explore new attractions such as the recent unveiling of the National Center for Civil and Human Rights, which opened near the Centennial Olympic Park, and the Georgia Aquarium. The story also referenced the Atlanta Streetcar linking to the Martin Luther King Jr. National Historic Site and the adjacent College Football Hall of Fame, which documents the history of the beloved sport.

In recent years, downtown Atlanta has benefitted from significant federal subsidies which are part of the New Markets Tax Credit Initiative. These funds have been earmarked to support economically and socially distressed areas. Under federal law, cities are allowed to employ special tax credits to support subsidies for projects that can help uplift deteriorating conditions. In the case of Atlanta, the downtown has been included in the physical boundaries eligible to qualify for this type of economic assistance. Invest Atlanta, an entity which is part of the Atlanta Development Authority, has guided these investments. The organisation has identified the growth of the downtown to be a critical part of its mission which aims to strengthen Atlanta's economy by improving its global competitiveness. In late 2014, $80 million in tax credits were funnelled in this direction. About $12 million in credits aided the redevelopment of a historic building (200 Peachtree) into an entertainment venue with restaurants, corporate function event spaces, a health and wellness spa, and other venues which brings thousands annually to downtown Atlanta. Over $13 million from the

New Markets Tax Credit Initiative aided the finance of the National Center on Civil Rights and Human Rights, and $25 million was expended on the expansion of the Georgia Aquarium. The latter was specifically used for staging the impressive AT&T Dolphin Tales, a Broadway-style extravaganza. It should be noted that these types of tax distributions have received quite a bit of criticism since it has been argued that the benefits primarily proved to advance corporate interests (Mariano, 2014).

This extensive, rapidly developing infrastructure of new amenities is not only available to tourists but also proves attractive to new residents. Hundreds of housing projects were recently completed or are currently under construction and aim to expand residential options in the downtown area. In the autumn of 2015, 11 new residential projects in the downtown area (seven new and four renovations) have opened or were scheduled to open at a construction cost of $255 million. When in place, these will bring 2093 new housing units in the area. It is likely that more construction will be coming in the next few years. In October 2015, Atlanta Mayor Kasim Reed announced a deal to renovate Philips Arena, home of the Atlanta Hawks (of the National Basketball Association) at a cost of between $150 million and $250 million. During his announcement, Reed noted that the result of this investment is likely to produce a 'residential and commercial construction component around Philips Arena between $500 million and a billion' (Trubey, 2015).

Sports have also proved important to this renaissance. In addition to the Atlanta Hawks, the presence of the Atlanta Falcons National Football League franchise in downtown has been critical. The new 75,000 seat Mercedes Benz stadium is currently under construction at a cost of $1.5 billion. It is expected that the project will help fuel the rejuvenation of the struggling west site. Referencing the opening of a nearby Hard Rock Hotel, Mayor Reed noted 'in addition to serving tourists and visitors, this new hotel will serve as a powerful economic anchor, bringing new jobs and further investment to our downtown corridor and stadium neighborhoods' (City of Atlanta, 2015).

These developments have had significant implications on the population. According to the U.S. Census, between 2000 and 2010, the downtown population growth rate was 44.8%, while the adjacent areas experienced a 33.4% growth change. Additionally, the average family income in downtown Atlanta in 1990 was $20,066. By 2011, the average family income had increased by 46% making it to an average of $47,088 (U.S. Census, 2010) and 'with 118,000 daytime workers which account for 31.5% of the city's total employment, downtown has the highest concentration of jobs per square mile in the entire metro area (30,547)' (Southerland, 2012, p. 12). In addition, census data points to other demographic changes such as the substantial growth in the number of well-educated young adults who are choosing to live in urban neighbourhoods. This national trend is fuelled by increased urban amenities. Ranked 12th in this category in the nation among 51 metropolitan areas, Atlanta saw a 39% increase from 2000 to 2010. This has meant that talented young adults are playing a key role in driving the urban revitalisation (Cortright, 2014). It should also be noted that the Atlanta metropolitan area continues to grow. In 1970, according to the Atlanta Regional Commission, the metro area was home to 1.5 million residents. In 1990, the number had grown to 2.5 million and it reached 4.1 million by 2010. In 2015, the number had surpassed the 4.3 million mark (Atlanta Regional Commission, 2015).

Conclusion

Atlanta's quest for a new status meant that in order for the city to be successful, a series of key steps ought to take place to ensure that outcome. Hosting the 1996 Summer Olympic Games and the construction and aggressive expansion of the airport proved critical to establishing a foundation that would assist the city's efforts to become nationally and internationally recognised. In the last 20 years, the Atlanta metropolitan area population grew significant as it became a commercial and transportation hub of the southeast. In recent years we are able to observe a renewed focus on redeveloping and in the process reorganising the role and function of the downtown. In the midst of a sprawling and rapidly expanding metropolitan area, downtown Atlanta started to deteriorate. A strategy focusing on sport, tourism and business convention events/activities is geared toward creating an associated infrastructure. Although the downtown Atlanta area has experienced robust growth that has included population and household growth, these trends could foster some setbacks as well. With urban growth comes issues associated with gentrification, which ultimately leads to displacement, especially in the downtown area. For example, public housing demolitions have brought about a new housing stock to meet the needs of a socially and economically evolving area. Accelerated residential renovations have also played an important role in order to accommodate the influx of new residents.

The case of Atlanta reveals that the restructuring of urban space is driven by multiple factors. These include: (1) the quest for global city status via competition which aims to distinguish one locale from another, (2) urban drivers, in this case culture in the form of sport, events and tourism development, which play a key role in aiding urban distinctiveness and finally (3) realisation agents which includes the elements of an urban regime which contributes to the fulfilment of this strategy.

References

ACVB. 2015. http://www.atlanta.net/acvb/.

Antrobus, M. (2006). Ambassador Force celebrates 10th anniversary. *Atlanta business chronicle*, 27 March.

Atlanta Better Buildings Challenge Reaches Milestone Savings. (2014). *Central Atlanta progress*, http://www.atlantadowntown.com/article/atlanta-better-buildings-challenge-reaches-milestone-savings.

Atlanta Marketing Plan 2014. *Atlanta.net*, http://news.atlanta.net/about/annual-report-business-plan.

Atlanta Regional Commission. (2015). Population estimates for the Atlanta region: Another steady year of growth (http://www.slideshare.net/ARCResearch/population-estimatesaugustsnapshot2015slidedeck/1).

Atlanta Streetcar (2014). Atlanta streetcar. 9 September. http://www.atlantadowntown.com/initiatives/atlanta-streetcar.

Bessonette, C. (1971). Atlanta international. *Atlanta journal constitution*, 18 November.

Chappell, K. (1996). The 3 mayors who made it happen. *Ebony*, 1 July.

Central Area Study I (CAS/I) Summary. (1971). City of Atlanta. http://www.atlantadowntown.com/_files/docs/cas1.pdf.

Central Atlanta Progress, Atlanta Downtown Improvement District, *Central Atlanta Progress*. http://www.atlantadowntown.com/.

Central Atlanta Transportation Study (1999). 13 December. http://www.atlantadowntown.com/_files/docs/cats-report-small.pdf.

Central Area Study II (CAS II) (1988). Summary. 17 February. http://www.atlantadowntown.com/_files/docs/cas2.pdf.

City of Atlanta. (2015). City of Atlanta announces Hard Rock International to build new Hard Rock Hotel Atlanta. Press release, 2 November.

Cortright, J. (2014). City report: The young and restless and the nation's cities. *City Observatory*, http://cityobservatory.org/wp-content/uploads/2014/10/YNR-Report-Final.pdf.

Cruichshank, D. (1981). Hartsfield Atlanta international airport. *Geography*, *66*, 60–63.

DeLoach, D. (2015). Areas around Woodruff Park begin transformation. *Atlanta business chronicle*, 27 March.

Harvey, D. (1989). *The condition of postmodernity: An enquiry into the origins of cultural change*. Cambridge, England: Blackwell.

Knox, P. (1997). Globalization and urban economic change. *Annals of the American academy of political and social science*, *551*, 18–27.

Payne, M. (2006). *Olympic turnaround: How the Olympic Games stepped back from the brink of extinction to become the world's best known brand*. London, England: Praeger.

Pierre, J. (2015). Varieties of capitalism and varieties of globalization: Comparing patterns of market deregulation. *Journal of European public policy*, *22*, 908–926.

Pieterse. J. (2015). *Globalization and culture: Global mélange*, New York, NY: Rowman & Littlefield.

Sealover, E. (2015). Denver continues to rise in ranking of convention cities. *Denver business journal*, 11 August.

SGR. (2013). http://www.sgrlaw.com/clients/profiles/atlanta-convention-visitors-bureau/.

Stafford, L. (2015). Hotel occupancy nearing peak years in metro Atlanta. *Atlanta journal constitution*, 16 October.

Monthly Air Traffic Report. (2012). *Hartsfield Jackson Atlanta International Airport*. http://www.atlanta-airport.com/fifth/atl/operation_statistics.aspx.

Monthly Air Traffic Report. (2014). *Hartsfield Jackson Atlanta International Airport*. http://www.atlanta-airport.com/fifth/atl/operation_statistics.aspx. 52 Places to go in 2014. (2014). *New York times*, 5 September.

Stone, C. (1986). Partnership new south style: Central Atlanta progress. *Proceedings of the academy of political science*, *36*, 100–110.

Stone, C. (1989). *Regime politics*. Lawrence, KS: University of Kansas Press.

Southerland, R. (2012). Downtown Atlanta: The heart of the city. *Georgia Trend*, November.

Mariano, W. (2014). Atlanta steers subsidies to downtown projects. *The Atlanta journal constitution*, 27 December.

Martin, H. (1987). *Years of change and challenge, 1940–1976*. Athens, GA: University of Georgia Press.

Mossberger, K. & Stoker, G. (2001). The evolution of urban regime theory: The challenge of conceptualization. *Urban affairs review, 36*, 810–835.

Trubey, S. (2015). Downtown Atlanta about to see $500 million-plus round of development? *Atlanta journal constitution.* 26 October.

Vesey, S. (1996). Post-Olympic city courting foreign market visitors bureau hopes legacies of games will sell 'New Atlanta'. *The Atlanta journal constitution,* 20 November.

Vesey, S. (1995). ACVB gears up to promote fun and games. *The Atlanta journal constitution,* 8 January.

U.S. Census (2010). Atlanta. http://www.atlantadowntown.com/_files/docs/downtown_counts_people-v2.pdf.

9　Events within Asia's integrated resorts

Glenn McCartney

Introduction

Tourism landscapes have been changing more than ever before. New virtual and manufactured environments are being created not only to cater to larger numbers of travellers, but to deliver a greater experience that will meet the contemporary consumer demands and expectations of travellers. The artificial, adapted and recreated worlds and themes within the gaming and entertainment industry have helped invent this possibility for unique visitor experiences with the importance and prominence of natural or historical locations diminishing in importance, and for the most part scenery as tourists search for exceptional entertainment and enjoyment opportunities (Gosar, 2009). Rising out of this demand for enhanced experiences have been integrated resorts (IRs), termed also destination resorts due to their sheer physical presence and impacts to the location. IRs are some of the largest hospitality, entertainment and event complexes globally. With apprehension over perceived social impacts, public policy often dictates that IRs be built away from, or be on the fringes of, urban settings. Even in remote locations the substantial numbers employed and supplying these mega-structures, its physical footprint, global partnerships, ongoing communication programmes and influence on destination image means they can be a major catalyst to economic and tourism regeneration. The awarding of casino concessions to internationally renowned entertainment companies and their commitments to build IRs significantly and rapidly reversed Macao's stagnating tourism fortunes in early 2000. Citing Macao as a case study, McCartney (2005) has suggested that casinos, if appropriately regulated, introduced and managed, can be used as a product to benefit tourism destination redevelopment. While substantial casino tax revenues can aid regeneration, diversified tourism regeneration would need to ensure the inclusion and growth of non-gaming elements such as the events, entertainment and meetings industries. The Singapore government instructed that an IR would have less than 10% of the gross floor space for the casino with the rest of the resort used for theatres, convention centres, theme parks, accommodation, retail, food and beverage outlets and other non-gaming components (MacDonald & Eadington, 2008). The expansion of the IR concept and its portfolio of events and entertainment have in the past few decades meant that it is increasingly a contender for destination introduction and beyond Asia.

The event portfolio offering across gaming and non-gaming departments within each IR is substantial and continuous. Citing construction and opening costs of each as over $1 billion (all monetary figures in US dollars), Eadington and Collins (2009) provide examples of destination resorts in various regions in the world. In the United States these include Bellagio, Wynn Las Vegas, MGM Grand, the Mirage, The Venetian and Caesars all in Las Vegas as well as Foxwoods and Mohegan Sun in Connecticut, Sun City in South Africa and Jupiter's in Australia. In Asia, Wynn Macau and The Venetian are cited as well as Genting Highlands in Malaysia. However, the growth of Asian IRs has endured, some in cluster settings such as The Cotai Strip in Macao and in Manila Bay. Both locations continue to construct and open IR properties. Others by more restrictive government sanction take a different model in permitting a few individual licenses such as Singapore with the Marina Bay Sands and Resort World Sentosa properties both opening in 2010. A previous anti-gambling establishment had felt it necessary and justified legal casino gambling and the construction of two IRs in order to rejuvenate, maintain destination competitiveness and reach international tourism arrival targets (Henderson, 2012).

Casinos and the substantial gaming revenues generated are core to the success of Asia's IRs (Loi & Kim, 2010; Henderson, 2012). The events and entertainment components are minor components of revenue creation, and in some cases at cost, but are still seen and widely used as critical marketing and attraction tactics to create reasons for first or repetitive visits by casino patrons as well as loyalty creation and competitive brand positioning (McCartney, 2008a). Macao's global leadership in the casino industry was reinforced in 2012 when its gross gaming revenues of $44 billion surpassed the aggregate revenue of all of the United State's commercial casinos (McCartney, 2016). Although capped at two casinos, Singapore's revenue had reached $5.9 billion in 2012 narrowly behind the Las Vegas Strip (Stutz, 2014). A common feature on communicating to casino patrons has been the lure of an event be it a casino tournament or across non-gaming such as accommodation, retail, food and beverage, or a mass attendance or VIP focused concert or show. Global western iconic brands now reinforce event hosting in IRs with movie franchises and movie studios such as Universal, Fox Studios, Marvel, Dreamworks and RatPac Entertainment all in collaboration with Asian IRs. In 2013, soccer star David Beckham signed on as an endorser for Sands China Ltd with their two IRs, Marina Bay Sands and sister property The Venetian, Macau, where he appeared at several events between the two properties. With gambling advertising banned in China, a major audience for both properties, the decision was also a tactical one with the company hoping to leverage Beckham's celebrity appeal in China (Tomlinson, 2013). The non-gaming IR events programme continues to be a significant component of casino companies marketing in China and Hong Kong where casino gambling is illegal or in the case of Hong Kong with restrictions.

Permitting the introduction of Asian IRs by governments and their ensuing lobby to gain local community support has been on the premise of emulating to some degree the success of Las Vegas in hospitality diversification with its mix of gaming, entertainment, meetings and events offerings. Such sizeable enterprises though have created challenges for the destination to absorb, testing the capabilities and competencies of governments to manage responsibly as well as destination resource needs such as trained talent and suppliers. The global proliferation of legal casino gambling justified through the sizeable rents and competitive advantage that can transpire often create political and social controversy based on social costs, crime, problem gambling and immorality arguments (Eadington, 1999). The often political and socially charged debate for and against casinos can lead to a string of regulatory and restrictive measures on what would be uncommon across any other tourism product. Paradoxically, such measures could render the resort at a competitive disadvantage to casino resorts in overseas jurisdictions. Eadington (1999) concludes that subject to legitimacy and political acceptance, the concept of a destination resort with a casino at the core surrounded by entertainment activities is a popular concept for experience seeking audiences less willing to take on physically challenging activities.

The marriage of casino and event hosting

Asia's IR development due to its casino element is an exclusive club by government invitation only, through a tendering and review process that has attracted some of the largest casino and entertainment companies globally. In the past decade Asia has experienced notable IR growth to which the event industry has benefited in tandem with a significant event and entertainment portfolio being constantly staged throughout. Holding one of the six concessions and sub-concessions awarded by the Macao Government, Sands China Ltd has close to 10,000 hotel rooms with The Venetian, Four Seasons, Conrad, Sheraton and St. Regis hotel brands, 100 different food and beverage outlets and 650 shops in a mall with 3 canals and gondola rides. Larger events are hosted in the 15,000-seat Cotai Arena and 1,800-seat Venetian Theatre, and at 1.2 million square feet one of the largest convention and exhibition halls in Asia. Its new 'The Parisian Macao' expansion will add 3,000 rooms with additional casino, retail, event and convention space (Sands China Ltd., 2016a). It is a rare exception that an IR operates without a casino or gambling permit. One such example is Sunway Resort City outside Kuala Lumpur built from 800 acres of derelict mining with a Sunway Lagoon multi-park attraction using the ancient Egyptian theme throughout, shopping mall, hotels, and Sunway Pyramid Convention Centre (Sunway Property, 2016).

In contrast to a gaming saloon, city or rural casino, the IR justifies the larger capital investment due to the diversity of products and services beyond gaming (Eadington & Collins, 2009). Attending events within the IR has the potential to produce financial spill over effect where event attendees may exit the event to gamble, stay in a hotel room, shop or go to a spa. Suh and West (2010) found a positive correlation between Las Vegas showroom attendance and increased food and beverage spending. The portfolio of events spill over research would be important to determine which type of event (sport, art, music, celebrity) induced the longest stay and greatest spend in which gaming and non-gaming product, as well as visitor profile. Tracking casino and hotel patron loyalty or whether the event stimulated a first time or repeat visit can be useful in determining event investment worth. IRs have 3- or 4-tiered casinos with hotel loyalty programmes and databases which can also be readily linked to event ticket purchase and possible tracking.

Sports are a commonly used event theme within IRs with the ability to appeal to a wide audience and aimed at encouraging greater spending within the resort. Sports event strategy, where the IR can host in several internal venues such as an arena, theatre or convention centre, will include sports celebrity appearances, extreme sports events, as well as competitions. Celebrity visits can be targeted at high net worth individuals as well as performing community assignments visiting local schools or sports centres. Contests held to encourage mass viewing can be one-off generated by the IR or have global recognition. Professional boxing titles are often contested within IR settings. Manny Pacquiao won the WBO International Welterweight title at The Venetian in Macao in 2013 against Brandon Ríos, later losing the title in 2015 to Floyd Mayweather, Jr. at MGM Grand Garden Arena, Las Vegas, a popular professional boxing venue. The Mayweather versus Pacquiao fight was estimated to generate $500 million from direct ticket sales and pay-for-view (Isidore, 2016). Naturally the economic impacts of the event at The Venetian and MGM would multiply into other non-gaming and gaming revenues during the events. Although some iconic Western soccer, basketball, tennis and boxing events and stars have been staged at Asia IRs, this must be in line with the level to which Western sports has progressed into Asian audiences, to what sport, team and who is recognizable. An influencing factor for the rising popularity of sporting events for Asian audiences will be the increasing numbers of Asian stars successfully becoming established across international sports.

The casino and event alliance previously has been suggested as a highly unlikely one. Fenich and Hashimoto (2004) discuss the focus of Las Vegas beforehand on casino gambling with MICE tourism only being gradually accepted by the casino industry due to concerns over destination competitiveness to secure gamblers, as well as seeing the revenues that business delegates could generate by paying for rooms and non-gaming amenities, instead of the complimentary system used by the casino. With significant portions of Asia's IRs revenue stream generated from the casino, gaming still exerts significant influence over IR event hosting (McCartney, 2008a). In contrast, in mid-2014 to the Las Vegas Strip's gaming to non-gaming revenue split of 47%/63%, all of Macao's IRs generated less than 10% non-gaming revenues, with events and entertainment consigned to support roles for casino development (McCartney, 2015).

Yet Asian governments with casino resorts are pushing for a greater diversity in products beyond gambling. In recent years, the Chinese government has been emphasizing the need for Macao to diversify into non-gaming events in order to be less reliant on casino revenues (McCartney, 2015). The Singapore government granted two casino concessions to Genting and Las Vegas Sands on the premise that they would be a catalyst for tourism development with an emphasis on integrated resort development and the prominence of non-gaming entertainment and leisure (Henderson, 2012). The nature of the event can also influence spill over effect. In their discussion of the complexity of IR settings, Whitfield *et al.* (2012) highlight the importance of ensuring that what is being created within the IR is aligned for potential audiences and the delivery of their expectations. As well as catering for international audiences, the IR also host events for domestic visitation. The Solaire Resort & Casino in Manila staged *Les Misérables* at its 1,740-seat theatre in 2016 with the local Filipino audience in mind with the show's songs popular to Filipinos (Solaire Resort & Casino, 2016). Local communities and residents employed within the IR will often be given the opportunity to attend and purchase event tickets at a discount. This can be a substantial audience base especially when extended to family members. Lower priced event ticketing is part of the employee benefits for the over 28,000 staff working at the IR complex at The Venetian, Macao (The Venetian Macao, 2016).

The future of the event industry within Asia's IRs is secured not only as the on-going support pillar to casino patronage and loyalty inducement, but in its recent elevation in importance through Asian governments and destinations on the wish to present a competitive, diversified tourism economy. Unique to the IR, it is a portfolio of several small and major regular and special events hosted across the property in various venues and settings.

Event portfolio within integrated resorts

The term IR received greater prominence in 2004 when the Singapore government mandated that a small proportion of the physical facility be for casino purposes. This was set at less than 10% of gross floor space with the rest being non-gaming such as hotels, theatres, convention centre, retail, food and beverage facilities, theme parks and museums (MacDonald & Eadington, 2008). The positive image perceptions displayed by the family-friendly IR rather than a casino complex has also attracted global luxury brands and partnerships. Leading event and entertainment companies in recent years have increasingly put their product and branding within IRs. It also presents a lucrative foothold potential and gateway to China's huge event and entertainment potential. Dreamworks at City of Dreams, Manila launched 'Dreamplay' an interactive experience for children and in the evenings, corporate groups, to 'Play, Create, Learn' through famous movie themed settings such as *Kung Fu Panda, Shrek*, and *Madagascar* (City of Dreams Manila, 2016). Based in Shanghai, Dreamworks teamed up with Chinese companies to form Oriental Dreamworks producing *Kung Fu Panda 3* (Oriental Dreamworks, 2016). Animation and events hosted with animated characters can be readily adapted to local languages and cultural elements. Asian and Chinese elements are also increasingly integrated as part of international event and entertainment company development so as to have greater appeal to Asian audiences.

As a mega-complex of events, entertainment and leisure, a combination of gaming and non-gaming events and entertainment is cornerstone to IR marketing efforts and audience interaction. Figure 9.1 highlights the typology (with each described in Table 9.1) of possible events hosted within an Asian IR with varying degrees of magnitude depending on IR size, venue capacities, product offerings and communication strategy. Event teams in the various casino and non-gaming departments such as retail, arena and destination marketing can initiate and stage the event. However, several objectives can be possibly secured such as revenue creation, branding, community relations, media publicity and government relations. IR event stakeholder collaboration can be more challenging given not just the sheer physical size of an IR complex but also in ensuring relative departments are communicated to or are optimally engaged within the event.

Given the multitude of products and service within an IR, an IR event will often collaborate with an internal hotel, retail or restaurant brand partner given that the audience could have a similar demographic. Each can also cooperate on costs and marketing resources. A popular yet expensive tactic is the engagement by the IR to external celebrity appearances and endorsements to reinforce event and marketing campaigns which they feel are recognizable and appealing to the target audience, with Chinese stars such as Tony Leong and Chow Yun Fat used by IRs in Macao (McCartney & Pinto, 2014). Shown at the grand opening of

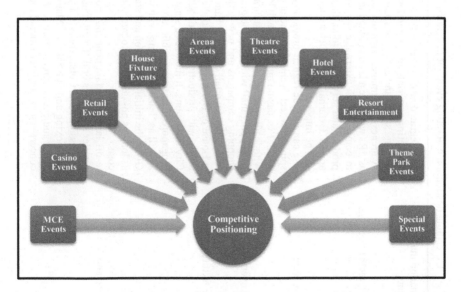

Figure 9.1 A typology of integrated resort event hosting looking at a number of destination marketing events.

Table 9.1 Describing destination marketing events at integrated resorts as per Figure 9.1

Destination marketing events	With integrated resorts seen as the destination, these events encompass the complete property, integrated into general marketing materials and promotions throughout the property. They can include cultural and arts festivals, external lighting shows and exhibitions and may or may not be charged for patronage. The objectives can vary such as brand awareness and image, community relations to attracting visitation and spending within the IR.
MCE Events (meetings, conventions, exhibitions)	Most IRs will have a level of meeting space (including meeting space within IR hotels). The IR and IR hotel will need to compete with external convention centres and standalone hotel properties. With a significant entertainment, product and service portfolio, the IR has multiple ways to design and budget for a meeting making, increasing appeal. External issues such as destination image, safety, security, accessibility, transportation and landscape will still be important.
Casino events	These can include regular promotions such as lucky draws, tournaments (e.g.slot, poker, baccarat or mahjong) and spin the wheel events for general mass casino patronage. With premium gamblers an important segment within Asian IRs, casino marketing will host regular events. To differentiate each event, this will often include alignment with leading retail brands, restaurants, drinks brands and celebrities.
Retail events	The shopping mall within the integrated resort will usually have space to host events aimed at key seasonal themes, shopping campaigns and new outlet openings including flagship outlets. Smaller bespoke VIP events are hosted within luxury retail outlets or banquet halls at casino premium customers.
House fixture events	The House of Dancing Water ticketed show, considered the World's Largest Water Extravaganza (City of Dreams, 2016), with production costs of $250 million, was purpose built with a 270 degree 2,000 seats theatre at Macao's City of Dreams. It includes a stage pool of 3.7 million gallons of water. Two fixed regular shows at Resort World Singapore, are staged outside using mechanical cranes and audio-visual effects (Crane Dance), as well as 'Lake of Dreams' with water, lighting and fire elements choreographed (Resort World Singapore, 2016). Given the initial production and staging costs, a major challenge is keeping these events relevant and appealing for as long as possible. Due to purposely built features, only minor alterations are possible without occurring greater costs.
Arena events	One-off large entertainment and sports events can be hosted. The sporting format and seating can be changed for smaller audiences or different stage presentations. Flooring changes means ice-skating, tennis and basketball area all possible. The Cotai Arena at The Venetian, Macau has hosted internationally renowned artists as well as world title boxing and martial arts. Major Chinese, Korean and Taiwanese stars also perform to appeal to the tastes of major audiences. Arena event teams at IRs will need to compete with neighbouring destinations with standalone concert venues for international touring artists.

Theatre events	With a reduced capacity (a few thousand seats), smaller entertainment and cultural events can take place. These venues can appeal to regional and global theatre shows, several of which are beginning to tour within Asia sees growing interest from Asian audiences with familiar/popular music with recognizable characters with appealing and understandable scripts.
Hotel events	The IR will normally have its own branded hotel. A growing number are globally recognised brands, these hotels will follow the international chain events commonly linked to food and beverage, loyalty programmes and hotel openings, refurbishments and business meetings. Poolside is a popular outdoor and evening venue at the IR luxury hotel appealing for events hosted by the casino, MCE and special events. The Hard Rock Hotel at City of Dreams Macau incorporate rock' and roll into wedding events and regular pool parties (Hard Rock Hotel Macau, 2016).
Resort entertainment	IRs may have artists and entertainment groups wondering around the property or standing in fixed points, mostly in non-gaming locations such as retail, hotel lobbies and arrival and exit points. Dressed in theme, they sing, dance, perform and interact with guests.
Themed studio events	International entertainment companies are increasingly establishing presence within IRs, such as Universal Studios at Resort World Singapore, Fox Studios at Resort World Malaysia and Dreamworks at City of Dreams, Manila. The ongoing series of popular movies keep the theme relevant and appealing with revenues created through new merchandising, themed rides and special events such as movie launches and seasonal link events (Christmas, Chinese New Year and Halloween). Some IRs self-theme, using local cultural themes or those popular overseas.
Special events	The constant expansion, renovations and rejuvenation initiatives within IRs provide opportunities to celebrate openings, product launches or to announce a new collaboration. Most Asian IRs follow both Western and Lunar calendars to celebrate events and occasions. Local commemorative days and festivals are also hosted in the IR to appeal to local communities, media, government and employees. A specific special event team may be purposely arranged and later disbanded, drawn across departments to spread benefits and have a common marketing message.

Studio City Macau, in October 2015, the 15-minute movie/advertisement 'The Audition' directed by Martin Scorsese, produced by Brett Ratner and starring Brad Pitt, Robert De Niro and Leonardo DiCaprio was estimated to cost the IR $70 million (Makinen, 2015). With the absence of Brad Pitt, all the celebrities connected to the movie arrived in Macao for the grand opening of Studio City appearing on stage to introduce the movie.

Even with the casino occupying less than 10% of floor space, it still has the ability to generate a disproportionate contribution to EBITDA (earnings before interest, taxes, depreciation and amortization) (MacDonald & Eadington, 2008). This permits investment in events and entertainment at the Asian IR that may not have been otherwise possible. With events within IRs produced with competitive positioning and market share in mind (Figure 9.1), there is increasing scrutiny on the types and ability of IR events to generate visitation, greater stay and spending. While participation at any IR event can meet the potential for greater stay and spending, events also play a key role in accessing markets where casino marketing is sensitive or banned. All of Asia's IRs lobby for the highly lucrative Chinese visitor. Reaching those in China where casinos are illegal and any marketing strictly prohibited, or with gambling marketing heavily restricted in Hong Kong, means that events take on an important marketing role.

The Chinese consumer's interest in events and entertainment

Outside China and its two SARs (special administrative regions) of Hong Kong and Macao, the Chinese community is present in Asian countries with IRs or in close neighbouring jurisdictions to those who have. It would therefore be incorrect to assert that the Chinese all think the same and therefore produce an event or marketing programme for a singular Chinese audience (McCartney, 2008b). Events are built around manufacturing experiences and given that the lifecycle and demise of an event tactic could be hastened when it no longer aligns to audience's motives to attend it, a greater understanding of the Chinese participation tastes towards the IR event portfolio (as observed in Figure 9.1) is needed.

Chinese travel and consumer tastes are becoming more sophisticated than a few decades ago when outbound leisure travel was at its infancy. China is now the largest travel source market in the world. In 2014, outbound tourism grew by 20% to 117 million and spent $4,000 on average (Plowright, 2015), although the majority still travel within Asia and historically mainly to Hong Kong and Macao. Chinese companies are increasingly making significant purchases of overseas hospitality and leisure brands. The Chinese company Fosun International Limited through its Happy Lifestyle operations owns Club Med, Atlantis (Sanya, Hainan), movie company Studio 8, and Cirque du Soleil from Canada. The company also has shareholders in companies such as Thomas Cook and other international retail and sports and leisure brands (Fosun, 2016). Cited as the world's largest property company with 133 Wandas Plazas and 84 hotels, Wanda Group owns over 6000 AMC cinemas throughout Asia and the United

States and through its Cultural Industry Group division is China's biggest film company, and with its Sports Holdings the rights to the Ironman Triathlon event and various global skiing and football activities (Wanda, 2016).

Understanding event content (such as storyline, food and beverage offerings, celebrity presence, language, fung shui and service touch-points) across Chinese communities will be important, but with that ticket distribution and payment method as well as the link to event communication. With an increasing number of Chinese travellers moving online, by September 2015, for example, daily WeChat app users in China had reached 570 million – the most globally (China Internet Watch, 2015). WeChat is now widely used across Asia's IR developments. The Chinese version of WeChat also has special interactive features not on Western versions such as sending lucky money Red Packet (Lai See) showing the need to adapt to cultural values.

Continued integrated resort expansion to the benefit of events

IR expansion is now part of Asia's hospitality and tourism landscape, with IRs now firmly established or under development in destinations such as Malaysia, Singapore, Macao, Philippines and Korea. Others such as Japan, Taiwan and Thailand continue to mull and debate over the idea of casino legalization and through this the onset of IR construction. These mega-complexes are home to a vast portfolio of varying magnitude of regular, special and one-off events. IR presence requires huge investment, confidence in government commitment and stability, and a comfortable return on investment period for investors and operators. The IR becomes a significant hub of economic activity and event hosting across gaming and non-gaming facilities. With each new IR will normally be the presence of more significant investment, resource needs, physical size, brand partnerships and glamour than the previous IR in the competing landscape, gradually becoming a significant hub of activity and impact for the local community.

While any hospitality or event expansion project can potentially generate negative sentiment perhaps due to incursion on environmental, community or historical sites or the perceived cost to the public purse versus potential benefits, there is particular debate and controversy surrounding IR development linked primarily to the presence of casinos. Yet events through signalling diversification beyond gaming are needed to divert government and policy interference and over-regulation that essentially make the IR and therefore the location under-competitive to the possible benefit of neighbouring jurisdictions.

Restrictive legislative and codes can be and are often applied to casinos, while IRs however offer an optimum landscape for a portfolio of events attracting an increasing number of international family event and entertainment companies, brands and celebrities. This alignment provides event knowledge, talent and know-how to the destination further legitimizing the benefits of IR presence. While a city or town may have a stadium, convention centre, theatres, and various other event venues, the IR has created all this within one location. Facilities and infrastructure at the IR such as car parks, hotels, restaurants, including banks, medical facilities, security and post offices have all been resourced and gauged to accommodate vast numbers and various visitor needs all under one roof. The integration concept further extends to transportation modes with coach, limo, ferry and airport services being provided by the IR. As notable and reported in Manila and Macao, lagging infrastructure at entry and exit points and congested road access means that casino and tourism tax dollars have not translated down to public sector investment or construction in tandem to the needs of the IR. IRs cannot operate as islands with overall destination appeal important for visitation decision-making. This too will impact the event industry, particularly those events which can be hosted outside IR settings in competing cities.

The beneficial relationship between the events industry and Asian IRs will continue. Sharing event experiences have increasingly moved online too with social and fantasy games. The future will therefore mean incorporating more innovation and creativity in events to stay relevant and with competitive advantage to lure new patronage and repeat visitation given this surreal and manufactured environment for staging events at IRs.

Events within IRs as part of regeneration strategy: From bystander to participant

IRs can and have shaped the direction of tourism development not only due to physical size and destination recognition but on the economic impacts that result. Large portions of the community will be employed or will supply or partner with the IR. Indirectly multiple visitor services will benefit and grow around the IR. McCartney and Nadkarni (2003), in their analysis of the growth of gaming in Macao within its historical backdrop, warned over a decade before that an overreliance on the tax revenues of the casino industry, many of which are now housed within Asia's emerging IRs, could relegate culture and heritage conservation on importance and attention. With the significant revenues generated from casinos essentially financing a major portion of government conversation actions, the hand that assisted could paradoxically be the one to cause the other's downfall. As a regenerating mechanism, IRs should be carefully considered on their expectations and the landscape that is anticipated to unfold. The event industry essentially plays a support role and marketing function to Asian IRs and the importance of casino revenue creation. As a consequence, there could be limited regeneration on local sports, cultural and music events as this is essentially not a part of IR event strategy.

Assigning a major portion of an IR physical space for non-gaming, be it an arena or meeting space, is no guarantee that similar will follow in terms of tourism diversification and the advancement of other services such as events and conventions. In fact, this study has shown in Macao and Singapore, especially, smaller casino spaces have significant capability to generate remarkable revenues compared to the rest of the casino resort. The past few decades though have shown the event and entertainment industry and the casino industry to be compatible within IR settings. While it is the activities of the IR that regenerate, the direction is not influenced to any great extent by non-gaming services such as events. Challenged with ensuring tourism and economic diversification occuring in the destination, Asian governments that have IRs are now tasked to elevate the importance of non-gaming. The issue remains equally moot for those governments in Asia considering IR introduction. The issue will be on how to take the IR's current engagement with the global event industry and event hosting and cultivate this further within the destination and local communities.

References

City of Dreams. (2016). The house of dancing water. http://www.cityofdreamsmacau. com/en/entertainment/detail/the-house-of-dancing-water.

China Internet Watch. (2015). WeChat daily active user reached 570 million in Sep 2015. http://www.chinainternetwatch.com/15287/wechat-users-insights-2015/.

City of Dreams Manila. (2016). Dreamworks. http://www.cityofdreams.com.ph/ entertainment/dreamplay.

Eadington, W. (1999). The spread of casinos and their role in tourism development. In D.G. Pearce & R.W. Butler (Eds.). *Contemporary issues in tourism development.* London, England: Routledge (pp. 125–140).

Eadington, W.R. & Collins, P. (2009). Managing the social costs associated with casinos: Destination resorts in comparison to other types of casino-style gaming. In W.R. Eadington & M.R. Doyle (Eds.). *Integrated resort casinos: Implications for economic growth and social impacts.* Reno, NV: University of Nevada (pp. 55–82).

Fosun (2016). Industrial operations. http://www.fosun.com/en/investment/investment_1.html.

Gosar, A. (2009). Gaming tourism in the context of modern tourist flows. In W.R. Eadington & M.R. Doyle (Eds.) *Integrated resort casinos: Implications for economic growth and social impacts.* Reno, NV: University of Nevada (pp. 193–205).

Fenich, G.G. & Hashimoto, K. (2004). Casinos and conventions: Strange bedfellows. *Journal of convention and event tourism, 6,* 63–79.

Hard Rock Hotel Macau. (2016). Event & banquet. http://www.hardrockhotelmacau.com/ event-and-banquet.php.

Henderson, J.C. (2012). Developing and regulating casinos: The case of Singapore. *Tourism and hospitality research, 12,* 139–146.

Isodore, C. (2016). Mayweather-Pacquiao rakes in a record $500 Million, *CNN money,* http://money.cnn.com/2015/05/12/news/companies/mayweather-pacquiao-revenue/.

Loi, K-I. & Kim, W.G. (2010). Macao's casino industry. Reinventing Las Vegas in Asia. *Cornell hospitality quarterly, 51,* 268–283.

MacDonald, A. & Eadington, W.R. (2008). The case for integrated resorts. http:// www.urbino.net/bright.cfm?specificBright=THE%20CASE%20FOR%20 INTEGRATED%20RESORTS.

Makinen, J. (2015). Did a Chinese casino really just pay $70 million for a 15-minute Martin Scorsese film? *Los Angeles times,* 27 October.

McCartney, G. & Nadkarni, S. (2003). *Heritage versus gaming: Odds on winning a piece of the tourist pie.* 2nd DeHaan Tourism Management Conference, Nottingham University Business School.

McCartney, G. (2005). Casinos as a tourism redevelopment strategy–The case of Macao. *Journal of Macau gaming research association, 2,* 40–54.

McCartney, G. (2008a). The CAT (Casino Tourism) and the MICE (Meetings, Incentives, Conventions, Exhibitions): Key development considerations for the convention and exhibition industry in Macao. *Journal of convention & event tourism, 9*, 293–308.

McCartney, G. (2008b). Does one culture all think the same? An investigation of destination image perceptions from several origins. *Tourism review, 63*, 13–26.

McCartney, G. (2015). When the eggs in one basket all cracked. Addressing the downturn in Macao's casino and VIP junket system. *Gaming law review & economics, 19*, 527–537.

McCartney, G. & Pinto, J.P. (2014). The impact of celebrity endorsement in influencing destination selection on outbound Chinese travelers. *Journal of vacation marketing, 20*, 253–266.

Oriental Dreamworks. (2016). About us. http://www.oriental-dreamworks.com/odw-about-our-film-studio.

Owen, C. (1990). Tourism and urban regeneration. *Cities, 7*, 194–201.

Plowright, M. (2015). Overseas spending by Chinese tourists nears S500bn. http://www.ft.com/intl/cms/s/0/044217d2-ed01-11e4-a81a-00144feab7de.html#axzz40PqGkjg7.

Sands China Ltd. (2016a). Sands China Ltd. http://www.sandschina.com.

Solaire Resort & Casino. (2016). Les Misérables. https://solaireresort.com/entertainment/les-miserables/.

Stutz, H. (2014). Singapore casinos produce $6 billion in gaming revenue in 2013; market still trails Las Vegas Strip. *Las Vegas review-journal*, 21 February.

Suh, E. & West, J.J. (2009). Estimating the impact of entertainment on the restaurant revenues of a Las Vegas hotel casino: An exploratory study. *International journal of hospitality management, 29*, 570–575.

Sunway Property. (2016). Sunway Resort City. http://www.sunwayproperty.com/malaysia-properties/malaysia-property-detail/sunway-resort-city/id/190dd4f0-572b-688c-a7be-ff000068ef51/type/1.

The Venetian Macao. (2016). Your ideal career at Sands China. https://www.venetianmacao.com/hotel/about-us/careers.html.

Thomas, R. & Long, J. (2001). Tourism and economic regeneration: The role of skills development. *International journal of tourism research, 3*, 229–240.

Tomlinson, S. (2013). David Beckham signs deal to plug hotels in China's gambling capital as Las Vegas firm looks to cash in on this popularity in the Far East. *Daily mail*, 23 December.

Wanda. (2016). Cultural Industry Group. http://www.wanda-group.com/businesses/culture/.

Whitfield, J., Dioko, A.N., Webber, D.K. & Zhang, L. (2012). Attracting convention and exhibition attendance to complex MICE venues: Emerging data from Macao. *International journal of tourism research, 16*, 169–179.

10 Urban elements that facilitate sport and physical activity in regenerated public spaces

Barcelona's waterfront

Sacra Morejon, Sixte Abadía and
Xavier Pujadas

Introduction

This chapter identifies urban elements that facilitate sport and physical activity in regenerated public spaces in Barcelona. Focusing specifically on Barcelona's waterfront, the port area was regenerated to create a new central area for the city based on sport as a leisure activity (Nel·lo, 1992; Novoa, 1998; Benach, 2000; Fava, 2003). City waterfronts were chosen as the object of study because these areas have shown themselves to be not only particularly dynamic, but also historically symptomatic of change in productive models and lifestyles (Norcliffe, 1981; Jauhiainen, 1995; Fava, 2003; Jones, 2010; Gonçalves & Thomas, 2012; Kostopoulou, 2013). In most cities that have a direct relationship with it, water is initially a key element of the productive system and a means of economic and political exchange. Waterfronts have since retained their strategic position and become spaces where their regeneration can be seen as a kind of general urban restructuring, in which the image of these areas is associated with a city's presentation (Jauhiainen, 1995).

Changes in urban planning have also led to a modification of central areas, defined traditionally by the productive system, then by the administrative sector, and finally by the commercial and recreational sector (Norcliffe, 1981). Because of the transformation of waterfront spaces into spaces for consumption (basically centred on sport and culture as leisure activities), it is important to bear in mind that, in the new definition of them, a design that promotes their recreational use must be chosen. In order to identify elements that facilitate sport and physical activity in this design, it is necessary to reference those studies that associate urban planning with the promotion of a more active lifestyle, given that mobility and the pursuit of sport and physical activity play a key role within it (Rodriguez *et al.*, 2006). According to the *Código Urban Sasoi* (Ayuntamiento de Irún, 2014), facilitative environments must be created in order to promote healthier lifestyles, which in turn bring social, educational, environmental, economic and, of course, health benefits.

Given the complexity of addressing the regeneration of urban space from the perspective of physical activity, the study presented in this chapter is divided into four sections. First, an overview of urban planning in cities with waterfronts is proposed. The aim of doing so is to find points in common and to consider some degree of extrapolation. Second, the fact that the urban regeneration of these spaces provides public authorities with an opportunity to take a sustainable approach and the chance to improve citizens' quality of life is underscored. Third, the case of Barcelona's waterfront is presented: the first phase of the study is descriptive and the second uses topographic tools to get an in-depth understanding of the area under study and to determine the elements that facilitate sport and physical activity. Fourth and last, the conclusions are given.

Port cities and urban evolution

Most cities with waterfronts share common traits in a process that ranges from their conception to their regeneration, which started in North America in the 1960s and in Europe a decade later (Jauhiainen, 1995). Certain regeneration projects of former industrial ports, like Baltimore's Inner Harbour, for instance, have served as successful models to be imitated (Kostopoulou, 2013). According to Fava (2003), there is considerable interest in redeveloping and integrating unused spaces left over from previous port activity into urban life. City areas like these are not only seen as a problem in terms of the relationship between a city and a port, but also as places where a city's historical structural processes are defined.

Focusing on these transformations, it should be possible to analyse them by taking into consideration a time division that may be common to all cases. According to Braudel (1969), this division corresponds to the rhythm of time of the social structure and the economic system of civilisation: the industrial city and the post-industrial city. The first is a city where the main purpose is production and the consequent accumulation of capital, in a world dominated by free market forces. The second is a city subjected to factors like the 1970s' oil crisis and changing demand, where the third sector and the information industry gain ground over traditional industry. Norcliffe (1988) explains this shift by saying that this new productive sector is located along major roads and requires less storage space.

In 1999, Han Meyer, an urban planning expert, presented a temporal structure of port-city development in five stages, comparing the different stages of urban development to that of a port. The first stage corresponds to the emergence of the industrial city, and the coexistence of city and port; in the second, infrastructure becomes important and the port becomes a port of transit – rather than being in the centre of the city, it is adjacent to it; in the third, and coinciding with an increase in mobility, the development of industrial ports away from the central area is encouraged; the last two stages include the globalisation and the internationalisation of industry, where the port becomes the node of a connected distribution network. In the last stage, the port is rediscovered by the city as part of the urban landscape. Transformed, it becomes a potential logistics and communications hub. A city area where major port infrastructure associated with industry has disappeared thus becomes a privileged space from the viewpoints of landscape and exchange. It therefore displays its potential for regeneration and for the location of a new central area there, one that is linked to leisure and consumption (Gonçalves & Thomas, 2012).

Beyond the original port, the waterfront takes on another dimension and creates a renewed relationship with the city on water (river, canal or sea), where it is no longer a city-port contact space, but rather an entire urban system. Fava (2003) states that a city's waterfront can be thought of as an aspect of globalisation, understood as a place for economic and political exchange, which naturally responds to the physical characteristics of the place itself. Hence, it is an interesting field of experimentation because it allows the relationship between local (influenced by a city's history and geography) and global (a place for exchange and consumption) to be observed. Benach (2000) analyses the case of Barcelona with the intention of explaining how new spaces for consumption help to build the city's image. According to her presentation, the production of a city's images is a key component of many cities' urban policies. Indeed, certain interventions become symbols of revitalisation: they provide new uses, they want to make the city attractive and they have high levels of acceptance among citizens.

It is possible to see that waterfronts largely meet these requirements and thus become a city's image. The change in urban functions, with a shift from production to consumption, opens the door to potential new uses for public space and, at the same time, demands a new image of a city in order to promote, project and look after it. The construction of new spaces for leisure (sport and cultural events) and for tourism is part of an attempt to project a renewed image of a city (Jones, 2010).

Barcelona's waterfront

After a careful review of the literature and meetings with several experts (Josep Parcerisa, architect and professor in the Barcelona School of Architecture at UPC-BarcelonaTech, and coordinator of the Urbanism Laboratory of Barcelona), a description of the process of building and transforming Barcelona's waterfront is given. It explains how the city went from being an industrial city enclosed within walls to a city open to the sea, whose waterfront was gradually redeveloped through several urban planning interventions driven by universal expositions and mega-events (in 1888, 1929, 1992 and 2004). In order to render this description suitable for use in studies of other cases, the reference to common elements described in the generic approach to the planning and analysis of port cities was not overlooked.

After that, the pre-existence of urban planning policies aimed at promoting sport and physical activity. Then, urban policies concerning physical activities in public spaces, identification of facilitative elements and localisation of said elements were addressed. In order to establish what these urban elements were, the basis was a previous study that analysed the ideal characteristics of the location of sports spaces (see Morejon, 2010). This study analysed the situation of these facilities to determine their suitability, where 'situation' is understood as being the way in which they relate to other urban elements within their surroundings.

The process of building and transforming Barcelona's waterfront

As an industrial city in the late nineteenth century, Barcelona had a twofold contradictory relationship with the waterfront: on the one hand, the city's most representative and important landmarks (Santa Maria del Mar, Les Drassanes, La Llotja and Palau de Mar) had been built near the sea yet within the city walls and, on the other, there was an entire area that was both unsafe and marshy between the walls and the sea, where functions considered unfit to be contained within the city were located (Fava, 2003). Furthermore, the first railway line in Spain was built in 1848. This line, which connected Barcelona to Mataró, ran along the coastline, thereby restricting access to the city from the sea along its entire length.

In Barcelona, the city's new productive sector was located along major roads thereby reducing the industrial port's storage spaces. The shift towards a post-industrial city coincided with the demolition of the wall separating the city from the sea and the need to give the city a new waterfront. The demolition of the city walls (1854) provided considerable space for the new health and hygiene culture's transformation, and a plan to expand Barcelona was approved in 1859 for that sector. Around the same dates, Ildefons Cerdà was commissioned with Barcelona's new growth project, which involved extending the city outwards (1860). Cerdà believed that a port was the centre of action of any maritime city, as was the river of any fluvial city.

Initial interventions: The universal expositions of
La Ciutadella (1888) and Montjuïc (1929)

The area of La Ciutadella (located on the edge of the walled city, next to the port) became a disputed place, and it was in 1888 when the first Barcelona Universal Exposition was organised that intervention focused on the regeneration of this space as a leisure area. This area had already been the object of a redevelopment project by Josep Fontserè i Mestres (1871), and it represented an important node connecting the old walled city to the new extended city, in the area closest to the sea.

Barcelona's waterfront was shaped by its port (the port infrastructure was renewed in 1874 and connected to the new free zone project), which became a quintessentially representative place. It was the space chosen by the city to exhibit its progress, development and, in short, its modernity. At the same time, projects like those by Cerdà or Jaussely chose to create a new central area for the city, and both concurrently considered the growing interest expressed by European society in sport as a leisure activity when envisioning the new Barcelona (Pujadas, 2001). Then, between 1888 and 1929, the role of the Passeig Colom Boulevard on the seafront was boosted. It thus became the city's area of leisure that, in turn, connected two other areas that had been the centres of intervention for the two universal expositions: La Ciutadella and Montjuïc. Both interventions meant that a new relationship between the city and the sea was being intentionally developed. According to Fava (2003), the waterfront at that time was mainly occupied by productive activities (port and industry) and by an incipient water-related recreational activity: together, the development of a culture of wellbeing and concerns about hygiene and health meant that a series of new bathing, swimming and sailing facilities was created. These included Club Català de Regates (1879), Club de Regates de Barcelona (1881), Club Nàutic (1903), Club del Mar (1913), Natació Barcelona (1907), Club Natació Atlètic (1913) and Club Natació Barceloneta (1929).

The Pla Macià was then submitted in 1933. This was a project by GATCPAC (Grup Arquitectes i Tècnics Catalans per el Progrés de l'Arquitectura Contemporània [Group of Catalan Architects and Technicians for the Progress of Contemporary Architecture]) which, together with Le Corbusier, proposed a shift towards the functional city. In this project, the waterfront was analysed from a landscape perspective as a whole. Beyond the relationship that the city established with the sea via its port, special plans began to be drawn up for several specific areas of the waterfront (1964, southeast area of Montjuïc, and La Ribera Plan), which took a new approach to the city's waterfront. The 1955 Mediterranean Games put Montjuïc firmly on the map as a public space for the pursuit of sport within the city (Pujades & Sánchez, 2002).

Given the changes in maritime technology and the desire to give the port of Barcelona an international dimension, the port's redevelopment and enlargement was considered in 1966. According to Lluís Cantallops (an urban planner), the need to solve certain problems associated with the city's waterfront had already been identified in 1971. These problems were access to the beaches, the lack of bathing facilities and a marina, and the port's congestion. One of the first interventions aimed at solving the problems identified was the transformation of the quay called Moll de la Fusta into a space open to the public (Solà Morales, 1980), where a new section of the seafront promenade was considered. Environmental issues, artistic heritage, the need for public space for tourism, the citizens' recreation and leisure time and urban redevelopment policies were addressed in this project (Fava, 2003).

The great transformation: The Olympic Games (1992) and the Universal Forum of Cultures (2004)

In the candidature process to become the host city of the 1992 Olympic Games, Barcelona's 1986 bid already considered some of the major structural changes that the city needed to open itself up to the sea once and for all (Novoa, 1998). Besides the partial projects that had been developed, a stretch of Barcelona's waterfront continued to be very run down. Railway lines blocked access to the sea, and the factories that had been built in that area gradually became obsolete and derelict. This area was considered a potential site for a waste disposal facility (Fava, 2003). The Special Plan for the Olympic Village envisaged running the railway lines underground, designing a coastal bypass (providing fast entrance and exit routes for port traffic), as well as structuring and planning the beaches, and creating parks and the marina. The Olympic Village adhered to the grid structure of the Cerdà project, and architects who had won a Fostering Arts and Design (FAD) award were commissioned with the design of the buildings (Nel·lo, 1992). The Spanish Coast Act (1988) allowed the physical space of the waterfront to be recovered and a promenade that joined up the various routes leading to the sea to be built. This transformation affected 120 hectares of land with different uses (parks, infrastructure, facilities, beaches, open areas and the Olympic Village), which are now totally integrated into the city. It is a very significant and cohesive urban space that promotes relationships among citizens (Novoa, 1998).

The last intervention on Barcelona's waterfront, which again took advantage of a universal exposition to take the construction of the city's structural projects forward, was specifically for the Universal Forum of Cultures held in 2004. In this case, the event was used to plan the northern stretch of the city's waterfront from the Olympic Village to the River Besòs. The neighbourhood suffered from considerable problems, and it had to be revitalised with a major capital investment and a change of land use. The General Metropolitan Plan of the 22@ sector was proposed. This plan placed considerable emphasis on centralising activities associated with new communication technologies, and the urban strategy was the policy of recovering industrial architectural heritage and the installation of cultural activities (Selfa, 2005).

The effects of the Olympic Games and the Universal Forum of Cultures were reflected in both the urban transformation of the city and the development of tourism. Indeed, the evolution of Barcelona's tourism is evidenced by an increase in the number of tourists and overnights in hotels since 1990 (which was less than 4 million) to 2013 (increasing to more than 16.4 million) (Turisme de Barcelona, 2014). The first period of major tourism growth was between 1992 and 1995 as a direct consequence of the 1992 Olympic Games. The second period was between 2001 and 2007. In just six years, the number of tourists had risen from 3 to 7 million (Bové & Guim, 2013). This improvement in Barcelona's position as a tourist destination cannot be understood without taking into account a change of strategy made by the city from 1992, which was based on an increase in hotel supply, on the creation of first-rate cultural infrastructure, on the urban restructuring of the city's industrial and waterfront areas, and on the creation of a public-private body to promote tourism (Duro & Rodríguez, 2015). Created in 1993, this new organisation called *Turisme de Barcelona* is still 'the organisation responsible for promoting Barcelona as a tourist destination' (Turisme de Barcelona, 2014). Over the past 20 years, Barcelona has gone from being a city with tourism to a touristic city. Rather than being a complementary activity, tourism has become a structural component of the city's productive system and of its metabolism, a feature of everyday life that leaves none of its citizens indifferent.

In fact, it has shaped the image of the city by which it is internationally recognised (López Palomeque, 2015, p. 486).

The city's image and the official discourse on new uses

These changes in urban functions, which took place on Barcelona's waterfront from 1986, were an attempt to project a renewed image of the city and largely responded to the Barcelona brand. The images created from these new urban spaces have helped to reinforce the citizens' sense of belonging, and the public authorities have made the most of such images to symbolise and showcase a model city. These new spaces for consumption have an impact on the construction of the city's image, which serves internally to strengthen social consensus in regard to Barcelona's urban planning policy, and externally as an indicator of quality of life (Benach, 2000).

Parallel to this, the early twentieth century saw the emergence in Europe of a tendency to use public space for the pursuit of sport. Bach (1993) explains the characteristics of this process and states that the places where these new pursuits develop are not sports facilities, but instead urban spaces designed for other uses. He explains that this situation conditions the application of policies for improving quality of life in urban and residential areas, and this concurrently leads to an increase in legislation on these new ways of doing exercise and recreational activities. From the 1980s, ways of doing physical activity that were more recreational began to emerge in Barcelona. People took to doing them in 'de-sportivised' spaces like urban public spaces (Pujades & Sánchez, 2002). At that time, it was necessary to rethink how the city would incorporate the citizens' desire to pursue modern sports outside conventional sports spaces (running, cycling or beach sports) on the one hand, and other extreme sports (such as skateboarding or roller-skating) using the newly created public space (beaches, parks and the seafront promenade) on the other. With the development of sport and leisure activities brought about by the change of public space use, the public authorities had to take a stance on such use by regulating it. In order to present the public authorities' official stance on public space use for sport and physical activity, particularly on the waterfront, reference must be made to the city of Barcelona's various Strategic Plans for Sport.

These plans are instruments used by Barcelona City Council to define the action strategy for improving the city's entire sports system, and they have been created by means of a participatory process involving various sectors, actors and stakeholders. The first Strategic Plan (2003) proposed that one of the key aspects was to consider Barcelona as a city that facilitates and promotes sport, and that such sport should foster the city's social construction. This initial Strategic Plan set out the main lines of action. Of those applicable to the waterfront, worthy of mention are: making the city the setting for the pursuit of sport and physical activity by providing and developing the city's own urban and natural spaces to achieve that; promoting Barcelona's relationship with the sea and aquatic space by turning the sea into an opportunity to improve the city's inhabitants' quality

of life; strengthening the international projection of the Barcelona brand by hosting major European and global sports events that bring benefit to the city; making
Barcelona a tourist destination of choice for sport.

A few years later, the Barcelona Sports Institute, through a second participatory process of sports planning in the city, produced a new Strategic Plan
(2012–2022) based on six dimensions, one of which is *Sport, City and Wellbeing.*
The main assets and shortcomings are identified in this section. Among the assets are the use of the city's unique spaces as settings for the pursuit of sport,
the increase in the number of people independently doing sport on the streets,
the promotion of spaces like parks and beaches, and the Barcelona brand as a
point of reference for sport because of the city's geographical location (the sea,
hills and the climate). One of the shortcomings mentioned is the need to improve
public spaces for sport and physical activity in open spaces, connecting them to
public facilities.

The need to keep beach services going outside the summer season is to ensure
that they can be used year-round for sport and leisure activities – and for the purpose of events and subsequent tourism opportunities. Attracting and organising
cultural and sporting events therefore conforms not only to a desire to have more
appeal in terms of tourism, but also to a rationale of reinforcing the leadership
and international projection of cities like Barcelona. So much so that another of
the current strategic dimensions of Barcelona's sports policy is the city's international profile which focuses on strengthening the city as a true world capital of
sport (Ajuntament de Barcelona, 2016).

Determining the elements that facilitate sport and physical activity

In the analysis of the best urban location for a sports facility, the opportunity or
threat that other nearby urban elements represent is identified. It is considered
that opportunity takes into account those elements that facilitate its pursuits,
and threat takes into account those that make difficult its development (Morejon,
2010). Previous research concerning ideal implementations of sports spaces
concluded that the parameters represented by urban elements of opportunity
(i.e. those that facilitate the pursuit of sport are the urban fabric, uses, services
and accessibility). The proximity of the urban fabric facilitates sport and physical
activity (Gelabert & Fàbregas, 1994), and one of the strengths of sports facilities
is how close they are to homes, shopping centres and places where there is a high
residential density (Bökemann, 1993). Foremost, to learn about the configuration
of the urban fabric around the waterfront, all the area under study was delimited, determining the boundaries by specifying the natural and built elements,
describing the various urban fabrics (neighbourhoods/districts) making up the
area, and providing information about the general parameters thereof (surface
area, inhabitants and density). Then, three areas were distinguished according to
how they reach the sea.

When analysing the uses, it must be noted that there is a correlation between mixed use and the fostering of active lifestyles (Rodriguez *et al.*, 2006;

Ayuntamiento de Irún, 2014). Thus, from a quantitative perspective, the land use of the neighbourhoods forming part of the waterfront was broken down, by percentage, into facilities, urban parks and the road network, and the percentage for each was compared to the city's mean values. In order to get a qualitative view, a mapping exercise was performed for facilities (those that, in one way or another, fostered, organised or prescribed physical activity were taken into account) and for parks (to see how much of the area was given over to isolated green areas or whether there was an interconnected network across the territory). According to the Master Plan for Sports Installations and Facilities in Catalonia (*PIEC*) (Generalitat de Catalunya, 2005), the existence of complementary or subsidiary facilities increases a place's attractiveness (Bökemann, 1993), and the proximity of green areas helps to add to sport and leisure offerings and provide the area of influence with certain healthier environmental conditions. The parameter of services that facilitate sport and physical activity involved the observation of certain urban elements (that have connotations of health, safety and attractiveness), sports equipment and the commercial. Finally, accessibility to the area under observation by both public and private transport was studied.

Boundaries of the area under study

In the case of Barcelona, the waterfront is delimited by Montjuïc hill to the south and the River Besòs to the north (see Figure 10.1). Both are natural boundary elements because they are obstacles in the way of the urban fabric. The city's administrative boundaries are the left channel of the river and the free zone (Zona Franca) beyond Montjuïc. The latter of these two areas has not been regenerated in accordance with the previously described parameters. It is still a logistics area associated with the productive sector and serving the industrial port (there is no public access to it).

Three of Barcelona's districts have waterfronts: Montjuïc, Ciutat Vella and Sant Martí. All three have similar surface areas, ranging from 400 to 500 hectares. Despite that, it is worth noting the significant differences in the number of inhabitants and, consequently, the density of the population. This ranges from 88 inhabitants per hectare in Montjuïc to 237 inhabitants per hectare in Ciutat Vella (148 inhabitants per hectare in Sant Martí). Each district is made up of a number of neighbourhoods, and in each case, it is possible to find a distinct urban structure, which establishes a particular way of relating to the waterfront. In the case of Montjuïc district, only one neighbourhood, Poble Sec (5) has access to the sea. However, accessibility to it is reduced because of the topography of the hill and the adjacent location of the commercial port. Visual contact with the sea can only be gained from certain altitudes of Montjuïc Park, and it is impossible to reach the waterfront via public spaces. In the case of Ciutat Vella district, only four neighbourhoods have access to the sea. They are: Raval (1), Barri Gòtic (2), Sant Pere, Santa Caterina and La Ribera (3) and Barceloneta (4). Each one has a specific urban fabric, meaning that a clear distinction can be made between the respective relationships they have with the city's waterfront. Only the

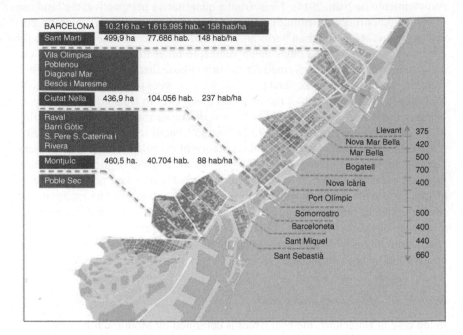

Figure 10.1 Barcelona's waterfront area, with general data for the districts and neighbourhoods forming part of it. It also includes the different beaches in the
area, with the length of each one.

Barceloneta has access to the waterfront via beaches, while the others have different degrees of access to it via Port Vell (now a marina). Finally, in Sant Martí
district, there are four neighbourhoods in contact with the sea. They are Vila
Olímpica (6), Poblenou (7), Diagonal Mar (8), and Besòs and Maresme (9). All of
them have easy access to the waterfront via the various beaches that were laid out
in relation to the large rainwater collectors built in Barcelona as part of the works
done as a result of the 1992 Olympic Games being awarded to Barcelona. In the
delimited area, there are 10 beaches ranging in length from 375 to 700 metres.
At the southerly end is the industrial and commercial port (Montjuïc), in the middle a marina (Port Olímpic in Vila Olímpica), and at the northerly end another
marina that is smaller than the former (Port del Fòrum in Besòs i Maresme). It is
possible to walk, run, cycle, and so on along nearly all of the city's coastline by
taking one stretch of the seafront promenade after another.

Land use: facilities and parks

The analysis of the waterfront from the perspective of elements that facilitate
sport and physical activity on Barcelona's waterfront was also performed by taking into consideration uses, both quantitatively (percentages compared to the
city) and qualitatively (characteristics and location of the facilities). By taking

this approach, the land use of the neighbourhoods making up the waterfront was broken down, by percentage, into facilities, urban parks and the road network compared to the entire city, with very significant values in all three cases. While the area under study represents approximately 13% of the city (in terms of both the number of inhabitants and surface area), the proportionality in terms of uses is not maintained, as the percentage in respect of uses that facilitate physical activity is higher. Thus, in respect of land use, the means for the area under study are 12% for facilities, nearly 21% for urban parks, and 28% for road networks (compared to 10%, 12% and 22%, respectively, for the entire city) (Table 10.1).

Focusing on facilities, those that, in one way or another, foster, organise or prescribe physical activity were taken into account, such as sports, educational and health facilities. Figure 10.2 locates the sports facilities in the area under study. It was found that the activities they encompassed were very diverse and linked to sports that could be classified as modern (basketball, football, futsal, swimming, *frontenis* [similar to squash], badminton, gymnastics, volleyball, tennis, handball, sailing and athletics), post-modern (yoga, martial arts, fitness training and padel tennis) or traditional (pétanque).

Regarding facilities, it was felt appropriate to consider education centres too. There is a clear relationship between physical activity and such centres, and this had a positive impact when it came to assessing the level of sport and physical activity done. Both curricular activities usually taking place in school playgrounds and extracurricular activities taking place outside school times were considered. Twenty-one education facilities dedicated to different levels of teaching were identified, including preschool, primary, secondary and even university-level centres.

Last, health facilities can also be considered as elements providing opportunities in the environment analysed, as they are places where physical activity is usually prescribed for either disease prevention or treatment purposes. In this case, very few centres were found – only one hospital, one health park and one primary care centre. Urban parks were located on the map in Figure 10.3 to see how much of the area was given over to isolated large green areas or whether there was a large, more extensive network of small parks scattered across the territory in a more or less uniform manner.

Services and accessibility

In the analysis of the parameter of services that facilitate the pursuit of sport, several aspects related to urban elements, sports equipment or the commercial sector were found. Of the urban elements representing a facilitative aspect of sport, it is worth highlighting the following: planters, public benches, children's play areas, recreation spaces, public fountains, ornamental fountains and trees along the street. A count of these elements in the neighbourhoods found that the presence of elements that facilitated the pursuit of sport was approximately 40% of the total for Barcelona, in all cases. It is worth recalling that in terms of size (number of inhabitants and surface area), the neighbourhoods that make up the waterfront only represent 13% of the city.

Table 10.1 General data and land use for each neighbourhood and urban elements for each district in Barcelona

	Barcelona	Ciutat Vella (1–4)					Sants-Montjuïc (5)	Sant Martí (6–9)				
	Total	1	2	3	4	$\bar{X}$	5	6	7	8	9	$\bar{X}$
General Information												
Population	1.615.985	48.485	17.257	15.674	22.632		40.704	9.191	32.208	12.289	23.998	**13,8**
Area (ha)	10.216	109,8	84,2	131,4	111,4		460,5	94,3	154,5	123,7	127,4	**13,7**
Land use (percentage)												
Residential	25,2	45,4	40,5	9,9	29,0		7,8	25,7	27,6	18,6	20,7	25,0
Facilities	10,7	13,8	11,3	11,4	10,5		27,0	7,5	10,6	8,3	12,9	12,6
Urban parks	11,9	11,6	7,1	7,9	31,7		47,6	14,3	14,3	36,7	17,8	21,0
Industry	13,6	9,5	12,0	31,7	4,8		1,6	15,8	16,6	9,5	14,8	12,9
Road network	22,7	19,8	28,6	38,9	23,9		15,9	36,7	30,9	26,8	33,8	**28,4**
Forest parks	15,9	0	0	0	0		0	0	0	0	0	0,0
Urban elements (units)												%
Planters	4.686		949				895		387			47,6
Public benches	33.031		1.750				4.608		8.043			43,6
Playgrounds	746		27				65		178			36,2
Recreational areas	117		3				12		14			24,8
Public fountains	1.658		101				195		335			38,1
Ornamental fountains	301		22				109		31			53,8
N. of trees in the streets	158.896		6.924				16.428		29.555			33,3

(Legend marker at top right: scale ● from 1 to 9, x)

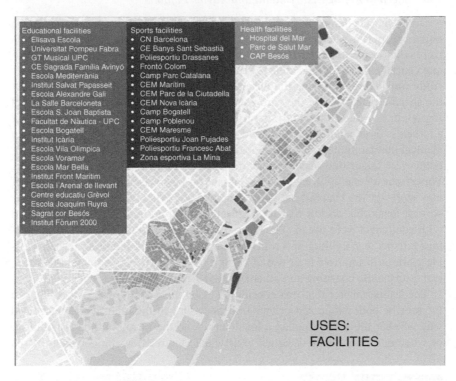

Educational facilities
- Elisava Escola
- Universitat Pompeu Fabra
- GT Musical UPC
- CE Sagrada Família Avinyó
- Escola Mediterrània
- Institut Salvat Papasseit
- Escola Alexandre Galí
- La Salle Barceloneta
- Escola S. Joan Baptista
- Facultat de Nàutica - UPC
- Escola Bogatell
- Institut Icària
- Escola Vila Olímpica
- Escola Voramar
- Escola Mar Bella
- Institut Front Marítim
- Escola l'Arenal de llevant
- Centre educatiu Grèvol
- Escola Joaquim Ruyra
- Sagrat cor Besós
- Institut Fòrum 2000

Sports facilities
- CN Barcelona
- CE Banys Sant Sebastià
- Poliesportiu Drassanes
- Frontó Colom
- Camp Parc Catalana
- CEM Marítim
- CEM Parc de la Ciutadella
- CEM Nova Icària
- Camp Bogatell
- Camp Poblenou
- CEM Maresme
- Poliesportiu Joan Pujades
- Poliesportiu Francesc Abat
- Zona esportiva La Mina

Health facilities
- Hospital del Mar
- Parc de Salut Mar
- CAP Besós

USES:
FACILITIES

Figure 10.2 Location of education, sports and health facilities that organise, encourage or prescribe physical activity.

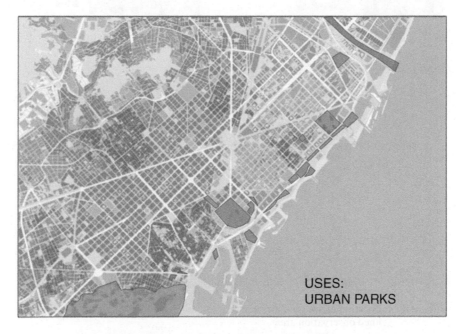

USES:
URBAN PARKS

Figure 10.3 Location of urban parks on Barcelona's waterfront.

Of the sports equipment in the area under analysis, elements that facilitate the pursuit of sport in public spaces were identified (such as goals, baskets or nets), as were other elements that, in their own right, configured the sports space (pétanque courts and table tennis areas). The location of these spaces in the area under study was identified during the observation phase, providing information about the specific places where they are usually situated (Figure 10.4). It was deemed important to perform an analysis of the commercial sector that, in one way or another, is associated with sport and physical activity, as it was considered an element that facilitates activity. Shops selling, hiring and repairing sports equipment were taken into account, identified and located in the area under study. Waterfront regeneration has had an impact on businesses, with the creation of new stores or the transformation of a number of existing ones. In some cases, several firms that do not restrict themselves to providing a service associated with equipment were found. They also offered guides to take people out on certain circuits (e.g. cycling and roller-skating circuits) and monitors to help people learn or to improve their use of certain pieces of sports equipment (surfing, stand-up paddle boarding and other sea-based activities).

The last parameter that was considered essential to study was accessibility to the area by both public and private transport. One of the main issues addressed was whether the area provided a local service to the neighbourhoods within it, or whether it was a zone designed to articulate the relationship between the sea

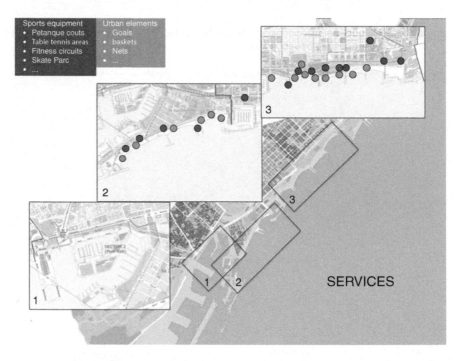

Figure 10.4 Location of sports equipment and urban elements for sport in the three defined observation areas.

and the city as a whole. Therefore, in order to demonstrate that it was accessible to all citizens, an analysis was performed of both public and private transport. Regarding public transport, a study located the stops of 24 urban bus routes on the waterfront (see Figure 10.5). In order to establish the extent to which they enabled people to get to other parts of the city, a graphic representation was produced of lines connecting the located stops with the ends of each line. By doing so, a fan-like structure covering the entire city was obtained. Moreover, the structure showed that there were connections with other neighbouring cities like Sant Adrià, Hospitalet and El Prat, among others. The same was done for the underground network, although only two lines have stops in the area under study (lines 3 and 4). As there is an integrated transport fare system in place, other lines that have stops connecting to those identified previously were also mapped. This enabled a tree-shaped graph to be obtained, showing that it was also possible to connect to other urban lines (1, 2, 5, 6 and 7), thereby encompassing the entire urban fabric. Regarding the bicycle public transport service, *bicing* (this is the official name of the bike sharing programme) stations were located along the city's urban waterfront, and it was found that none of the areas was unserved. In the same way as for public transport, only the closest stations were of interest, but it was felt appropriate to map them all because of an often-encountered problem of arriving at a station, only to find that it is full (people then have to go the nearest one with free spaces).

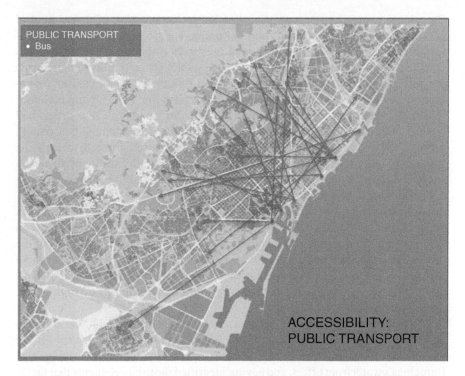

Figure 10.5 Analysis of the different urban bus routes of Barcelona that have a stop at the waterfront.

Regarding private transport, two things had to be checked. First, ease of access via the road network and, second, ease of parking (both cars and bicycles were considered private transport). Having analysed cycle lanes, it was found that there is a specific lane along the entire length of the waterfront, thus configuring what could indeed be called a green bypass. Cycle lanes in other areas of the city can be accessed via several cross-city roads (Paral·lel, Drassanes, Les Rambles, Ciutadella, Marina, Ciutat de Granada, Diagonal and Rambla Prim). Regarding roads for access by car, accessibility to Barcelona's entire waterfront was found to be very easy because the Ronda Litoral (B-10, with four exits to the area under study) runs all the way along it. The Ronda Litoral is a highway free from traffic lights that bypasses the city. Parking was found to be a little more complicated because there are only 12 public car parks in zones 1 and 2 (Port Vell and Barceloneta) and just one in the Fòrum area. Cars have to be parked on the road in other areas of the waterfront. Despite the fact that there are roads along most of its length, their capacity is insufficient to absorb the numbers of cars present in the summer season, when the beaches fill up (in the area stretching from Port Olímpic to Fòrum, there are three lines of surface parking along the Passeig Marítim promenade).

Conclusions

Barcelona's waterfront regeneration has led to the creation of a new central area for the city based on sport and culture as leisure activities. These transformation processes began in Europe in the 1970s (Jauhiainen, 1995), and this coincided with the growing tendency to use public space to pursue new forms of sport and physical activity (Bach, 1993). In Barcelona, the waterfront regeneration process is considered to have started after the 1992 Olympic Games were awarded to Barcelona although a tendency to 'sportivise' the streets had already begun in 1980 (Pujadas & Sánchez, 2002). Barcelona City Council, through successive Strategic Plans for Sport, expressed its will to turn the waterfront into an opportunity to improve citizens' quality of life by fostering sport and physical activity. Since the urban design of public spaces has been shown to facilitate a more active lifestyle among residents (Rodriguez et al., 2006; Fusco, 2007), the aim of this study was to identify the indicators of such an opportunity. Barcelona's waterfront was found to have a series of urban elements that facilitate sport and physical activity, such as the proximity of the urban fabric, mixed land use (with a significant presence of facilities, parks and roads), the existence of facilitative services (sports equipment and shops associated with a particular sport) and very good accessibility by both public and private transport.

The redevelopment of Barcelona's waterfront has been praised for its ambition and innovation, and for focusing on the creation of open public space for the pursuit of leisure activities (Jones, 2010). In short, beyond the final image that Barcelona's waterfront offers, and having identified the urban elements that facilitate sport and physical activity, now it is time to consider potential extrapolation to other urban experiences. Given the approach taken to this study, transfer is a suitable formula in all urban regeneration of public spaces, and this is so for urban waterfronts where the memory of productive model transformations and city links is concentrated. It is, of course, an analysis tool, but in addition, it is an instrument for use by public authorities when devising plans that aim to promote a more active lifestyle among citizens.

References

Ayuntamiento de Irún (2014). *Código Urban Sasoi.* Irun: Ayuntamiento de Irún and IrunKirol.

Bach, L. (1993). Sport without facilities: The use of urban spaces by informal sports. *International review for the sociology of sports, 28,* 281–296.

Benach, N. (2000). Nuevos espacios de consumo y construcción de imagen de la ciudad de Barcelona olímpica. *Estudios geográficos, LXI,* 189–205.

Bové, M.A. & Guim, M. (2013). La eclosión turística de Barcelona: Política de planificación vs cooperación público-privada. *XXXIX Reunión de estudiós regionales/ international conference on regional science.* Oviedo (Asturias).

Bökemann, D. (1993). Sports technology and choice of location: Individual evaluation of sports facilities. *International Review for the sociology of sport, 28,* 299–310.

Braudel, F. (1969). *Ecrits sur l'histoire.* Paris, France: Flammarion.

Duro, J.A. & Rodriguez, D. (2015). Barcelona como municipio turístico: algunos datos evolutivos y elementos de futuro. *Documents d'anàlisi geogràfica, 61,* 507–538.

Fava, N. (2003). *Projetti e processi in clonflitto: Il fronte marittimo de Barcellona* (doctoral thesis). Barcelona, Spain: ETSAB-UPC.

Fusco, C. (2007). "Healthification" and the promises of urban space: A textual analysis of place, activity, youth (PLAY-ing) in the city. *International review for the sociology of sport, 42,* 43–63.

Gelabert, J. & Fàbregas, F. (1994). *Els equipaments esportius a Catalunya. Documents del Pla Director d'instal·lacions i equipaments esportius de Catalunya. Actuacions de la Secretaria General de l'Esport en matèria d'equipaments esportius.* Barcelona, Spain: Secretaria General de l'Esport.

Generalitat de Catalunya. (2005). *PIEC. Pla director d'instal·lacions i equipaments esportius de Catalunya.* Barcelona, Spain: Generalitat de Catalunya, Consell Català de l'Esport.

Gonçalves, A. & Thomas, H. (2012). Waterfront tourism and public art in Cardiff Bay and Lisbon's Park of Nations. *Journal of policy research in tourism, leisure & events, 4*(3), 327–352.

Jauhiainen, J.S. (1995). Waterfront redevelopment and urban policy: The case of Barcelona, Cardiff and Genoa. *European planning studies, 3,* 3–21.

Jones, A. (2010). Issues in waterfront regeneration: More sobering thoughts – a UK perspective. *Planning practice & research, 13,* 433–442.

Kostopoulou, S. (2013). On the revitalized waterfront: Creative milieu for creative tourism. *Sustainability, 5,* 4578–4593.

López Palomeque, F. (2015). Barcelona, de Ciudad con turismo a Ciudad turística. Notas sobre un proceso complejo e inacabado. *Documents d'anàlisi geogràfica, 61,* 483–506.

Morejon, S. (2010). *Pautes de disseny de les instal·lacions dels clubs de tennis de Catalunya* (doctoral thesis). Barcelona, Spain: FPCEE Blanquerna-UPC.

Nel·lo, O. (1992). *Les repercussions urbanístiques dels Jocs Olímpics de Barcelona'92.* Barcelona, Spain: CEO-UAB.

Norcliffe, G.B. (1981). Industrial change in old port areas, the case of the Port of Toronto. *Cahiers de géographie du Québec, 25,* 237–254.

Nóvoa, M. (1998). Una reflexión sobre la reciente transformación de Barcelona. *Revista da faculdade de letras–geografía,* Series I, *XIV,* 61–75.

Pujadas, X. (2001). L'espai d'ús esportiu en la formació de la Barcelona metròpoli (1870–1936). *L'avenç, 257,* 44–47.

Pujadas, X. & Sánchez, R. (2002). *Desarrollo urbano y usos deportivos y recrativos de la Ciudad: El caso de la Barcelona contemporània.* Congress of the Asociación Española de Ciencias del Deporte. Madrid, Spain: INEF.

Rodriguez, D.A., Khattak, A.J. & Evenson, K.R. (2006). Can new urbanism encourage physical activity? *Journal of American planning association, 72,* 43–54.

Selfa, J. (2005). Procesos de transformación urbana en la Barcelona postolímpica desde la perspectiva de la nueva geografía cultural. *Treballs de la societat Catalana de geografía, 60,* 109–125.

Turisme de Barcelona (2014). *Turisme a Barcelona. Informe anual 2014.* Barcelona, Spain: Turisme de Barcelona.

11 Economic effects of sports development strategies

Regeneration to support urban event and tourism strategies in five cities across the United States

Sangkwon Lee

Introduction

Using sport, events and tourism to stimulate economic growth in certain areas is a popular development strategy that a variety of levels of government have employed. These strategies have focused on regenerating urban areas and enhancing the image of city or country to attract tourists as a means of economic growth. Sport is an essential part of everyday life in American society, and the size of the sport industry is huge enough to affect noticeably some level of economy. Sport-driven development strategies have been increasingly popular to elected officials, developers and owners of professional sports organizations.

This chapter will discuss the relationship between sport, events and tourism development and urban regeneration in Arlington (Texas), Cleveland (Ohio), St. Louis (Missouri), Indianapolis (Indiana) and Santa Clara (California) and describe the role of public investment in the sport development strategies; explain the economic effects of public investment in the targeted community; and address how the economic consequences are distributed across different groups in the communities.

Urban regeneration and sport, events and tourism

Many cities in the United States have tried to use sport as a catalyst to regenerate urban downtown areas beset by a variety of problems such as manufacturing collapse, a perceived unsafe environment and a low quality of education. Local governments focused on how sport events can be utilised for economic growth in the local communities and provision of better quality of life and supported urban revitalization efforts, often focusing on sport, events, tourism and wider entertainment industries. Policy makers at various levels of government have looked towards sport not only to spark urban regeneration but also to reestablish the cultural importance of the downtown. Although sport facilities and sporting events are unlikely to generate huge economic impacts, they could contribute to the redevelopment of a certain area (Santo, 2010).

Urban regeneration through sport has been a popular and promising development strategy in the United States. In particular, the cities that experienced severe economic decline from the loss of manufacturing jobs and residents aggressively adopted sport development strategies to regain the sound economic status they had previously enjoyed for a long period of time. Cities that had numerous steel mills and oil refinery factories have tried to convert their manufacturing dependent economies into service dependent economies by focusing on sport, events, tourism, hospitality and entertainment. The deindustrialization, globalization and population loss partly forced policy makers to pay attention to sport, events and tourism as an alternative tool for economic growth. Attracting professional sports teams to these areas was a key to the development strategy. Many cities tried to create tourist attractions and places of consumption through sport-led development strategies.

Sport tourism is typically defined as 'leisure-based travel that takes individuals temporarily outside of their home communities to participate in physical activities (active sport tourism), to watch physical activities (event sport tourism), or to venerate attractions associated with physical activities (nostalgia sport tourism)' (Gibson, 1998, p. 49). Advocates of sport-led economic developments address that sport tourism brings economic benefits to host communities as a result of visitor's spending in accommodation, food and beverages, admission fees, transportation and other spending in the communities (Weed & Bull, 2009). The impacts of sport tourism are mostly measured in terms of its contribution towards the urban regeneration of the host community.

Sport tourism-led regeneration is the way sport is used in regenerating an area economically, socially, physically, and environmentally (Smith, 2007; Larissa, 2010) and events are increasingly recognised as an integral part of this. While sport facility projects did not produce regional economic growth, despite substantial public subsidies, local and state governments were convinced that such facility development would bring business, residents and tourists to downtown areas and generate a positive economic impact on the community. Sports became a development strategy to spur the local economy and public policies surfaced to embrace the new opportunity for downtowns (Turner & Rosentraub, 2002).

Many cities in the United States, like Cleveland and St. Louis, have built new sports facilities in their respective downtown areas with the expressed intention to bring economic prosperity. New sports facilities, however, have not historically provided resurgence in local economic activity. For example, Baade and Sanderson (1996) found that local communities were not likely to benefit from the construction and existence of a new sports facility. From a tourism perspective, Eisinger (2000) addressed that cities are justifying expenditures on global sporting events and professional sports facilities to attract tourists to the city and that leveraging of these events has little to do with the residents of surrounding communities. Instead, sports teams and facilities generate a very small scale of economic activity and cannot reverse the decentralization of residential and business activity that plagues most cities' downtown areas. Only a few studies have suggested that small-scale sporting events contribute to economic benefits for host economies (e.g. Jarvie, 2003; Wilson, 2006; Gibson *et al.*, 2012). In general, because new sports facilities have little success in regenerating a city's downtown area, critics question the validity of the sport development model to spur economic growth.

The usage of sports facilities is a major factor whether such facilities could bring economic benefits. Meeting the occupancy rate of sports facilities and diversifying entertainment and activity base is a key to financial success of new sports facilities and this is where there is a greater focus on the potential of events beyond the usual sports matches that are the primary function of such stadia. The frequency of the games and events attract more people to the downtown area, increasing expenditure and tax revenue in the targeted development area. For example, the Staples Center in Los Angeles, which has three professional sports tenants, typically hosts approximately 280 events per year and attracts over 4 million patrons (Crompton, 2014).

Arlington (Texas), Cleveland (Ohio), and St. Louis (Missouri) are all great examples of how cities have used sport as a key catalyst to boost economic growth. Additionally, the cases of Indianapolis (Indiana) and Santa Clara (California) will also be discussed when addressing sport, tourism and event related development strategies.

Arlington, Texas

Arlington is a city in Tarrant County, Texas located in the Dallas-Fort Worth metropolitan area. It has a population of 375,600 making it the 50th largest city in the United States. It has a very diverse economy supported by manufacturing, hospitality and tourism, logistics and trade, healthcare and life science, and professional services (City of Arlington, 2016). Arlington has two major sporting venues, AT&T Stadium (home of the National Football League [NFL] franchise Dallas Cowboys) and Globe Life Park (home of the Major League Baseball [MLB] franchise Texas Rangers).

The city of Arlington has aggressively adopted sport, tourism and event related development strategies. The Arlington Sports Facilities Development Authority, which was an institution in charge of building the sport facility, issued floating rate notes (a type of government bond) in 1992 ($70 million with a 4.35% initial interest rate) and 1993 ($60 million with a 4.3% initial interest rate). In 1993, the city sold $135 million (71% of total cost) in bonds to build a ballpark (now Globe Life Park) for the Texas Rangers. The bond would be covered by a 0.5% increase to the general sales tax. Although the ballpark did not serve as an anchor for additional economic development, the 20-year debt was paid off 10 years early. Revenue generated by the sales tax increase, due to a thriving economy in the mid-to-late 1990s in the Dallas-Fort Worth metropolitan area, combined with annual $3.5 million rental payments from the team, allowed the city of Arlington to retire the bonds and expire the tax increase 10 years ahead of schedule in 2001.

The AT&T Stadium opened in 2009 and cost $1.3 billion to build with a partial public subsidy. In 2004, voters in the city approved a sales tax increase to subsidise a 30-year, $325 million bond package designed to pay for the new stadium. The new stadium would provide thousands of jobs and expanding sales tax revenue.

Additionally, the new revenue stream with the $500,000 from the Cowboys' naming rights deal with AT&T was expected. The city officials also expected more than 100,000 people to spend money in the Arlington area from hosting a variety of sport and entertainment events such as the Super Bowl, the 2014 National Collegiate Athletic Association (NCAA) Men's Final Four, the NCAA College Football Playoff and the Cotton Bowl. While the bonds are expected to be retired in 2021, AT&T Stadium is on pace to be paid off 14 years early. The value of the Cowboys, the most valuable team in the NFL, is approximately $2.1 billion and the owner of the team has a net worth of $2.7 billion (Cluck, 2013). The state-of-the art stadium (e.g. luxury suite, personal seat license) plays a crucial role in increasing the financial benefits to the players and owner of the professional sport team.

Mills *et al.* (2014) found that Arlington's aggressive development strategies have resulted in the city's ability to export tax revenue used for its investment. The net positive economic outcome for the area is less clear than the simple change in tax revenues. While sales tax revenues increased with the tax rate increases, economic activity decreased within Arlington. The residents in Arlington could pay more for goods and services and reduce their consumption of these goods due to the sales tax, or they must absorb higher transportation costs to travel to retail centers where the extra sales tax is not charged. Local retailers may also have suffered from lower revenues. The study concluded, 'Arlington's experience with sport facilities identifies an instance where positive fiscal outcomes from a public investment for some cities could exist, but the economic impact on the private sector and/or consumers within the city as a whole was less desirable' (Mills *et al.*, 2014, p. 151).

Recently, to enhance economic activity in the surrounding area, the city of Arlington and the Texas Rangers began collaborating on a $200 million mixed-use development near Global Life Park. The development agreement, which would be a public-private partnership between the city and the Texas Rangers, includes about 100,000 square feet of restaurant, retail and entertainment space near the ballpark. The developer is requesting $50 million worth of development incentives from the city for the project, and the Texas Rangers would pay the rest of the cost. If the project succeeds, the city would give the Texas Rangers performance-based incentives including income from property, sales, mixed beverage and hotel occupancy tax for 30 years. It also would include hotel occupancy and sales tax income from the state for 10 years (Cardona, 2015).

In terms of the effectiveness of economic contribution, the sport facilities in Arlington have provided little economic benefits to the community. Given the circumstances the sport facilities in Arlington are facing, a facility cannot be a catalyst for economic development if it is an island surrounded by parking lots (Baade & Dye, 1988). Similar to Arlington, many new stadiums do not stimulate surrounding economic development because they are not physically interwoven with other components of the urban fabric (Crompton, 2014). Because of the locations of sport facilities, their urban integration is often limited to supplying parking facilities close to the downtown business district.

Cleveland, Ohio

The Central Market Gateway Project (Gateway Project) initiated by the city of Cleveland is a sport development strategy to regenerate its downtown area. The project included an MLB park (now Progressive Field) and a new arena (now Quicken Loans Arena) to attract the Cleveland Cavaliers (National Basketball Association franchise) back to the downtown area of the city. *Cleveland Tomorrow*, a council of the chief executives of the region's large corporations, contributed to construction costs, and local business interests helped develop a $1 million campaign to support a tax referendum to fund the project. The Gateway Project was finally approved in 1990 and both facilities were opened in 1994.

The sports facilities in Cleveland are part of a huge downtown revitalization push that included the Gateway Complex, the Rock and Roll Hall of Fame and Museum, and the Science Center and IMAX theatre built nearby on the downtown lakefront. The true backbone of Gateway's success has been its emergence as a neighborhood. Ten housing projects incorporating 16 historic buildings have yielded 698 units, putting the neighborhood only slightly behind Cleveland's thriving warehouse district, which reached sufficient size to begin attracting restaurants and other traditional retail outlets.

After using the sport facilities for the last two decades, the professional sports teams in Cleveland constantly requested the local governments to subsidise the renovations of existing sports facilities. In 2014, the Cuyahoga County voters approved a 20-year extension of the sin tax (alcohol and cigarette), which took effect in August 2015. The sin tax is expected to raise a total of $260 million for Progressive Field, Quicken Loans Arena, and the FirstEnergy Stadium (home of the NFL franchise Cleveland Browns) to pay for the sport facilities' upkeep and to pay off sport facilities-related debt. The annual payments to cover principle and interest are estimated to be approximately $6.5 million. The county borrowed $120 million in 1992 and 1994 to build Quicken Loans Arena and Progressive Field and still owed $55.1 million as of January 2015. Cuyahoga County Council plans to sell 10-year, $65 million bonds to pay for improvements to Progressive Field and Quicken Loans Arena.

Cleveland has been able to make the image of the Gateway district and the downtown vibrant urban center by using sport development strategies. The Gateway Project is often considered a worthy investment for the municipality. The downtown revitalization associated with Cleveland's sports facilities has been frequently cited an example of sports facilities acting as catalysts for urban renewal and development. First, the financial deal provides for a fair split of stadium revenues to enable the city to cover its debt payments and for the team to improve its profits. Second, the new sport facilities have been successful in economic growth and job creation. Third, the city has been successful in regenerating its respective downtown area through the sport development projects. Finally, the project has succeeded because its developers and stakeholders were able to integrate existing structures, rather than starting from scratch, offering tax breaks to those who rescue historic buildings (Muret & King, 2004).

It is worth noting that the development project has some drawbacks. The largest criticism is that although 800 units of housing, intending to attract middle to high-income residents, have been added to the downtown and the Gateway district, it is unaffordable to low-income households. Such relatively high housing costs caused the area to displace residents. While the success of the site has spilled over into the downtown area and connected the city, this spillover effect has been limited because it has caused other areas to be abandoned. In addition to the displacement of residents, affordability and unequal distribution of economic benefits from the development are major problems. Cleveland's experience indicates that sport facilities can play an important role in urban revitalization efforts, catalyzing district redevelopment in the form of hotels, residences and retail businesses (Chapin, 2004).

St. Louis, Missouri

St. Louis had attracted the Rams (NFL franchise) away from Los Angeles with an appealing stadium deal that has now turned into nothing short of a fiscal disaster for the region and the state of Missouri. The Edward Jones Dome construction was funded by 50% financing from the state and 25% from the county and city, respectively. The three governments paid $24 million annually to cover debt and stadium upkeep. In 1995, the city of St. Louis opened the Edward Jones Dome for the St. Louis Rams. The stadium was financed in part by $126 million in a series of bonds that would ultimately cost $720 million issued by the state of Missouri, the county of St. Louis, and the city of St. Louis (Waldron, 2012). The revenue sharing component of the financial agreement between the three governments and the Rams is lopsided in favor of the team. The agreement provides for the Rams to receive all $74 million generated by the sale of personal seat licenses (PSLs), 100% of the revenue generated by the Edward Jones Dome's 122 suites and 6200 club seats, and 75% of the stadium's advertising revenue. The city, county and state governments, however, only collectively receive $250,000 in annual rent, an estimated $1 million in annual admission taxes, and 25% of the stadium's advertising revenue. In this case, it is clear that the Edward Jones Dome was not a sound investment for the taxpayers. The stadium was wholly financed just 17 years into its 30-year lease. The Rams asked for major renovations to the stadium thanks to a deal that requires the city to maintain its 'first tier' status, meaning the sport facility must be considered among the top quarter of all NFL facilities.

Decades later, St. Louis was able to resist having significant public funds go into the construction of new Busch Stadium. However, after seven years, construction was finally completed on the $100 million phase of Ballpark Village, a Cardinal-themed consortium of restaurants and a team museum (Leichenger, 2014). The downtown regeneration project employed tax-increment finances (TIF). TIF subsidies typically take a portion of tax revenue generated from development projects and put them back towards paying off the construction debt. Therefore, if a facility does not keep pace with its expected revenue, then taxpayers are likely to pay the cost (Leichenger, 2014). Lipsitz (1984) indicated that the mid-1960s construction of Busch Memorial Stadium (the old home of the St. Louis Cardinals) brought profit to corporations at the expense of residents. While city services declined and families and resources fled to the suburbs, St. Louis' urban renewal commission, *Civic Progress*, made blighted areas downtown into tax-free zones for development.

The city, county and state governments tried to keep the St. Louis Rams, threatening relocation to Los Angeles after the 2015–16 season. The St. Louis Stadium Task Force proposed spending more than $470 million in city, county and state tax dollars to build a new stadium for the Rams. However, in 2016, the St. Louis Rams moved to Los Angeles after constantly threatening relocation to the city. As of January 2015, city and state taxpayers still owed more than $100 million in debt on the bonds used to finance the Edward Jones Dome, which the city, the county and the state spent $280 million in public funds in 1995. The sport facility and new team had no noticeable effect on tax revenue, aside from a small increase in income tax receipts. As for urban regeneration, the Bottle District, immediately north of the stadium, is an empty lot (Miller, 2015).

Public subsidy and economic impact of sports development on local economies

In the United States, the total investment in sport facilities for professional sports teams in the four major leagues in the past two decades was approximately $37 billion. The public sector's contribution was approximately $20 billion (Crompton, 2014). It means that 54% of total investment was funded by public money. The NFL's 29 stadiums have received public money for construction or renovation. Over the last two decades, taxpayers across the country have spent nearly $7 billion on stadiums for the league that surpassed $10 billion in revenue in the 2014 season. Taxpayers contributed an average of $262 million to each NFL stadium built between 1990 and 2010, about $60 million more than the average MLB ballpark received (Waldron, 2015).

One of the unique characteristics of financing sports facilities in the United States is that a majority of sports facilities exclusively used or operated by professional sports team owners have been funded through public subsidies. Local and state governments have used a variety of public money to help build sports facilities that were considered a powerful tool for economic growth and urban redevelopment or regeneration of their communities (Santo, 2010). The economic rationale of sport related development, which advocates of sport development strategy heavily rely on, is that new money from out of town visitors' spending would increase sales, tax revenues, and employment in the area.

Some studies, nevertheless, reported that there are no or little economic benefits derived from professional sports franchises and sporting events to the communities (e.g. Baade, 1996; Baade & Sanderson, 1997; Noll & Zimbalist, 1997; Coates & Humphreys, 2003). Researchers have found that professional sports franchises have civic pride and quality of life benefits for local residents, but it has also found that spending pubic money on the stadiums has little economic benefits and rarely creates the jobs. Even though most major sport facilities do not directly generate tax revenues for a city, they serve as catalysts, which stimulate proximate retail, commercial and residential development. Hosting sporting events showed different outcomes concerning economic benefits depending on the scale of the event. In general, while hosting mega-events such as the Olympic Games and the FIFA World Cup made little contribution to economic benefits, hosting small-scale events such as local and regional tournaments brought economic benefits to the host communities.

There are two distinct groups that contrast results on economic benefits associated with the economic impact of sport, tourism and event related developments. The ex-ante economic impact studies conclude that sport developments typically bring economic benefits to the targeted areas. Advocates of sport development maintain that sports facilities contribute to make a city create a positive image and provide economic benefits by increasing tourism and urban regeneration. The ex-post economic impact studies, however, address that sport developments rarely contribute to economic growth. This contrast in economic consequences mainly comes from analysis methods the researchers select. The studies that employed input-output analysis-based methods typically produce economic benefits while the studies that used econometric-based methods show little or no economic benefits (Baade & Matheson, 2004; Delaney & Eckstein, 2007; Eckstein *et al.*, 2010).

Proponents of sport development strategies often claim that revenue generated from the lease of sport facilities, taxes, and other sources such as naming rights and parking fees will be sufficient to cover a city's expenditures. However, numerous studies conducted by sports economists presented that economic contributions to local economies from sport teams, events and facilities are exaggerated (e.g. Siegfried & Zimbalist, 2000; Crompton, 2006; Porter & Fletcher, 2008; Matheson, 2009). In reality, sports facilities do not generate any new revenue and they are costly to maintain. It is important for cities that a certain level of economic activity is generated from sporting events. Sports economists note that money spent on sports would have otherwise been spent on other leisure and entertainment activities. This substitution effect does not create any new net income for the city and its businesses that would not have existed but for the presence of the sports facilities. Proponents of sport development strategies also address that the development create jobs. Although the number of jobs increases because of the development, the types of jobs that new sports facilities create tend to be low-wage, part-time and seasonal. These facts suggest why sports development strategies do not induce the same magnitude of economic activity as other types of public investments such as public infrastructure and education. Austrian and Rausentraub (2002) examined whether sport development strategies affect urban regeneration. The authors pointed out the difference between such effects and effects on overall economic activity in the area:

> If the justification for using public resources to build downtown sport facilities is that these structures will shift economic activity to an area that needs redevelopment, then the issue is not whether overall economic activity increased or decreased, but whether the vitality or centrality of the downtown area was enhanced or sustained.
>
> (Austrian & Rausentraub, 2002, p. 551)

Many new sports facility deals do not provide the respective host cities with sufficient revenue to meet financial obligations. Therefore, cities try to seek to collect enough revenue from the new sports facility to cover their debt service payments and up-front costs. In addition, cities should seek to gain economic benefits such as job creation, downtown revitalization and additional tax revenue from various businesses. Cleveland, Indianapolis, Los Angeles and San Diego have been regarded as cities in which sport projects have been an effective catalyst for urban regeneration. The main factor of the success was that the investments in these cities were concentrated in a relatively small area (Crompton, 2014).

Distribution of economic consequences: Winners and losers

It is worth noting the fact that even if there are some economic benefits generated from sport facilities and sporting events, an unequal distribution of economic consequences among different groups in the communities is another concern from an equity perspective. Because sports facilities were funded with public money, equity across different groups in distributing resources should be seriously considered. Thus, the public subsidy of sport facilities and events has been one of main topics of interest to researchers, policy makers, and practitioners in the sport, tourism and event management fields.

There are always winners and losers in the distribution of economic consequences associated with sport tourism and event related developments. As mentioned above, using sport developments as catalysts is one of the popular economic development strategies for local and state governments in the United States. The winners, benefiting economic consequences from the developments, include elected officials, developers and owners of professional sports organizations (Swindell & Rosentraub, 1998). Most other stakeholders, including residents, lose out, especially when public money is used to subsidise building sport facilities and hosting sporting events. In particular, the burden of public subsidy falls disproportionately on small cities that are the least able to bear the cost.

In 2014, the San Francisco 49ers (NFL franchise) moved from the Candlestick Park Stadium to the $1.3 billion Levi's Stadium in Santa Clara, a suburb of San Francisco, California. In 2007, to lure the San Francisco 49ers, the city council began negotiations with the team owners, with promises that no new taxes would be needed and that the huge and luxurious stadium would bring additional revenues without liability. On 8 June 2010, Measure J was passed with 15,000 voters in favor and 10,000 against. The advocates of building the sport facility persuaded the voters with the following language in the ballot:

> No use of City General and Enterprise Funds for construction; no new taxes for residents for stadium; private party pays all construction cost overruns; no City/Agency obligation for stadium operation/maintenance.

Within a year, however, that ballot language had been changed. Twelve percent of the cost of the $1.3 billion stadium was provided by the city, with another

$330 million to be borrowed by the city's Stadium Authority. That would bring the taxpayers' costs for the Levi's Stadium to more than $200 million, not counting any obligation incurred by the Stadium Authority. As a result, Santa Clara taxpayers ended up on the book for over $200 million in public subsidies – an amount that exceeds the entire city's annual budget of $140 million. The public subsidy for a new stadium costs a small city approximately $1,650 per resident.

On the other hand, thanks to the Central Market Gateway Project in Cleveland, owners of the professional sport organizations gained increased revenues from the new facilities equipped with many revenue-focused features. Downtown business interests and landowners witnessed renewed and vibrant economic activities helped increase property values. These benefits were quite concentrated on a handful of people and the favorable lease terms negotiated with the professional sport organizations have limited the direct financial benefit of the project to the public with the small overall economic impact of the project. Cleveland is generally regarded as one of the successful sport developments compared with other cities in the United States. In terms of the distribution of economic consequences, there is a huge gap between groups in the community. Collins and Grineski (2007) also maintained that sport facilities do not generate wealth, but rather redistribute it for a handful of business operators. Additionally, sport development strategies often result in the displacement of the poor living in the cities. The main purpose of government investments is to strengthen a city's tax base through attracting richer residents to the targeted area. The increasing gentrification of sport is a key cause not only to replace working classes with wealthier residents, but also to attract more affluent businesses. It also contributes to enhancing a city's image. Therefore, it is apparent that economic benefits and costs from sport, tourism and event related developments are disproportionately distributed across different groups.

Sport development and public subsidy

Is it acceptable to continue supporting sport development through taxpayers' money? Sport, tourism and event related development strategies are also open to questions regarding efficiency and opportunity costs (Santo, 2010). When selecting public policy strategy, the opportunity costs should be considered as a critical factor. Opportunity costs are the benefits that would be forthcoming if the public resources committed to a sport development project were redirected to other public services or retained by the taxpayer (Crompton, 2014). In other words, opportunity costs are the notion of how the public money has been spent on the next best alterative. The city of Indianapolis shows why considering opportunity cost is important in public policy:

> To pay off the initial Pacers arena cost and a new stadium for the Colts, Indianapolis' Capital Improvement Board had cut off all of its arts and tourism grants. In addition, the city not only funneled city property-tax revenues to the board but also asked to reduce library hours and close public pools due to budget shortfalls
>
> (deMause, 2013).

In the cities that used pubic subsidy for sports facilities and sporting events, state and local governments removed or reduced public services, reducing education budgets, and selling local hospitals, even while they asked taxpayers to pay for new and existing sports facilities. It is, therefore, not recommended to use sport development strategies for the regeneration of a city, and numerous studies indicate that sport development strategies are not effective tools to boost the local economies (e.g. Siegfried & Zimbalist, 2000; Baade & Matheson, 2004; Collins & Grineski, 2007). In addition, the strategies made the distribution of economic consequences worse across different stakeholders in the area.

Another important factor that affects public policy strategy is a policy maker's perspective. Which perspective should be taken as public policy makers: For the few or the majority? It is critical to consider how public resources are distributed to different stakeholders in implementing public policies. If policy makers focus on a small number of stakeholders such as elected officials, property developers and the owners of professional sport teams, they are more likely to use taxpayers' money to subsidise the construction of sport facilities that rarely contribute to economic growth. On the other hand, if policy makers take care of ordinary residents, they are more likely to use public money to enhance the quality of life of residents through providing quality public services such as public education, parks or recreation facilities. From a public consumption perspective, critics of new sports facilities point out that ticket prices for major league sporting events have risen to the point where many local residents cannot afford to take advantage of the new facility. A new sports facility would provide access to fewer people in the community than a pubic park and recreation facility. As a result, critics argue new sports facilities are inefficient public investment options. When sporting facilities or events are presented as part of urban policy agendas, stakeholders typically pay attention to both positive economic and social impacts that can be derived from sporting facilities or events. Therefore, selections to use public resources on sport facilities or sporting events are justified as being for the greater good of residents (Misener & Mason, 2006).

Conclusion

This chapter described the relationship between sport, tourism and event-led development through urban regeneration and the role of public investment. In addition, the economic effects of sport, tourism and event related development, focusing primarily on sport facilities, were discussed. Finally, this chapter addressed the distribution of economic consequences from the sport, tourism and event developments across diverse stakeholders. Although many studies highlight little positive economic impacts from sport, tourism and event developments, many local and state governments still have a tendency to use sport developments as catalysts for economic growth and urban regeneration. As a result, they are likely to provide a variety of economic incentives to lure and keep professional sport organizations. Public investment and tax-exempt status policy are widely used economic incentives while many local residents cannot afford to attend professional sporting events because of the high costs of tickets, parking and food, beverage and souvenir concessions. Public subsidy for private professional teams inevitably brings a significant controversy on equity across groups in a community.

The experiences obtained from the past sport, tourism and event developments require a different approach that aims for a more equitable distribution of economic consequences. Procedural and distributive justice should be considered during the entire planning, implementing, and controlling phases. A 'community benefits agreement' is one of the practical approaches that policy makers need to adopt to solve current problems associated with sport, tourism and event developments in relation to urban regeneration. Community benefits agreements are referred to as contracts negotiated between private developers and community-based coalitions (Cain, 2014). Since the late 1990s, community benefits agreements have been adopted as a strategy to proportionally distribute the economic consequences of sport developments between groups in a community. Based on many academic and practical resources, it is imperative to find an equitable and effective approach for successful urban regeneration through sport, tourism and event development strategies.

References

Austrian, Z. & Rosentraub, M.S. (2002). Cities, sports and economic change: A retrospective assessment. *Journal of urban affairs, 18*, 1–17.

Baade, R.A. & Dye, R.F. (1988). An analysis of economic rationale for public subsidization of sport stadiums. *The annals of regional science, 22*, 37–47.

Baade, R.A. & Matheson, V.A. (2004). The quest for the cup: Assessing the economic impact of the World Cup. *Regional studies, 38*, 343–354.

Baade, R.A. & Sanderson, A. (1996). Field of fantasies. *Intellectual ammunition*, March/April.

Cain, C. (2014). Negotiating with the growth machine: Community benefits agreements and value-conscious growth. *Sociological forum, 29*, 937–958.

Cardona, C.Z. (2015). Arlington considering $200 million proposed development near Rangers ballpark. *The Dallas morning news*. 12 December.

Chapin, T.S. (2004). Sports facilities as urban redevelopment catalysts. *Journal of the American planning association, 70*, 193–209.

City of Arlington (2016). http://www.arlington-tx.gov/business/ecodev/arlington-overview/.

Cluck, R. (2013). Big win for Arlington, thanks to Dallas Cowboys. 13 September, http://www.billmoyers.com.

Coates, D. & Humphreys, B.R. (2003). Professional sports facilities, franchises, and urban economic development. *Public finance and management, 3*, 335–357.

Collins, T.W. & Grineski, S.E. (2007). Unequal impacts of downtown redevelopment: The case of stadium building in Phoenix, Arizona. *Journal of poverty, 11*, 23–54.

Crompton, J.L. (2014). Proximate development: An alternate justification for public investment in major sport facilities? *Managing leisure, 19*, 1–20.

Crompton, J.L. (2006). Economic impact studies: Instruments for political shenanigans? *Journal of travel research, 45*, 67–82.

Delaney, K.J. & Eckstein, R. (2007). Urban power structures and publicly financed stadiums. *Sociological forum, 22*, 331–353.

deMause, Neil. (2013). Do cities gain from subsidizing sports teams? *Aljazeera.* 21 August.

Eckstein, R., Moss, D. & Delaney, K.J. (2010). Sports sociology's still untapped potential. *Sociological forum, 25*, 500–518.

Eisinger, P. (2000). The politics of bread and circuses: Building the city for the visitor class. *Urban affair review, 35*, 316–333.

Gibson, H. (1998). Sport tourism: A critical analysis of research. *Sport management review, 1*, 45–79.

Gibson, H.J., Kaplanidou, K. & Kang, S.J. (2012). Small-scale event sport tourism: A case study in sustainable tourism. *Sport management review, 15*, 160–170.

Gratton, C., Shilbli, S. & Coleman, R. (2005). Sport and economic regeneration in cities. *Urban studies, 42*, 985–999.

Jarvie, G. (2003). Communitarianism, sport, and social capital: Neighbourly insights into Scottish sport. *International review for the sociology of sport, 38*, 139–153.

Larissa, D. (2010). Sport and economic regeneration: A winning combination? *Sport in society, 13*(10), 1438–1457.

Leichenger, A. (2014). St. Louis, stadium funding and urban renewal that doesn't actually renew. *BEACON,* 16 December.

Matheson, V.A. (2009). Economic multipliers and mega-event analysis. *International journal of sport finance, 4*, 63–70.

Miller, J. (2015). Falling prey to the fallacy of tailgate economic. *Heartland institute,* 23 April.

Mills, B.M., Rosentrau, M.S., Winfree, J.A. & Cantor, M.B. (2014). Fiscal outcomes and tax impacts from stadium financing strategies in Arlington, Texas. *Public money & management,* March, 145–152.

Misener, L. & Mason, D.S. (2006). Creating community networks: Can sporting events offer meaningful source of social capital? *Managing leisure, 11*, 39–56.

Muret, D. & King, B. (2004). Sports-driven projects a tough sell. *Street & Smith's sports-business journal,* 15–21.

Noll, R.G. & Zimbalist, A. (1997). *Sports, jobs, and taxes: The economic impact of sports teams and stadiums.* Washington, DC: Brookings Institution Press.

Parlow, M.J. (2014). Publicly financed sports facilities: Are they economically justifiable? A case study of the Los Angeles Staples Center. *University of Miami Business Law Review, 10*, 483–545.

Porter, P.K. & Fletcher, D. (2008). The economic impact of the Olympic Games: Ex ante predictions and ex poste reality. *Journal of sport management, 22*, 470–448.

Santo, C.A. (2010). The economic impact of sport stadiums, teams and events. In C.A. Santo & G.C.S. Mildner (Eds.). *Sport and public policy: Social, political, and economic* perspectives. Champaign, IL: Human Kinetics (pp. 49–64).

Siegfried, J. & Zimbalist, A. (2000). The economics of sports facilities and their communities. *The journal of economic perspectives, 14*, 95–114.

Smith, M.K. (2007). *Tourism, culture and regeneration.* Oxfordshire, UK: CAB International.

Swindell, D. & Rosentraub, M.S. (1998). Who benefits from the presence of professional sports teams? The implications for public funding of stadiums and arenas. *Public administration review, 58*, 11–20.

Waldron, T. (2015). Taxpayers have spent a staggering amount of money on NFL stadiums. *The Huffington post*, 10 September.

Waldron, T. (2012). Foul play: Five cities that want taxpayer money to finance pro sports stadium boongoggles. http://thinkprogress.org/economy/2012/06/12/496136/foul-play-five-cities-that-want-taxpayer-money-to-finance-stadium-boondoggles/.

Wilson, R. (2006). The economic impact of local sport events: Significant, limited or otherwise? A case study of fur swimming events. *Managing leisure, 11*, 57–70.

12 The role of sports tourism and events to regenerate and sustain off-season tourism in Istria, Croatia

Addressing perspectives from industry managers and planners

Nicholas Wise, Marko Perić and Tanja Armenski

Introduction

Istria County, positioned in the north and westernmost part of Croatia along the northern Adriatic coast, is a popular destination among tourists from central Europe. While the Istria region has existing tourism infrastructures already well developed, it is still important to consider regenerative strategies and attempts to diversify tourism and promote tourism during the off-season. Tourism managers and planners in Istria seek to create opportunities to maintain the regions competitive advantage. Sports tourism has been a focus in this region for some time, and across the region there have been numerous investments and plans aimed at regenerating sports infrastructure to attract more tourists and support events. The Mediterranean climate makes the region attractive to tourists during the warm dry summer months. For the sports tourist, the moderate climate and range of amenities enable year-round sports activity. Regenerating towns and cities to update sports tourism products, facilities and infrastructures represents an approach to develop year-round tourism. According to the Croatian Ministry of Tourism, in 2015 Istria County accounted for 23.5% of the total tourist arrivals and 29.3% of the total tourist overnight stays in Croatia (Ministry of Tourism, 2016). These are observed as slight decreases from previous years, which were just over 24% and 30%, respectively (Ministry of Tourism, 2015). Investing in new sports tourism opportunities and new facilities represents not only an attempt to increase tourism, but a strategy to establish new enterprises and benefits for a range of stakeholders.

For this study, we conducted an open-ended survey with seven industry managers (from the tourism, sports tourism and hospitality industries). To protect the identity of survey participants, we have not referred to peoples' names, using instead Participant 1–7. The objective of this chapter is to focus on strategic regeneration and management plans involving sport, tourism and event opportunities in Croatia's Istria Region, with much of the focus on Medulin and Pula. This part of Croatia has recently seen new investments in sport and events facilities. Observed as an attempt to regenerate the industry, this chapter builds on foundation research concerning Medulin (Wise & Perić, 2017). The purpose of our wider research is to discuss how different investments in a variety of sports create new opportunities. This is seen as developing and sustaining off-season tourism and also considers how locals can and will benefit. For locals involved or employed in tourism and the service sector in Croatia, employment is often limited during the winter months when tourism drastically declines or operations cease. Responses from sport and tourism industry managers from Medulin and Pula are presented here to show how sports tourism products are being developed and delivered to practically frame the direction of sports tourism-led regeneration efforts. This chapter will first discuss sports tourism-led regeneration in Istria before addressing perspectives from industry managers. Subsequent sections look at the need for upgraded facilities, tourism strategy and social impacts. These sections are followed by concluding remarks and some directions for future research.

Sports tourism regeneration in Medulin and Pula

Several cities on the Istrian Peninsula have developed sport-led tourism programs that are attracting visitors during the off-season months. Participant 7 referred to the need and 'desire to extend the season' and hinted that the industry required new investments to sustain the sports tourism and sports events industry in the future. Destinations across Istria are ideal for attracting both active and passive sporting tourists in the winter months according to one manager. Participant 2 suggests Istria 'is one of the most ideal in the region' for sports tourism. Participant 2 then refers to Medulin as a destination with 'perfect conditions for the development of winter sports tourism.' This participant referred to winter sports tourism, but they are referring to sports tourism during the winter months as the destination does not accumulate the amount of snowfall nor have the Alpine climate and environment as neighbouring countries to the north have (e.g. Slovenia, Italy and Austria).

Sports tourism initiatives and opportunities are contributing to the creation of an alternative, or niche, tourism agenda for the region. For instance, in Medulin, the regeneration of sports tourism infrastructure was recently completed in 2014 and the initiative is to generate tourism opportunities during the low tourism seasons from November to April. During these months, due to the winter temperatures, it is not ideal for sea/sun tourists, but the cooler temperature can be attractive for sports tourism and winter training. For example, football training in this area is attractive to clubs based in central and northern Europe (Austria, Germany, Slovenia and clubs around Croatia). The focus on sports and events is important in this region and there is a long tradition of sporting events and activities in this part of Croatia – an example being tennis camps and events in Istrian destinations such as Pula and Umag (see Perić & Wise, 2015). Cycling is also important and there has been a focus on further developing biking and running trails for subsequent leisure and recreational opportunities. Because cycling trails are improved along coastal and inland areas, this also benefits locals who can easily access biking and hiking trails. Concerning local social regeneration, this will help support infrastructure for locals and encourage wellbeing through recreational activity.

Discussing the importance of sport for destinations in Istria, Participant 2 acknowledges:

> Medulin is a recognised destination of winter sports tourism that generates tens of thousands of overnight guests, with their primary reason to visit being sport. This type of tourism in the long run held here, following the trends of modern sport and the needs of athletes. Since our goal is to become a regional leader in the gathering of professional and amateur athletes from different sports, we are forced to constantly invest in sports facilities and service.

Sports tourism and regular events during the winter play an important role in the local tourism and hospitality industries. A number of hotels in Istria would otherwise close during the winter months without sports tourism and events, and new investments in sports tourism facilities and sporting events represent an opportunity to keep more hotels open all year-round. In Medulin specifically, football training facilities have existed since the 1970s, but this recent development aims to attract more clubs to further develop the local sports tourism industry – creating a market niche that will help brand sports tourism in Istria. This is comparable to Spring Training for Major League Baseball in the United States, where teams train in Florida and Arizona because winter temperatures in many northern cities are not ideal. In Medulin six football pitches have been upgraded (these are managed by the hotels) to attract football clubs. Similarly, tennis facilities in Medulin and Pula allow for tennis camps and training activities. Regardless of the sports activity during the traditional off-tourism season, the expansion of this niche form of tourism helps the local hotel industry and the local population who are employed in tourism and supporting service sector industries.

Sports clubs and those who organise training camps for football or tennis now have more options, in addition to the upgraded fields and courts. Participant 2 added: 'We believe that the more content and better services will bring us more direct income in the winter times (low season) when it is very difficult to attract guests.' Adding more services is what several hotels in Medulin and Pula did. In addition to upgrading the spaces for sports activity, they also improved changing facilities, storage space for equipment, fitness/weightlifting facilities and some also employ nutritionists who work with sports clubs to ensure dietary requirements are met. There are also new conference/meeting rooms for strategic planning and skills teaching. In terms of organisation and investment, sports development is organised by Arenaturist and the Park Plaza Belvedere and their affiliates maintain the sporting facilities and rent the spaces in both Medulin and Pula. An important intention here is that such investments will create opportunities to sustain tourism in the off-season and assist with unemployment or underemployment. In addition to such economic benefits, there is the potential for well-being benefits for locals to make use of the new facilities to encourage active-healthy lifestyles (see Wise & Perić, 2017). There are numerous debates concerning how such investments will impact locals, but public initiatives and private investments are a step towards year-round tourism in this region, which relate to wider tourism strategies in Istria. The next section looks at perspectives concerning the need to upgrade sports facilities in the region.

The need to upgrade sports facilities

As noted above, sports tourism is not a new industry in Istria. However, as other similar destinations invest in new sporting facilities and infrastructures, for a destination to maintain its competitive advantage, this requires periodically improving facilities and infrastructures to ensure clients do not go elsewhere. This was clearly noted by one participant who mentions:

> The hotels have a rich history of sports tourism, but in recent years due to a lack of investment by the hotels in the sports facilities we observed a decline in arrivals of athletes. Those who came were from lower national sports leagues and had less purchasing power. We thought the reconstruction of the hotel to 4-Star standards and new investments in sports facilities allow us the possibility to extend the sports season and attract clubs. After the first season this proved to be correct. Clubs have a choice, to stay in the hotel of the lower category (3-Star) and train on the courts of the sports centre. This has a positive effect on our occupancy rates and sports during the winter season for all hotels, both 4-Star and neighbouring 3-Star facilities. (Participant 1)

Participant 6 noted the need to allow for an 'extension of work in accommodation in the winter period,' which is important to keep local people engaged and continually employed in the industry. Carrying on this discussion, managers pointed to a number of reasons why improvements were needed to help sustain tourism during the off-season months:

> Generally the development of sports and, even more further extension of the season the development of sports tourism which will benefit not only the hotel company, but the whole destination. Preparations football teams, for example taking place precisely in those months when staying in Istria, the smallest number of guests, so it is this form of tourism very welcome in the region. (Participant 3)
>
> Investment in the development and growth of the sport and of sports tourism which is in preparation of athletes creates the conditions for a year-round tourist season. (Participant 4)
>
> The investment was not too much, except for roads. The decision of managers is the main reason for investing in facilities and to up star ratings of hotels, and sport extends the tourism season. Medulin is known as a sporting destination. (Participant 5)

These responses speak to the need, and point to maintaining a competitive advantage if the region is going to ensure it attracts sports tourists in the future.

Despite having a history of sports tourism, planners in Istria looked at the growth and development of sports tourism in competing destinations. Participant 2 emphasised, 'We keep track of new trends, needs and our competition too; and certainly before any investment we made, we weigh the benefits to look at which investment will bring us more guests.' Participant 4 notes the importance of 'keeping track of how other places and countries invest in sports tourism and sports infrastructure. We analyse examples of good practice in these areas including cases of best applications' for the intention to deploy such practices in Medulin to improve the value and delivery of their sports tourism product. Several participants spoke about Turkey as a close competitor in the region:

> When planning a sports centre in Medulin, the Department of Marketing and Sales made a survey of sports destinations located in the neighbouring countries including Turkey. Research on the destinations included the following: category, number of accommodation units, distance from the nearest international airport, the number of football pitches and the distance from the hotel facilities, whether the football pitches have: lighting, dressing rooms, toilets, space for the spectators (such as grandstands), parking for visitors. The data collected helped us plan for needed facilities and services in the sports centre in order to be successfully positioned on the market. (Participant 1)
>
> Referring to investors, I believe that they are all aware of the importance of this segment (sports tourism and events) to destinations in the Mediterranean. While, for example, on the Adriatic Sea, during the winter months most hotels are closed. In Antalya during this period, the tourism industry earns billions. It is estimated that annually visit the region over 1,400 sports teams, and only in February almost 500 football clubs. A cluster of cities and towns in northwest Istria are making great efforts to develop sports tourism – specifically biking, football and tennis. (Participant 3)

Another participant, however, was quite critical of the upgraded facilities in Istria, and suggested that more in-depth monitoring is needed. They are concerned that these facilities are a result of 'copying and pasting (from one hotelier to other hoteliers) with no real goal' (Participant 5). The same participant also feels they are 'blending market segments' (Participant 5) and they recommend that the need to work on clustering in different parts of Istria, for instance focus on developing some areas that cater more to families and children, such as sports camps, and designate others more for extreme sports and/or more specifically for training. As observed above in the comment by Participant 1, looking to other examples is necessary to look at existing regional industry benchmarks to ensure new developments meet the current demands of clubs.

With the need to regenerate the industry, and a close consideration of competition in the proximate region, participants were asked to identify and express their concerns and limitations linked to the recent sports tourism facility and infrastructure developments. Participant 7 was particularly concerned about infrastructural developments due to costs and the amount of finances needed to invest extensively in new facilities and subsequent amenities to ensure market capture could be achieved to ensure future growth is possible. Beyond the tangible expenses are also marketing and branding expenses. Participant 1 speaks to this point, noting: 'before the reconstruction all sports and hotel facilities, many were in a poorer condition, and now we need to invest a lot in marketing activities to promote Medulin as a top sporting destination.' Dedicating funds to market a destination adds supplemental costs on top of the finances needed to regenerate a destination. But in an increasingly competitive sports tourism market, it is essential that the hotels promote new facilities to sports clubs that want to train or organisations that put on events. Another concern is investing enough to ensure you can actually attract clients and clubs. Participant 2 notes although 'the limiting factor is financial, top sport does not tolerate mediocrity, but only the best most modern sports infrastructure, which is financially very demanding.' Participant 2 also added:

> Only one football grass pitch with the accompanying equipment can stand up to 500,000 euros, and the fee from renting cannot always return investment in the short term, but only through long-term stay of our guests in the hotels.

In other words, direct benefits are very low, but indirect benefits are manifested by overnight stay. Therefore, the physical regeneration of the sporting facilities and infrastructures that takes place needs to be strategic so that target demand can be met to ensure room occupancy rates are high during these winter months. Participant 3 adds 'hotel accommodation must be adapted for sports groups.' While it is difficult to alter the actual rooms, hotels have added extra facilities such as spas, weightlifting equipment, storage space and meeting rooms to cater to team sports which bring along equipment and require space for other necessary programmes.

While this section has looked at the need for upgraded sports facilities and offered insight into financial constraints, the final key point referenced was the need for cooperation and partnerships to ensure stronger and consistent management of sports tourism and the promotion of sporting events. Participant 3 stresses the need not only for 'institutional cooperation in the sphere of the public sector, but also through the establishment of vertical and horizontal forms of public-public, public-private and private-private cooperation.' The formation of public-private cooperation, especially, can lead to points of contention (Perić, 2009). One of the biggest challenges is communication, and this can be difficult when different ministries meet to discuss planning agendas and strategy. Participant 5's point of concern is the 'Medulin Tourist Board and Municipality Head of Medulin do not communicate and have no common strategy.' This participant also mentions that the 'Medulin Tourist Board is the long arm of Arenaturist' and there are disagreements among local officials and sports tourism managers over who is investing in the industry and who is managing the industry. When one commission invests, they want to see a return, but in some cases, those managing the development of the industry want a return even though they do not put forward any finances that go into the physical infrastructure. Although new investments in sporting infrastructures are needed, questions continue to arise over who should invest in it. Participant 5 believes there is enough accommodation capacity, and they also feel that Arenaturist should invest in public sport infrastructure and public infrastructure in general. Despite the fact that Arenaturist has invested a lot of money in sporting infrastructure (and accommodation), some local officials think it is not enough. Arenaturist's managers are more cautious with these types of investments because of questionable profit equations. Participant 4 contributes to this discussion again noting 'the low availability of capital and insufficient investment incentives,' but also speaks about the amount of time it takes to obtain the necessary permits and it takes 'too much time to reconcile between the state and local levels.' For this participant, these issues can make attracting quality investors difficult. It is surprising to see that Arenaturist (who already invested a lot of money within the area) is not always recognised as a partner; such views may be a result of relationships among stakeholders and investors. Whoever the investors, managing new as well as existing sporting facilities is a key process in delivering value to sports tourists, and therefore 'a must' for any serious sports tourism development (Perić & Wise, 2015; Wise & Perić, 2017).

Implications and management concerning sports tourism and events strategy

As discussed above, sport and events is part of the strategy to increase tourism in Istria during the off-season. Participant 7 stressed part of the strategy is for 'the development of active holidays.' Istria is well-regarded for its sea and sun tourism, but the tourism industry sees significant declines during the winter months. This takes a toll on the hotel and restaurant industry as well as the local population who are majorly employed in the tourism industry or work in jobs that align with the tourism industry. Therefore, diversifying sport, and sporting events, is central to the current tourism strategy concerning Istria at the national, regional and local levels, as noted by Participant 7 who refers to the Croatian Ministry of Tourism, Istria Tourist Board and the local municipality, respectively. Participant 4 mentioned other organisations such as the Croatian Olympic Committee, The Public Institution Kamenjak, Sports Office Medulin, and the Istria Sports Union. Having the support of a range of ministries and organisations can assist the development of a sports and sports tourism product and especially support events. Similarly, and with more detail, other participants remarked:

> The 'Tourism Development Strategy of the Republic of Croatia until 2020' stipulates sport as one of the critical points of Croatian tourism, and the need to upgrade the accommodation facilities (higher categories); recent investment in Medulin achieved this. (Participant 1)

It fits in the national Tourism Development Strategy and it fits in the 'Tourism Master Plan for the Istria Region 2015–2025.' (Participant 5)

Operating strategy of the Istrian Tourism Master Plan defines the priorities of product development, including the focus on the development of 'Sports and activities'; investments therefore very much fit into the overall strategy of the Istria Region. The 'Tourism Development Strategy of the Republic of Croatia until 2020' has been highlighted that sports tourism is an increasingly important and a rapidly growing group of products for which some operators reported growth of 30% per year. But the fact is that Croatia still does not use enough of its comparative advantages for the development of this product. (Participant 3)

Investments of the Municipality of Medulin in sports infrastructure contribute to the growth of sports tourism as a product which is in the Tourism Development Strategy of the Republic of Croatia until 2020 defined as a product with a strong development perspective but where, at the moment, Croatia insufficiently uses its comparative advantage. Investments of the Municipality of Medulin in sports infrastructure contribute to the strategic objectives of the 'Master Plan for Sustainable Tourism Development of the Municipality of Medulin from 2013 to 2018.' (Participant 4)

When discussing strategy, some participants offered insight that was particular to certain sports:

Tourism office of the Municipality of Medulin recognised in its strategy that sports tourism can extend the season. Since 2015, together with the cooperation with Arenaturist, tourism office organises international football tournament in order to promote Medulin as a sports destination to football clubs in the neighbouring countries. (Participant 1)

Investments at Park Plaza Belvedere fit with national strategy in the field of cycling as one of the fast growing 'type' of tourism in Europe, so it invested in facilities related to cycling tourism, and now the hotel is equipped with all necessary facilities and services for bike tourists stay. The strategy of Medulin is still to be developed as a sporting destination especially in sports such as football, athletics and triathlon. The latest investments in Medulin coincide with that strategy. (Participant 2)

Regeneration policy is often linked to a tourism strategy. As we see from the above comments, participants spoke about the significance of sport to diversify tourism opportunities. From a managerial standpoint now, to ensure regeneration and strategy are supported and delivered, cooperation is essential. We asked participants to discuss how the public sector organisations (or ministries) are working with the local tourism organisations when it comes to planning for sports tourism and hosting sporting events to attract visitors. Responses relate to the discussion of partnerships acknowledged above, but put more emphasis on strategic management:

The cooperation of all involved segments of the tourism workers is at a high level. For instance, the Ministry of Tourism funded a conceptual design project for the Sports Centre Kažela, Arenaturist with the help of the Municipality and Tourism Office of the Municipality participate in the organisation of numerous events (events as a reason for arrival of new guests). Only in 2015 we participated in the organisation of a dozen sporting events in various sports disciplines, and these events attracted thousands of athletes in Medulin. (Participant 2)

Tourism development strategy of the Republic of Croatia until 2020 and Strategic Marketing Plan for Croatian tourism (both indicating for instance golf tourism, cycle tourism, and sports tourism as key tourist products), and Tourism Master Plan for the Istria Region 2015–2025 provide inputs for planning. (Participant 3)

Indeed, sport and tourism managers can do a better job when they have clear directions and support from other strategic levels within the tourism system. In this way they can make 'best practice' and 'strategic-fit' decisions to ensure long-term sustainability.

Participant 5 sees this all differently, and claims 'there is no real plan. The University of Pula composed a tourism development strategy for the Municipality of Medulin but we are not completely satisfied with it. The new "Master Plan for Istria" is hard to get to see what they are planning.' It must be noted that when this survey was being conducted, the new 'Master Plan for Istria' was in the process of adoption, so it was not yet a public document. In most cases, plans on different administrative levels (national, regional and local) have been made by different parties. It seems there are plenty of opportunities to improve communications and collaborations between different stakeholders. More collaboration is needed at least between the regional and local levels, which are 'closer' to each other than compared to national bodies.

Concerning management and strategy, collaborations among private and public stakeholders can alter plans and agendas. Participant 7's main concern referred to how both the public and private sectors come to an agreement over finances. This concern is articulated by Participant 6 who speaks about differing interests: the 'public sector seeks to satisfy their constituencies while the private sector is largely motivated by profit.' Participants offered further insight, stating:

Institutional cooperation in the sphere of the public sector, as well as vertical and horizontal public-public, public-private and private-private are keys for the development of such a product. (Participant 3)

Often the problem lies in the legislation that complicates the funding and sponsoring sporting events as well as joint ventures in sports facilities. Coordination between the stakeholders themselves could be a challenge too. But in Medulin situation is not so bad and solutions that satisfy all parties (win-win) are always found. (Participant 2)

Attractiveness of the destination is the key to development of any branch of tourism, including sports tourism, and this is realised through the successful marketing of the destination, whose cost should be covered jointly by both (public and private) organisations. If public and private organisations do not cooperate successfully, the destination as such will stagnate, become unattractive to guests on the market, etc. At the end it will result with a negative impact on both organisations – decline of revenues (and guests), less employment, decrease in revenues from tourist taxes are a result of declines in tourist consumption. (Participant 1)

Participant 1 mentioned attractiveness; however, attractiveness does not guarantee results or success. Underperformance in a destination (in terms of the number of overnight stays and tourist spending) will have negative consequences for all stakeholders. For the public sector, local authorities and tourist boards, they will receive less money because they rely on the distribution of revenue from tourist tax added to each stay each night. From a managerial standpoint, strategy and marketing are key parts of ensuring a product is developed and delivered. Strategy is all about making choices based on long-term plans. It gives meaning and direction to how the business models are developed and utilised (see Casadesus-Masanell & Ricart, 2010) and focusing on value creation for customers (Mäkinen & Seppänen, 2007). Value creation and delivery is crucial for having satisfied customers. Delivery requires cooperation from the stages of tourism planning and strategy through to the stages of regeneration and the delivery of sports products and events.

Further, private companies are often the key generators who invest in sports tourism-led regeneration; however, a long-term focus is also required at both the organisational and socioeconomic levels (Stubbs & Cocklin, 2008). These companies should adopt a systemic approach that seeks to integrate and consider social impacts and sustainability in a manner that generates shared value creation for all stakeholders (McLennan *et al.*, 2012; Bocken *et al.*, 2015). This approach is formulated within frameworks of sustainable business models aimed at capturing value for a wide range of stakeholders (Bocken *et al.*, 2013). Arguably, this is why we need sustainable business models (SBMs) that incorporate a triple bottom line approach and consider a wide range of stakeholder interests, including the environment and society (community and local population). Moreover, sustainable business models capture economic value for itself while maintaining or regenerating natural, social and economic capital beyond its organisational boundaries (Schaltegger *et al.*, 2015). However, wider public support is needed, and local tourism industries need local businesses and local involvement to ensure growth is sustained over the long term (Wise, 2016).

Potential social impacts

This last section of the data deals with particular social impacts brought about by all this sports tourism regeneration in Istria to identify what opportunities industry managers see as benefits for local residents. Scholars have focused on the importance of social regeneration and social impacts (e.g. Chalip, 2006; Deery *et al.*, 2012; Smith, 2012; Richards *et al.*, 2013; Wise, 2016), but there is more work that needs to be done to address social impacts on local populations.

Smith (2012) discussed social impacts and regeneration and addressed social capital as an important area to consider. Harrison-Hill and Chalip (2005) found that sport and the host destination have to be cross-leveraged, meaning vertical and horizontal alliances need to exist such as providers, management, facilities and physical infrastructures to optimise the quality of experiences and attractiveness of a sports tourist destination. Moreover, the quality of new facilities, infrastructures and services at the destination provides essential support for the overall sports tourism experience and opportunities. To consider how local residents can gain from this we need to look at how infrastructures can support local well-being, engagement, involvement, and new employment opportunities for local residents. Wise (2016) argues that much of the focus has been on the activities themselves and more research that considers the people who live in the actual place is necessary. Therefore, in Istria, sport creates opportunities, not only for tourists, but for locals who reside close to these new facilities and infrastructures. However, it can be a challenge to manage social impacts. We asked participants some questions that addressed how sports tourism and events will impact the local community and residents.

With any industry, there needs to be support from the local population. Local businesses are important because they help ensure money is retained locally in the region, city, town or community. Participants were asked to discuss what entrepreneurial and enterprise opportunities have resulted from investments in sport, specifically in Medulin and Pula. When asking about what enterprise opportunities exist, or have potential, respondents mentioned:

> Specialised shops with sports equipment, for example shops for diving, water sports, cycling. (Participant 1)
>
> With every single overnight stay new opportunities for local entrepreneurs are generated. For instance, development of cycle tourism offers a possibility of development of a rent a bike business. (Participant 2)
>
> Turnover growth of existing restaurants, opening of new restaurants, accommodation occupancy hotels of the season, investing in the renovation and construction of new facilities, development activities, wellness services, investing in development of additional sports facilities and sports recreation such as fitness centres. (Participant 4)

Participant 6 was more critical and thinks that future enterprise opportunities may not exist because they see 'services mainly exist in hotels using their sports facilities.' However, most responders show how the business ventures they are aware of feed off of the product and support the hotels. The hotel companies that played a central role in the physical regeneration of the facilities to attract sports tourists and host events can also benefit from local businesses. This is because local businesses can supply sports and recreational products such as bicycles or equipment for other activities. While the opportunity to start a new enterprise exists for locals as a result of sports tourism regeneration, Participant 5 notes that Medulin still needs more dedicated sports shops. Participant 2 added that 'overall, most of the needs of athletes are satisfied with the help of local businesses because for the hoteliers [the] "core business" is accommodation.' It will be important that community stakeholders meet with hotel managers and investors to better understand what new products and enterprises are needed to support the industry and grow businesses locally.

While local business ventures are important, other social benefits such as training and volunteering opportunities can help support, or restore, peoples pride in place (Wise, 2016). This is more the case when places host events, because it gives a place a new recognition that helps to promote a destination. Participant 4 reinforced this point when they mentioned the importance of 'including volunteers, especially young people, in the organisation and implementation of various sporting events.' From the standpoint of managing sport and events, it is important that mangers seek ways to involve residents, may this be through volunteering opportunities, regular employment, or offering and supporting training and educational programmes to promote interest in the sport and events industries. We asked respondents to discuss what volunteer opportunities exist to get locals involved:

> Numerous sporting events like Race Kamenjak, Ironman, triathlon for an amateur in Medulin, cycling events in Medulin, Premantura and Banjole provide volunteering opportunities to many citizens. (Participant 1)
> Only in last year's Ironman race several hundreds of volunteers participated. This proves that the organisation of sports events creates opportunities for volunteering. (Participant 2)

The sports tourism industry is supported by the hotels and organisations such as Arenaturist. However, events, while they are also supported by the same businesses and organisations, require the use of volunteers. One of the challenges of the events industry is the lack of full-time employment opportunities, and the reliance on volunteers. While volunteering is seen as creating social benefits, it is the existence of training and educational opportunities that will ultimately help support and sustain the future of the industry and keep locals gainfully employed in sports tourism.

We asked participants to discuss educational and/or internship opportunities that exist for the local residents, but we see this is an area that needs to be addressed as there was no real substance or support in many of the answers. Some organisations may work closely with universities in the region; however, this works best when content delivered by educational institutions focuses on contemporary industry needs and demands. Participant 5 referred to the opening of a large educational centre, but there were no specific details as to where this centre was based or who supported it. Similarly, Participant 4 noted 'opportunities for education, training and internships for students, encouraging the local population to get involved in sports activities, promoting healthy lifestyles and active sports for all ages.' Referring specifically to Arenaturist, Participant 2 mentions this organisation 'employs more than 90% of the local population [in their organisation]. In this context, any investment that generates additional overnight stays opens up the possibility of new employment, internship, or practices for local people.'

Participant 2 seems to refer back to the first point about enterprise opportunities here because they link to possibilities of practices, referring to local businesses that can support the industry. This section attempted to understand some of the wider social benefits for locals, but this is an area that requires more depth and attention to better understand how locals benefit. This is the focus of some on-going research with local residents in Medulin specifically.

Concluding remarks

> Medulin will continue to develop as a centre of excellence for sports tourism (during the winter). There is a great opportunity for the destination Istria to step on the market as a whole, and this could potentially bring more visitors in the region and create a world known brand. (Participant 2)

During the summer months, Medulin, Pula and destinations across Istria are sea and sun destinations that attract families. However, as more destinations enter the market (both in Croatia, or Montenegro and Albania as neighbouring competitors), the strategic plan is to focus on sport during the off-season to create a market niche and fill hotels year-round for the benefits of local employment and to expand the tourism industry. Participant 5 sees this as a 'win-win situation to simultaneously work on our new facilities and improve accommodation capacities.' This participant further stresses the impact of regeneration, that the region anticipates more profit and development concurrently.

The findings and related discussions in this chapter will also have managerial implications for private companies which are key generators (i.e. investors) of sports tourism and event regeneration. First, it will influence the future business strategies of these stakeholders. As Schaltegger *et al.* (2012) argue, designing sustainable business models that enable the firm to capture economic value for itself through delivering social and environmental benefits is really a challenge for private stakeholders involved in sports tourism enterprises (and development). What's more, it is important to integrate social indicators into internal measurement systems to ensure the interests of all stakeholders are met. To conclude, the future intentions of this research are to spatially identify physical infrastructural regeneration and how this links to wider planning agendas aimed at further developing off-season tourism and attracting more events. This chapter begins this work and discussion of sport management planning and sports tourism/sporting events agendas in Medulin and Pula – and this work will extend to similar cases in Istria.

References

Bocken, N., Short, S., Rana, P. & Evans, S. (2013). A value mapping tool for sustainable business modelling. *Corporate governance*, *13*, 482–497.

Bocken N.M.P., Rana, P. & Short, S. (2015). Value mapping for sustainable business thinking. *Journal of industrial and production engineering*, *32*, 67–81.

Casadesus-Masanell, R. & Ricart, J.E. (2010). From strategy to business models and to tactics. *Long range planning*, *43*, 195–215.

Chalip, L. (2006). Towards social leverage of sport events. *Journal of sport & tourism,* *11*, 109–127.

Deery, M., Jago, L. & Fredline, L. (2012). Rethinking social impacts of tourism research: A new research agenda. *Tourism management, 33*, 64–73.

Harrison-Hill, T. & Chalip, L. (2005). Marketing sport tourism: Creating synergy between sport and destination. *Sport in society, 8*, 302–320.

Mäkinen, S. & Seppänen, M. (2007). Assessing business model concepts with taxonomical research criteria. *Management research news, 30*, 735–748.

McLennan, C.J., Pham, T.D., Ruhanen, L., Ritchie, B.W. & Moyle, B. (2012). Counterfactual scenario planning for long-range sustainable local-level tourism transformation. *Journal of sustainable tourism, 20*, 801–822.

Ministry of Tourism (2015). Republic of Croatia edition 2015 Ministry of Tourism Republic of Croatia: Tourism in figures 2014. http://www.mint.hr/UserDocsImages/150701_Tourism014.pdf.

Ministry of Tourism (2016). Turistički promet od siječnja do prosinca 2015. godine. http://www.mint.hr/UserDocsImages/160219_tpromet015.pdf.

Perić, M. (2009). Criteria for setting up the public-private partnership in Croatian tourism and selection of optimal public-private partnership model. *Poslovna Izvrsnost, 2*, 111–126.

Perić, M. & Wise, N. (2015). Understanding the delivery of experience: Conceptualising business models and sports tourism, assessing two case studies in Istria, Croatia. *Local economy, 30*, 1000–1016.

Richards, G., de Brito, M.P. & Wilks, L. (Eds.). (2013). *Exploring the social impacts of events*. London, England: Routledge.

Schaltegger, S., Lüdeke-Freund., F. & Hansen, E.G. (2012). Business cases for sustainability: The role of business model innovation for corporate sustainability. *International journal of innovation & sustainable development, 6*, 95–119.

Smith, A. (2012). *Events and urban regeneration: the strategic use of events to revitalise cities*. London, England: Routledge.

Stubbs, W. & Cocklin, C. (2008). Conceptualizing a "sustainability business model." *Organization & environment, 21*, 103–127.

Wise, N. (2016). Outlining triple bottom line contexts in urban tourism regeneration. *Cities, 53*, 30–34.

Wise, N. & Perić, M. (2017). Sports tourism, regeneration and social impacts: New opportunities and directions for research, the case of Medulin, Croatia. In N. Bellini & C. Pasquinelli (Eds.). *Tourism in the City: Towards an integrative agenda on urban tourism*. Berlin, Germany: Springer Verlag (pp. 311–320).

Conclusion
Future directions in the (re)generation game

John Harris and Nicholas Wise

Moving forward

This collection has outlined some of the key issues and pressing concerns relating to the area of regeneration with specific reference to the inter-related areas of sport, events and tourism. It has critically assessed the ways in which a variety of different stakeholders have used sport, events and/or tourism as a means of regenerating. As noted in the Introduction, the concept of regeneration is complex and is continually being debated within and across several disciplines. More work is needed in the area of social and economic regeneration to understand the impacts of change on urban and regional communities. As this collection clearly shows, the range of interdisciplinary approaches to regeneration concerning the holistic integration of events, sport and tourism evidences a vibrant field of research.

Much work has addressed sport tourism or event tourism, but it is also important to acknowledge how sporting events, which are often the basis of much regeneration led initiatives and strategies, are in effect also part of wider tourism development. The lines and boundaries between the three areas are imprecisely drawn. In bringing together findings from a range of international case studies from scholars in different parts of the world, this collection has critically assessed some of the key factors impacting upon regeneration initiatives beyond any narrow disciplinary framework.

In geographical terms, the cases in this collection engaged with various scales, from venue-specific analyses and immediate surroundings through to urban, regional and national configurations. Whilst each chapter incorporates a discussion of sport, events *and* tourism, depending on the specific issues most relevant to each case-study focus, authors may have directed their gaze more so at *one* of these but then linked in their discussions to address the broader interconnectedness of all three. As Editors we did not prescribe or impose a particular lens or scholarly approach to do this. Edited collections are sometimes criticised for the diversity of approaches within them, but we feel that rather than viewing this negatively, we recognise that such diversity is a positive aspect of research in an area as broad and complex as regeneration.

As outlined in the Introduction to this collection, there are a whole host of inter-related academic areas and a variety of different disciplinary perspectives that contribute to the work on regeneration. This is clearly evidenced here through analyses informed by, for example, economics, geography, cultural studies and management. Our authors come from many disciplinary backgrounds, and are located within a set of very diverse school and departmental structures. They also come from different parts of the world and each brings her or his own personal biography to scholarship with some living and/or working in the places that they are writing about. Some of these scholars have been at the forefront of research in developing our understanding of this broad landscape of sport, event and tourism-led regeneration (see, for example, Hall, 1992; Spirou, 2011). Such work provides the base upon which the scholars involved in this edited collection can be brought together to contribute to the further development of work in this area.

Collectively, we have tried to show how sport, events and tourism can make a positive difference. This though is also tempered by a commitment to a critical scholarship that tries to challenge and evaluate the worst excesses of marketing, polity and governance. There was no one prescribed way to look at regeneration in the international cases that are the focus of our contributors and, as noted above, in places we see that one of the three may receive a greater degree of discussion. The very different locations that are used as case studies within this collection show how regeneration initiatives have impacted upon a range of different locales. In looking at this subject 'in the round,' the different sites and diverse approaches have uncovered a variety of key issues that will shape further research in this area moving forward. Central amongst these is the need to better understand the ways in which different groups can work together to bring about significant change. Change moving forward therefore requires holistic understanding. Differing perspectives will challenge us, as scholars, planners, policy makers and students, to recognise that there are a variety of ways of thinking and collaborating. Recognising interdisciplinary approaches contributes to diverse critical thinking and challenges us to think about how we measure impact and inform social policy that is inclusive of the key issues specific to a particular city, region and/or nation.

Challenges and possibilities: Towards a more critical analysis

What then are some of the main challenges facing this subject? There are far too many examples of empty and dilapidated facilities in a range of Olympic Games venues. These were all built upon the promise and prevailing discourse of regenerating places, economies and societies. The huge costs associated with regeneration initiatives, and particularly those built around mega-events, mean that the actual impacts are often unclear and lost within a world of public relations and politicking. This is starting to receive more and more attention from academics in different regions and will continue to occupy the work of scholars for some time. On the other side of the coin, one of the key points highlighted in a number of the chapters is the undoubted power of events. Beyond the world of mega-events discussed above there is a growing recognition that small-scale events may actually have a greater positive long-term impact upon host communities (e.g., Gibson *et al.*, 2012). It is also important that local communities are actively involved in regeneration initiatives at all levels.

The pressure to predict eye-catching economic and social impacts means that any new sport, event or tourism-led regeneration initiative must gain the support of a variety of stakeholders. We have known for some time now that the majority of large-scale events are sold on a shaky platform of underestimated costs and overestimated benefits. Central to this is the pressure to deliver on new facilities with the attendant surrounding infrastructure within a definitive timeframe that will support a renewed sense of optimism. There is also a hope for areas that have suffered from long-term economic decline. More recently we have also seen a push to incorporate event-led regeneration in many emerging economies. It is important to recognise that regeneration and development in emerging economies is understood and approached differently in developed economies. Developed economies use, or have used, sport, events and tourism to establish a new service-oriented economic base as many post-industrial cities and countries were significantly impacted by economic restructuring. Emerging economies are using sport, events and tourism to diversify and/or plan for the future. While perceived or intended economic impacts are often at the forefront of discussions to host events, it is important to continue addressing the most pressing social challenges and impacts. As noted by some of the contributors to this collection, the reality is often very different and the expected, or promised, returns failed to materialise. The real legacy of many event-led projects was that they did not result in, for example, getting more people actively involved in sport or see any upsurge in long-term tourist numbers.

Some of the chapters in this collection have also specifically looked at the marketing and promoting of a particular image through sport, events and/or tourism. This (re)imaging and (re)imagining of place has become increasingly prominent in the event portfolios and tourism development initiatives of cities and nations across the globe. It is important that we continue to look at contemporary issues from different disciplines in order to come together to question and challenge the status quo. Rojek's (2013, p. 181) work is important here to highlight that beyond the stated hype, corporatisation and stated altruistic role of events, 'all that events are capable of breeding is event consciousness.' There is no one model of regeneration that guarantees the effectiveness of any particular sport, tourism or event-led initiative. What is important is that research looking at international cases from interdisciplinary perspectives continues to challenge and build upon existing scholarship as the sport, events and tourism industries continue to drive regeneration.

References

Gibson, H., Kaplanidou, K. & Kang, S. (2012). Small-scale event sport tourism: A case-study in sustainable tourism. *Sport management review, 15*, 160–170.

Hall, C.M. (1992). *Hallmark tourist events: Impacts, management and planning.* London, England: Belhaven Press.

Rojek, C. (2013). *Event power [How global events manage and manipulate].* London, England: Sage.

Spirou, C. (2011). *Urban tourism and urban change: Cities in a global economy.* London, England: Routledge.

Index